Second Edition

CAPE **LAW**

Text and cases: Contract law, Tort law and Real property

Veronica E. Bailey

authorHOUSE®

AuthorHouse™
1663 Liberty Drive
Bloomington, IN 47403
www.authorhouse.com
Phone: 1 (800) 839-8640

Published by AuthorHouse 01/04/2016

ISBN: 978-1-5049-5415-0 (sc)
ISBN: 978-1-5049-5414-3 (e)

Print information available on the last page.

This book is printed on acid-free paper.

Contents

CONTRACT LAW

REAL PROPERTY

TORT LAW

Table of Cases

HOW TO PREPARE FOR EXAMS

Before and during Exams

(1) Before the exam, know the "big ticket" topics.
(2) Have a template for writing out the issues.
(3) Do not get too caught up in your conclusions.
(4) You are engaging in studies to become a Lawyer, practice using the expressions or terminologies used within the profession (e.g., use "legal words").
(5) Look for verbal clues in the fact pattern.
(6) Answer the question you know best first.
(7) Answer the specific question asked - identify the issue presented, the relevant area or areas of law to be discussed, apply the law to the facts and conclude
(8) Give both sides to every argument.
(9) Use transition words (or "signposts") to guide the Marker. In other words, be coherent in your discussion of the exam question.
(10) After you have answered a question, let it go and move on to the next question as time is of the essence in an examination room

A Law Student's Advice – Felisha Holt

(1) Do methodical studying, flashcards, and creating your own outlines.
(2) Focus on what your Lecturer presented in class because this is the best clue about what may appear on the final examination.
(3) Take the time to make your own study guides.
(4) Eat a good meal and try not to stress or get too excited before the exam.

(5) If possible, take every single past paper and complete all relevant questions under similar time and examination constraints.
(6) Go with your gut about what works best for you, and do not adopt any specific approach to studying just because people around you are doing it.
(7) Get to the point and get to know what your teacher expects.

CONTRACT LAW

Chapter 1

INTRODUCTION TO THE LAW OF CONTRACT

A contract is a part of our everyday experience and could vary from buying a meal, newspaper, petrol, lunch in a restaurant to even securing a mortgage for the purchase of a house. Simply defined, a contract is a legally binding agreement between two or more parties for either performing or refraining from performing an act. Additionally, Sir Frederick Pollock (1950, p. 133) purports that, a contract is "a promise or set of promises which the law will enforce". This contractual agreement will therefore create rights and obligations that either party to the agreement may enforce in the courts. The normal method of enforcement is an action for damages (monetary compensation) for breach of contract, though in some cases the court may order specific performance by the party in default.

HOW ARE CONTRACTS CLASSIFIED?

Contracts may be classified broadly as *Special contracts* and *Simple contracts*

Special contracts

Often referred to as Specialty contracts, these are contracts made by deed. A deed is a written document that is signed, witnessed by a Justice of the Peace and delivered to each contracting party. It is often used to convey some right or interest in land or to create a legal obligation under a contract such as a Hire Purchase Agreement.

Simple contracts

As highlighted earlier, these are contracts that we are most familiar with and could include agreements such as the act of purchasing petrol for our motor vehicles and even purchasing a laptop. These are obligations that can be entered into orally, in writing or implied by the conduct of the parties. They are called Simple contracts.

You will also encounter the concepts of *bilateral contracts* and *unilateral contracts* throughout your studies as these are also examples of Simple contracts.

Bilateral contracts

In a bilateral contract, both parties make promises. It is a contract where a promise by one party is exchanged for a promise by the other. For instance, Isaac promises to pay $2500 and Kimeisha promises to wash his clothes on the weekend. Notice that promises are being exchanged. Each promise is deemed to be sufficient consideration and so this exchange is enough to render them both enforceable.

Unilateral contracts

A unilateral contract is one-sided in nature. It is one where one party promises to do something in return for an act by another party. Notice that there is no mutual promise being exchanged. It is a one sided promise being made. An example of a unilateral contract would be where Byron promises a reward to anyone who will find his lost turtle. The essence of the unilateral contract is that only one party, Byron, is bound to do anything. He is the only person making a promise. No one is compelled to search for the lost turtle, but if Carlton, having seen the offer, recovers the turtle and returns it, a unilateral contract is made and he will be entitled to the reward.

Chapter 2

FORMATION OF A CONTRACT

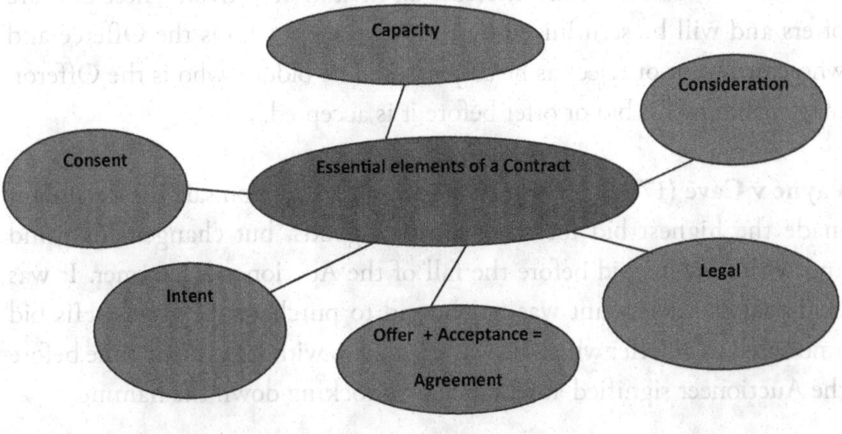

The first essential element of any contract is an agreement. This agreement consists of an offer and unconditional acceptance of all the terms of the contract. Generally, at least two parties are required: one party, the offeror who makes an offer which the other party, the offeree, accepts unconditionally.

OFFER

Treitel in his book defines an offer as 'an expression of willingness to contract on terms that are certain and made with the intention that it shall become binding on the offeror or as soon as it is accepted by the offeree'. (1999, p.8)

Not all 'expressions of willingness to contract' are offers. Some of these expressions are simply a request for information, a statement of intention and "invitation to treat". This latter unusual expression refers to the circumstances where a party is merely inviting offers, which he is then free to accept or reject. In other words, there is the opportunity to further negotiate in these instances.

The following are examples of invitations to treat:

AUCTION

An auction is a request for offers to be submitted to an Auctioneer. The Auctioneer's call for bids is therefore an invitation to treat. These bids are offers and will be scrutinized by the Auctioneer who is the Offeree and who can accept or reject as he so pleases. The bidder, who is the Offeror, may withdraw his bid or offer before it is accepted.

Payne v Cave (1789) 3 Term Rep 148 - at an auction sale the defendant made the highest bid for the plaintiff's goods, but changed his mind and withdrew his bid before the fall of the Auctioneer's hammer. It was held that the defendant was not bound to purchase the goods. His bid amounted to an offer which he was entitled to withdraw at any time before the Auctioneer signified acceptance by knocking down the hammer.

GOODS ON DISPLAY

Where goods are placed on display in a store or on a supermarket shelf with a price tag, this is not an offer to sell but an invitation for customers to make an offer to buy. Customers can further negotiate on price or even colour.

Fisher v Bell [1960] 3 All ER 731 - A shopkeeper displayed a flick knife with a price tag on the window. Legislation had made it an offence to 'offer for sale' a 'flick knife'. The shopkeeper was prosecuted …but the Justices declined to convict on the basis that the knife had not, in law, been 'offered for sale', but was merely 'displayed for sale'.

This decision was upheld by the Queen's Bench Divisional Court. Lord Parker CJ stated: "It is perfectly clear that according to the ordinary law of contract the display of an article with a price on it in a shop window is merely an invitation to treat. It is in no sense an offer for sale, the acceptance of which constitutes a contract."

Pharmaceutical Society of Great Britain v Boots Chemists [1953] 1 All ER 482 - The Defendant's shop was adapted to the "self-service" system. The question for the Court of Appeal was whether the sales of certain drugs were affected by or under the supervision of a registered pharmacist. The question was answered in the affirmative. Somervell LJ stated that "in the case of an ordinary shop, although goods are displayed and it is intended that customers should go and choose what they want, the contract is not completed until, the customer having indicated the articles and (possibly the colour and quantity) which he needs, the shopkeeper, or someone on his behalf, accepts that offer. It is then that the contract is completed."

An invitation to treat is therefore not an offer but is merely an invitation for interested persons to enter into negotiations for a purchase.

ADVERTISEMENTS

Advertisements of goods for sale are generally invitations to treat. The following cases illustrate this point:

Partridge v Crittenden [1968] 2 All ER 421. - The defendant had advertised in a periodical 'Quality Bramblefinch cocks, Bramblefinch hens, 25c each'. He was charged with 'offering birds for sale'. His conviction was quashed by the High Court. Lord Parker CJ stated that when one is dealing with advertisements and circulars, unless they indeed come from manufacturers, they will generally be construed as invitations to treat and not offers for sale. In a very different context Lord Herschell in **Grainger v Gough (Surveyor of Taxes) [1896] AC 325**, said this in dealing with a price list:

> *"The transmission of such a price list does not amount to an offer to supply an unlimited quantity of the wine described at the price named, so that as soon as an order is given, there is a binding*

> *contract to supply that quantity. If it were so, the merchant might find himself involved in any number of contractual obligations to supply wine of a particular description which he would be quite unable to carry out, his stock of wine of that description being necessarily limited."*

Where an advertisement is open for acceptance by the entire world and has a guarantee attached, it is an offer. You would have observed that this is an exception to the general rule that an advertisement is an invitation to treat. Acceptance of this type of unilateral offer will result in a unilateral contract.

Carlill v Carbolic Smoke Ball Co [1893] 1 QB 256

An advertisement was placed for 'smoke balls' which stated, if used as directed, would prevent influenza and offered to pay £100 to anyone contracted influenza after using the ball in the prescribed manner. The company deposited £1,000 with the Alliance Bank to show their sincerity in the matter. The plaintiff bought one of the balls but contracted influenza. It was held that she was entitled to recover the £100. The Court of Appeal held that:

a. the deposit of money showed an intention to be bound, therefore the advert was an offer;
b. it was possible to make an offer to the world at large, which is accepted by anyone who buys a smokeball;
c. the offer of protection would cover the period of use; and
d. the buying and using of the smokeball amounted to acceptance.

This particular advert was therefore a unilateral offer to the world at large which was accepted by the plaintiff through conduct.

PRICE QUOTATIONS

A request for information or asking for price of an item or goods does not amount to an offer.

Harvey v Facey [1893] AC 552 - The plaintiffs sent a telegram to the defendant, "Will you sell Bumper Hall Pen? Telegraph lowest cash price". The defendants reply was "Lowest price £900".
The plaintiffs telegraphed "We agree to buy ... for £900 asked by you".

It was held by the Privy Council that the defendant's telegram was not an offer but simply an indication of the minimum price the defendants would want, if they decided to sell. The plaintiff's second telegram could not be an acceptance.

Gibson v Manchester City Council [1979] 1 All ER 972 - The council sent to tenants details of a scheme for the sale of council houses. The plaintiff immediately replied, paying the £3 administration fee. The council replied: "The corporation may be prepared to sell the house to you at the purchase price of £2,725 less 20 per cent. £2,180 (freehold)." The letter gave details about a mortgage and went on "This letter should not be regarded as a firm offer of a mortgage. If you would like to make a formal application to buy your council house, please complete the enclosed application form and return it to me as soon as possible." G filled in and returned the form. The Labour party took control of the council from the Conservatives and instructed their officers not to sell council houses unless they were legally bound to do so. The council declined to sell to G.

In the House of Lords, Lord Diplock stated that words seem to make it quite impossible to construe this letter as a contractual offer capable of being converted into a legally enforceable open contract for the sale of land by G's written acceptance of it. It was a letter setting out the financial terms on which it may be the council would be prepared to consider a sale and purchase in due course.

INVITATIONS TO TENDER

Your school may need someone to make blouses and shirts for its students or it may need someone or a company to build a computer laboratory. In fact, if you have a Cafeteria on your school campus, your school would have initiated this relationship by way of an Invitation to Tender.

This intention to recruit the services of competent providers (of these services) is often communicated through invitations to tender. You will find these advertisements in the newspaper. This process is not an offer but is instead an invitation to treat as proposals are in response to the advertisement sent by the school and the school has the option to accept or reject. The parties who submit these proposals are called Bidders. The school will then accept the best or most suitable Bid as an offer. See the following cases:

Harvela Investments v Royal Trust Co. of Canada [1985] 2 All ER 966 - Royal Trust invited offers by sealed tender for shares in a company and undertook to accept the highest offer. Harvela bid $2,175,000 and Sir Leonard Outerbridge bid $2,100,000 or $100,000 in excess of any other offer. Royal Trust accepted Sir Leonard's offer. The trial judge gave judgment for Harvela.

In the House of Lords, Lord Templeman stated: "To constitute a fixed bidding sale all that was necessary was that the vendors should invite confidential offers and should undertake to accept the highest offer. Such was the form of the invitation. It follows that the invitation upon its true construction created a fixed bidding sale and that Sir Leonard was not entitled to submit and the vendors were not entitled to accept a referential bid."

Blackpool Aero Club v Blackpool Borough Council [1990] 3 All ER 25 - BBC invited tenders to operate an airport, to be submitted by noon on a fixed date. The plaintiffs tender was delivered by hand and put in the Town Hall letter box at 11am. However, the tender was recorded as having been received late and was not considered. The club sued for breach of an alleged warranty that a tender received by the deadline would be considered. The judge awarded damages for breach of contract and negligence. The council's appeal was dismissed by the Court of Appeal.

This decision may have been arrived at because the tender is an offer and an invitation to treat is not. Consequently, remember the 'Postal Rule' is only relevant to acceptance of an offer and not acceptance of an invitation to treat.

The Tender

A tender is an offer, the acceptance of which leads to the formation of a contract. However, difficulties arise when tenders are invited for the periodical supply of goods:

(a) Where X advertises for offers to supply a specified quantity of goods during a specified time, and Y offers to supply these, then acceptance of Y's tender creates a contract, under which Y is bound to supply the goods and the buyer X is bound to accept them and pay for them.

(b) Where X advertises for offers to supply goods up to a stated maximum, during a certain period, the goods to be supplied as and when demanded, acceptance by X of a tender received from Y does not create a contract. Instead, X's acceptance converts Y's tender into a standing offer to supply the goods up to the stated maximum at the stated price as and when requested to do so by X. The standing offer is accepted each time X places an order, so that there are a series of separate contracts for the supply of goods.

Great Northern Railway Co. v Witham (1873) LR 9 CP 16. - GNR advertised for tenders for the supply of steel and W replied 'I undertake to supply the company for 12 months with such quantities as the company may order from time to time'. The tender was accepted and orders were placed. When W later refused to supply, it was held that W's tender was a standing offer which GNR could accept by placing an order. W's refusal was a breach of contract but it also revoked W's standing offer for the future, so W did not have to meet any further orders.

ACCEPTANCE

According to Ewan McKendrick "an acceptance is an unqualified expression of assent to the terms proposed by the offeror". (2000, p. 42) The acceptance must be a "mirror image" of the offer for a contract to be binding. Where the offeree does not accept exactly what is offered then a counter offer may be the result.

However, in certain cases it is possible to have a binding contract without a matching offer and acceptance.

Brogden v Metropolitan Railway Co. (1877) 2 App Cas 666 - B supplied coal to MRC for many years without an agreement. MRC sent a draft agreement to B who filled in the name of an arbitrator, signed it and returned it to MRC's agent who put it in his desk. Coal was eventually ordered and supplied but after a dispute arose B said there was no binding agreement.

It was held that B's returning of the amended document was not an acceptance but a counteroffer which could be regarded as accepted, either when MRC ordered coal or when B actually supplied. By their conduct the parties had indicated their approval of the agreement.

Lord Denning in **Gibson v Manchester City Council [1979]** said that 'one must look at the correspondence as a whole and the conduct of the parties to see if they have come to an agreement.'

Percy Trentham Ltd v Archital Luxfer Ltd [1993] 1 Lloyd's Rep 25. - T built industrial units and subcontracted the windows to L. The work was done and paid for. T then claimed damages from L because of defects in the windows. L argued that even though there had been letters, phone calls and meetings between the parties, there was no matching offer and acceptance and so no contract.

The Court of Appeal held that the fact that there was no written, formal contract was irrelevant, a contract could be concluded by conduct. Plainly the parties intended to enter into a contract, the exchanges between them and the carrying out of instructions in those exchanges, all supported T's argument that there was a course of dealing between the parties which amounted to a valid, working contract. Steyn LJ pointed out that:

(a) The courts take an objective approach to deciding if a contract has been made.

(b) In the vast majority of cases, a matching offer and acceptance will create a contract but this is not necessary for a contract based on performance.

COUNTER OR SUBSTITUTE OFFERS

These offers are often referred to as 'counter offers' or 'return offers'. The effect of this type of offer is that it changes a specific term of the contract. It can be seen where an offeree may introduce a new term or varies the terms of the offer in his reply. This type of response will not amount to an acceptance and a "counter offer" is substituted to which the offeror can agree or refuse. When a counter-offer is introduced, it extinguishes the original offer which cannot again be later accepted. Let us use an everyday example: Edward has offered his car for sale for the sum of $300,000. Along came a prospective buyer who says he will purchase the car but will do so for $250,000. This prospective buyer has introduced a substitute offer which has effectively destroyed the original offer by Edward which cannot be reinstated. Edward, however, can choose to accept or reject the new offer.

Hyde v Wrench (1840) 3 Beav 334. - 6 June W offered to sell his estate to H for £1000;
H offered £950 instead
27 June W rejected H's offer
29 June H offered £1000. W refused to sell and H sued for breach of contract.

Lord Langdale MR held that if the defendant's offer to sell for £1,000 had been unconditionally accepted, there would have been a binding contract; instead the plaintiff made an offer of his own of £950, and thereby rejected the offer previously made by the defendant…a counter offer ensued that does not have to be accepted by the defendant.

However, a counter-offer should be distinguished from a mere request for information.

Stevenson v McLean (1880) 5 QBD 346 - On Saturday, the defendant offered to sell iron to the plaintiff at 40 shillings a ton, open until Monday.

On Monday at 10am, the plaintiff sent a telegram asking if he could have credit terms. At 1.34pm the plaintiff sent a telegram accepting the defendant's offer, but at 1.25pm the defendant had sent a telegram: 'Sold iron to third party' arriving at 1.46pm. The plaintiff sued the defendant for breach of contract and the defendant argued that the plaintiff's telegram was a counter-offer so the plaintiff's second telegram could not be an acceptance.

It was held that the plaintiff's first telegram was not a counter-offer but only an enquiry, so a binding contract was made by the plaintiff's second telegram.

CONDITIONAL ACCEPTANCE (Standard Form Contracts)
If A makes an offer on his standard document and B accepts on a document containing his conflicting standard terms, a contract will be made on B's terms if A acts upon B's communication, an example is by delivering goods. This situation is known as the "battle of the forms" and is illustrated in the case that follows.

Butler Machine Tools v Ex-Cell-O Corporation ***[1979] 1 WLR 401 CA*** - *Ex*-Cell-O requested information from Butler as he wished to acquire a machine being sold by Butler. Butler gave the defendants an invoice containing the price along with the terms of the sale which are standard. The invoice included clauses that would allow the seller to vary the contract and that the sellers' terms would undermine any terms submitted by a purchaser. Ex-Cell-O placed an order using their standard contract form which did not include the price variation clause. The contract was duly executed with Ex-Cell-O's document being the last to be signed by Butler. The machines were delivered but later Butler sought to enforce the price variation clause and demanded a price change of £2,893 above what was agreed. Ex-Cell-O refused to pay.

It was held by the court that the variation clause was not a part of the contract as Butler's contract was destroyed by a counter offer from Ex-Cell-O. When a standard contract document is being used, the last document to be signed will usually prevail and so it was on that basis that Ex-Cell-O's terms will have to prevail.

COMMUNICATION OF ACCEPTANCE

The business of engaging in a contract is absolutely not about reading minds and as such, acceptance generally has to be communicated. Where acceptance is not communicated then a contract does not exist.

Lord Denning in **Entores v Miles Far East Corp - [1955] 2 All ER 493** stated for example that If a man shouts an offer to another man across a river but the reply is not heard because of a plane flying overhead, there is no contract because the other person did not hear the offer. The offeror must wait until the noise passes then shout the offer again. Similarly, the offeree must wait and then shout back his acceptance so that the offeror can hear it. Further, acceptance must be communicated by the offeree or an authorized agent. Acceptance by anyone other than an authorized agent will not be valid and therefore a contract cannot be brought into existence.

Powell v Lee (1908) 99 LT 284 – The plaintiff applied for a job and was erroneously told by a member of the board that he was accepted. The board had in fact decided on accepting him but later changed their mind and appointed someone else. The plaintiff brought an action against the school alleging a breach of a contract to employ him that has caused him to suffer damages in loss of salary. The county court judge held and the decision was upheld by the King's Bench Division that there was no authorized communication by the board of their intention to contract with the plaintiff as the member of the board was not an authorized person to communicate the board's decision.

The decision in **Powell** was correctly decided as where an offeror forces a contract on the offeree on the basis of the offeree's silence, this contract will be seen as tantamount to extortion and the court will be unwilling to enforce such an arrangement. The following case also gives a very good illustration of the need to communicate acceptance.

Felthouse v Bindley (1862) 11 CBNS 869 - A nephew negotiated with his uncle for the purchase of a horse. He told him he expected to hear from him by the weekend and that where there is no communication, the horse will be his. The horse was stabled with an auctioneer who had mistakenly sold it against the uncle's instructions. The uncle commenced proceedings against the auctioneer for conversion. The action depended upon whether a valid contract existed between the nephew and the uncle. It was held that there was no contract as silence is not deemed to be acceptance and so the uncle could not sue successfully.

INSTANTANEOUS COMMUNICATION

Where you send an email, faxed message or any instantaneous message, when is this message received by the intended party?

Entores v Miles Far East Corp [1955] 2 QB 327 - The claimant made an offer by Telex to the defendants in Holland to purchase Cathodes. The defendant sent back a telex from Holland to the London office accepting that offer. The question for the court was at what point the contract came into existence. If it is enough that acceptance is effective from the moment it is sent to Holland, then the contract was finally executed in Holland. If the acceptance took place when the telex was received in London after being acknowledged by Holland then the contract would be governed by English law. It was held that in order to amount to an effective acceptance the acceptance needed to be communicated to the offeror. Therefore the contract was made in England. Have a look also at **Brinkibon v Stahag Stahl [1983] 2 AC 34 and The Brimnes [1975] QB 929** which are very instructive cases on instantaneous communication relevant to the making of a contract.

EXCEPTIONS TO THE COMMUNICATION RULE

(a) Acceptance by conduct is one exception to the general rule regarding communication of acceptance. This is relevant to unilateral contracts where an offer was made to the world at large and thus the need for communicating acceptance is implicitly waived.

(b) The offeror may expressly or impliedly waive the need for communication of acceptance by the offeree

(c) The Postal Rule - this is an exception to the general rule that acceptance takes place when it has been communicated. This position holds true even where the letter of acceptance is delayed, destroyed or lost in the post so that it never reaches the offeror. In light of so many alternatives to sending acceptance these days an acceptance by way of post has to be an appropriate and reasonable means of communication between the contracting parties.

Adams v Lindsell (1818) 1 B & Ald 681 The defendant offered wool for sale to the claimant by way of the post. He requested that acceptance should be communicated by way of the post as well. The defendant's letter to the claimant was delayed. Consequently, immediately upon receiving the offer (same day), the claimant posted an acceptance. The defendant lost patience and assumed the claimant no longer had an interest in the wool and sold it to a third party. The claimant sued for breach of contract and it was held that there was a valid contract executed when the letter of acceptance was placed in the post office.

This case established the "postal rule" and applies where:

(i) the post is the agreed form of communication between the parties; and
(ii) the letter of acceptance is correctly addressed; and
(iii) the letter carries the right amount of postage stamps.

The acceptance in these instances then becomes effective when the letter is posted and confirms that this mode of acceptance is an exception to the general rule.

Have a look also at **Household Fire Insurance Co. v Grant (1879) 4 Ex D 216** which illustrates the application of the postal rule.

It would appear that when the postal rule is relied on, withdrawal of an acceptance once a letter is dispatched would not be allowed. There is no clear authority in our jurisdiction as far as the writer knows but have a look at the case of **Dunmore v Alexander (1830),** a Scottish precedent which appears to permit such a revocation.

METHOD OF ACCEPTANCE

There may be specific instructions in the offer as to how acceptance should reach the offeror. Actual communication is generally required in these instances.

Holwell Securities v Hughes [1974] 1 All ER 161 – An option to purchase a house for Forty Five Thousand Pounds was given by Hughes to Holwell Securities. The option was to be exercised 'by notice in writing' within 6 months of becoming available. Sometime before the expiration of the 6 months period, Holwell exercised the option by sending the acceptance by mail. This letter was never received by Hughes. Holwell sued for breach of contract and asked the court for specific performance relying on the postal rule by stating that acceptance took place before the expiration of the option. It was held that by indicating that notice be given in writing Hughes needed to have received communication expressly and the postal rule was therefore ousted.

An equally advantageous alternative method of acceptance is adequate where a method is indicated that does not exclude any other mode.

Honeyman J in **Tinn v Hoffman (1873) 29 LT 271** posited that where acceptance was requested by return post "that does not mean exclusively a reply by letter or return of post, but you may reply by telegram or by verbal message or by any other means not later than a letter written and sent by return post." In other words, even where acceptance is requested by post, a superior or more efficient method can be used to communicate acceptance. See **Yates Building Co. v Pulleyn Ltd (1975) 119 SJ 370**

KNOWLEDGE OF THE OFFER

The criteria outlined in ***Carlill v Carbolic*** is also relevant to offers of rewards. This is evident in cases where a prized possession may have been lost and the owner is willing to offer monetary reward for its return. The general position is that an offer must be communicated as is the acceptance.

What happens when an offeree carries out what is an acceptance, that is, he performs, but the offer was not his primary reason for doing so? Can this act be seen as a valid acceptance? The authorities on this issue are conflicting if not a little confusing.

(a) An acceptance which is wholly motivated by factors other than the existence of the offer has no effect.

R v Clarke (1927) 40 CLR 227- The Government offered a reward for information leading to the arrest of certain murderers and a pardon to an accomplice who gave the information. Clarke saw the proclamation. He gave information which led to the conviction of the murderers. He admitted that his only object in doing so was to clear himself of a charge of murder and that he had no intention of claiming the reward at that time. He sued the Crown for the reward. The High Court of Australia dismissed his claim. Higgins J stated that: "Clarke had seen the offer, indeed; but it was not present to his mind - he had forgotten it, and gave no consideration to it, in his intense excitement as to his own danger. There cannot be assent without knowledge of the offer; and ignorance of the offer is the same thing whether it is due to never hearing of it or forgetting it after hearing."

(b) Where the offer somehow may have induced a required act, acceptance will still be valid.

Williams v Carwardine (1833) 5 Car & P 566 - The defendant offered a reward for information leading to the conviction of a murderer. The plaintiff knew of this offer and gave information that it was her husband after he had beaten her, believing she had not long to live and to ease her conscience. It was held that the plaintiff was entitled to the reward as she knew about it and her motive in giving the information was irrelevant.

HOW CAN AN OFFER BE TERMINATED?

Acceptance

When there is an unconditional acceptance of an offer, a binding contract is made and the offer expires.

Rejection
When the offeree rejects the offer explicitly or by way of a counter-offer, that is the end of the original offer.

Revocation
An offeror has the option to revoke or withdraw his offer at any time before acceptance. To be effective, the revocation must be communicated to the offeree.

Byrne v Van Tienhoven (1880) 5 CPD 344. - 1 Oct. D posted a letter offering goods for sale.
8 Oct. D revoked the offer; which arrived on 20 Oct.
11 Oct. P accepted by telegram
15 Oct. P posted a letter confirming acceptance.

It was held that the defendant's revocation was not effective until it was received on 20 Oct. This was too late as the contract was made on the 11th when the plaintiff sent a telegram. Judgment was given for the plaintiffs.

An offeror can revoke his offer through a reliable agent or third party.

Dickinson v Dodd (1876) 2 ChD 463 - Dodd offered to sell his house to Dickinson, the offer being open until 9am Friday. On Thursday, Dodd sold the house to Allan. Dickinson was told of the sale by Berry, the estate agent, and he delivered an acceptance before 9am Friday. The trial judge awarded Dickinson a decree of specific performance. The Court of Appeal reversed the decision.

James LJ in the Court of Appeal stated that the plaintiff knew that Dodd was not going to sell the property to him as it was already sold and this message was relayed to the plaintiff by a competent agent. The plaintiff acknowledged this in his own evidence. There could not have been an acceptance of the offer as the subject matter, the property, has already been sold.

An offer originally made to the world at large can be revoked in like manner.

Shuey v United States [1875] 92 US 73 - April 1865, the Secretary of War offered a reward published in the public newspapers for any information that leads to the arrest of wanted men. November 1865, the President revoked the offer of the reward in the same publication. In 1866 the claimant, unaware that the reward was revoked, found one of the named persons, and alerted the authorities. He sued for the reward but his suit was dismissed. It was held that the offer of a reward was withdrawn through the same channel in which it was made and it was of no consequence that the claimant was unaware of the revocation as the offer of reward was not directly made to him.

Where there is a unilateral offer and the offeree has started to act on this offer, the offeror cannot revoke his offer.

Errington v Errington [1952] 1 All ER 149 – A father secured a mortgage for his newly married son on the premise that if they paid off the mortgage, they could have the house. Unfortunately not long after the agreement took effect, the father died. His widow claimed the house. Following an appeal in the Court of Appeal, the daughter-in-law was granted possession of the house.

Denning LJ stated: "The father's promise was a unilateral contract - a promise of the house in return for their act of paying the instalments. It could not be revoked by him once the couple entered on performance of the act, but it would cease to bind him if they left it incomplete and unperformed, which they have not done. If that was the position during the father's lifetime, so it must be after his death. If the daughter-in-law continues to pay all the building society instalments, the couple will be entitled to have the property transferred to them as soon as the mortgage is paid off; but if she does not do so, then the building society will claim the instalments from the father's estate and the estate will have to pay them. I cannot think that in those circumstances the estate would be bound to transfer the house to them, any more than the father himself would have been."

Daulia v Four Milbank Nominees [1978] 2 All ER 557 - The defendant offered to sell property to the plaintiff on agreed terms. The defendant asked the plaintiff to attend at the defendant's office to exchange contracts. The plaintiff was informed upon arrival that the property was sold to a third party for a higher consideration. The plaintiff's claim was struck out and Goff L.J. had this to say obiter:

> *"In unilateral contracts the offeror is entitled to require full performance of the condition imposed otherwise he is not bound. That must be subject to one important qualification - there must be an implied obligation on the part of the offeror not to prevent the condition being satisfied, an obligation which arises as soon as the offeree starts to perform. Until then the offeror can revoke the whole thing, but once the offeree has embarked on performance, it is too late for the offeror to revoke his offer."*

Counter offer

See Substitute Offer above and **Hyde v Wrench (1840)** where it can be seen that a counter or substituted offer destroys the original offer.

Lapse of time

An offer can only be open for a reasonable period of time when no time limit is given by the offeror. Where a period of time is indicated by the offeror then the offer will lapse after that period of time.

Ramsgate Victoria Hotel v Montefiore (1866) LR 1 Ex 109 - Montefiore offered to purchase shares in the plaintiff hotel on 8 June. It was not until 23 November that the plaintiff accepted and by this time the defendant was no longer interested in the shares and so refused to pay. The hotel decided to sue but it was held that the six-month delay between the offer in June and the acceptance in November had resulted in a lapse of the offer and therefore could no longer be accepted. The defendant was not liable for paying the price of the share.

Failure of a condition

An offer may be made subject to implied or express conditions and is incapable of being accepted unless the conditions are met.

Financings Ltd v Stimson [1962] 3 All ER 386 – The defendant offered to take out a car on hire purchase from the plaintiffs through a dealer. He gave them his deposit and drove out his car. He later returned the car to the dealer's premises as he was dissatisfied with its performance. The car was later stolen from the premises and damaged. The dealer did not tell the plaintiffs that the defendant had returned the car and so they went ahead and signed the hire purchase agreement.

It was held by the Court of Appeal:

(a) That there was revocation of the offer by the defendant when he returned the car to the dealer even where the plaintiff was unaware.
(b) The defendant would have examined the car and determined that it was in good condition and that it should remain in the same condition until acceptance. The acceptance was therefore invalid since the condition was not fulfilled.

Death
Where the offeror dies, the offer cannot generally be accepted. However, where there is a personal representative, then the transaction can continue. This can be seen in instances where a property is being offered for sale and the offeror dies. The personal representative, for example the Executors, can complete the sale. The following case provides a very good illustration of this discussion.

Bradbury v Morgan (1862) 1 H&C 249 – JM Leigh requested credit and guaranteed an account for his brother HJ Leigh in the sum of One Hundred Pounds from Bradbury & Co. The brother was therefore given credit on the basis of the guarantee. Having no notice of JM Leigh's death, Bradubury continued to extend credit to the brother. The Executors of JM, Morgan refused to settle the outstanding bill, arguing that they were not liable as the debts were contracted and incurred after the death of JM. Judgment was given for the plaintiffs, Bradbury.

ACTIVITY SHEET

1. (a) With reference to decided cases, outline FOUR ways in which an offer may be terminated.
   (b) Sean's pet dog, Jokomo, has simply vanished. On March 20, she puts up posters in the neighbourhood shops, pharmacies and salons offering a reward of $1000 for Jokomo's return by March 25. She also advertises the reward for its return in the local newspaper. On March 23, Sean decides that she does not want Jokomo anymore because she received a called from the immigration department that she is to leave the island soon. The next day, she publishes an advertisement in the newspaper withdrawing the reward. Evan finds Jokomo that same day and sends an email to Sean claiming the reward and informing her she can collect Jokomo from his house. Sean opens the email March 26. Is Evan entitled to the reward? Support your answer with reference to case law.
2. In the law of contract, can an individual accept an offer about which he or she does not? know?
3. In June 2011, Javon started his own computer enterprise after graduating from college with a bachelor's degree in Management Information Systems. He enters into an agreement with Dacres, a supplier of games and programmes, to purchase items for his store. Javon accepted the items ordered but now disputes the price as being too high and refuses to pay. Price was omitted from the agreement. What are the obligations of both Dacres and Javon in this scenario?
4. Explain the rules relevant to acceptance using cases to support your response.

Chapter 3

INTENTION TO CREATE LEGAL RELATIONS

SOCIAL/DOMESTIC AGREEMENTS **COMMERCIAL AGREEMENTS**

INTENTION TO CREATE LEGAL RELATIONS

In order to establish what the contracting parties intended or whether they wanted to be legally bound, the court will apply an objective test and judge the situation based on all the circumstances. The court will make a decision based on whether the parties are families/friends or whether it is a business relationship.

1. SOCIAL & DOMESTIC AGREEMENTS

The law presumes that social agreements, that is, agreements among friends and family members are not intended to be legally binding.

Agreements between spouses living together as one household are presumed not to be intended to be legally binding, unless the agreement states the contrary.

Balfour v Balfour [1919] 2 KB 571- The defendant who worked in Ceylon, came to England with his wife on holiday where he left her because of health reasons and returned to Ceylon. The defendant promised to pay his wife, the plaintiff £30 monthly as maintenance, but discontinued the payment as their relationship broke up. The wife sued unsuccessfully and it was held that:

(1) she had provided no consideration for the promise to pay £30; and
(2) agreements between husbands and wives are not contracts because the parties do not intend them to be legally binding.

If an agreement made between families or friends will have severe or legal consequences the presumption that no legal relation is intended will be rebutted.

In **Merritt v Merritt (1970)** The husband had left the matrimonial home, which was owned by him, to live with another woman. The spouses met in the husband's car and he agreed to pay her 40 euros out of which she would keep up the mortgage payments on the house. The wife refused to leave the car until he signed a note of the agreed terms and an undertaking to transfer the house into her sole name when the mortgage was paid off. The wife paid off the mortgage, but the husband refused the transfer. Although this too was an agreement between a husband and a wife, there were obvious differences between this and **Balfour v Balfour**. The husband and wife here were not living in amity when the agreement was made, and the surrounding circumstances all suggested that there was an intention to create legal relations. This was a contract.

Where spouses are not living together in harmony the presumption against a contractual intention will not apply.

If an agreement made between families or friends includes reliance and will have serious or even legal consequences the presumption that no legal relation is intended will be rebutted.

Tanner v Tanner [1975] 1 WLR 1346 - A man promised a woman that the house in which they had lived together even before they were married should be available for her and the couple's children. Consequently, the woman moved out of her apartment which was rent controlled. It was held that they had entered into a legally binding contract and the man was not allowed to renege on his promise.

The authorities suggest that generally, agreements made between parents and children are not intended to be legally binding.

Jones v Padavatton (1969)
In 1962 Mrs. Jones encouraged her daughter to leave her job in America to study law in England. A monthly allowance was promised and Mrs. Jones bought a house in London which she leased to tenants in order to provide additional income and accommodation for her daughter as there were problems with housing in London at the time. Five years later their relationship broke down and Mrs. Jones claimed the house even though the daughter had not even passed half of her exams and so had not completed her studies.

It was held that the arrangement between the mother and her daughter was a family arrangement and not intended to be binding. Therefore, the mother was not liable as in any case, she had given the daughter a reasonable time to complete her studies and could also claim the house.

Parker v Clarke (1960)
Mrs. Parker was the niece of Mrs. Clarke. An agreement was made that the Parkers would sell their house and live with the Clarkes. They would share the bills and the Clarkes would then leave the house to the Parkers. Mrs. Clarke wrote to the Parkers giving them the details of expenses and confirming the agreement. The Parkers sold their house and moved in. Mr Clarke changed his will leaving the house to the Parkers. Later the couples fell out and the Parkers were asked to leave. They claimed damages for breach of contract.
It was held that the exchange of letters showed the two couples were serious and the agreement was intended to be legally binding because

(1) the Parkers had sold their own home, and
(2) Mr. Clarke changed his will. Therefore the Parkers were entitled to damages.

The court will look at all the circumstances where the parties are not related but are sharing the same household to determine whether there is an intention to create legal relations

Simpkins v Pays (1955)
The defendant, her granddaughter, and the plaintiff, a paying lodger shared a house. They all contributed one-third of the stake in entering a competition in the defendant's name. One week a prize of £750 was won but on the defendant's refusal to share the prize, the plaintiff sued for a third.

It was held that the presence of the outsider rebutted the presumption that it was a family agreement and not intended to be binding. The mutual arrangement was a joint enterprise to which cash was contributed in the expectation of sharing any prize.

2. COMMERCIAL AGREEMENTS (BUSINESS)

There is the presumption that there is an intention to create legal relations in the making of a contract in a business relationship. However, where an express statement is included to rebut the presumption, then there may not be an intention.

Rose and Frank Co v Crompton Bros Ltd [1925] AC 445 - The defendants were paper manufacturers and entered into an agreement with the plaintiffs whereby the plaintiffs were to act as sole agents for the sale of the defendant's paper in the US. The written agreement contained a clause that it was not entered into as a formal or legal agreement and would not be subject to legal jurisdiction in the courts but was a record of the purpose and intention of the parties to which they honorably pledged themselves that it would be carried through with mutual loyalty and friendly co-operation. The plaintiffs placed orders for paper which were accepted by the defendants. Before the orders were sent, the defendants terminated the agency agreement and refused to send the paper.

It was held that the sole agency agreement was not binding owing to the inclusion of the "honourable pledge clause". Regarding the orders which had been placed and accepted, however, contracts had been created and the defendants, in failing to execute them, were in breach of contract.

A participant may not recover his winnings from a football pool since they are generally stated to be "binding in honour only" and are not legally binding.

Jones v Vernon Pools (1938)
The plaintiff claimed to have won the football pools. The coupon stated that the transaction was "binding in honour only". It was held that the plaintiff was not entitled to recover because the agreement was based on the honour of the parties (and thus not legally binding).

Contractual intention may be negatived by evidence that "the agreement was a goodwill agreement made without any intention of creating legal relations" as can be seen in **Orion Insurance v Sphere.**

Drake Insurance [1990] 1 Lloyd's Rep 465
Where an ambiguous clause is inserted into a contract the court will be responsible for its interpretation.

Where a statement or promise is unclear, contractual intentions may be contradicted

JH Milner v Percy Bilton [1966] 1 WLR 1582 - A property developer reached an "understanding" with a firm of solicitors to employ them in connection with a proposed development, but neither side entered into a definite commitment. The use of deliberately vague language was held to negative contractual intention.

There are circumstances that prevent contract formation even where parties enter into a commercial agreement:

INDUCEMENTS (Representations or 'mere puffs')
For the purposes of attracting customers, tradesmen may make vague, exaggerated and subjective claims in advertisements which may even prove

impossible to verify. Such statements are essentially statements of opinion or "mere puffs" and are not intended to form the basis of a binding contract. They are made with the intention to attract customers. By contrast, more specific pledges such as, "If you can find the same holiday at a lower price in a different brochure, we will refund you the difference", are likely to be binding. Remember the **Carlill Case** mentioned above? The latter submission can be seen in that case while the former submission can be seen in a popular advertisement that intends to give purchasers "*wings*".

A statement will not be binding if the court considers that it was not seriously meant. This was the situation in **Weeks v Tybald (1605) Noy 11** where the defendant "affirmed and published that he would give £100 to him that should marry his daughter with his consent." The court held that "It is not reasonable that the defendant should be bound by such general words spoken to excite suitors.

The decision was also not favourable in the case of **Heilbut, Symons & Co v Buckleton (1913)** where the plaintiff said to the defendants' manager that he understood the defendants to be "bringing out a rubber company." The manager replied that they were, on the strength of which statement the plaintiff applied for, and was allotted, shares in the company. It turned out not to be a rubber company and the plaintiff claimed damages, alleging that the defendants had warranted that it was a rubber company. The claim failed as nothing said by the defendants' manager was intended to have contractual effect.

LETTERS OF COMFORT

This is a document supplied by a third party to a creditor, indicating information to the creditor on the debtor's ability to meet his potential obligations. They are opinions and do not give a guarantee as to the continued viability of a borrower. Letters of Comfort are generally not legally binding but gives a potential creditor some reassurance that a debtor will do business with the creditor.

LETTERS OF INTENT

This is a letter that is used by one party stating the intention to do business with another. A letter of intent is an instrument which is frequently used when there is uncertainty concerning the performance of a contract but there is no need to communicate with the other contracting party. Where the construction of the letter of intent is ambiguous, the court may be called upon to make a decision on whether the party expressing an intention to contract should be bound. The party stating his intention may be bound by law in an event where a person has acted on the document and may have incurred expenses in reliance on it. **Turriff Construction v Regalia Knitting Mills (1971) 22 EG 169** held that a letter of intent can be legally binding where there is a collateral contract for preliminary work.

ACTIVITY SHEET

1. Kalf and Eny are brothers. They both own cars. Kalf told Eny to sell his car and he will take him to and from work every day. Eny sold his car. However, very soon thereafter, Kalf became very unreliable in picking up his brother who is constantly late for work and is frequently at work late, waiting for his brother. Eny is now frustrated and is thinking about taking his brother to court.

Do you think Eny will be successful in his claim? Discuss using cases to support your answer.

2. Jeneve gave up her job on her mother's instruction and went back to school. She subsequently had financial problems regarding her school fees and her mother refuses to assist her in honoring her obligations with her school. She may not be able to sit her exams. Jeneve has filed a suit against her mother in order to force her to pay the fees. Jeneve believes that her mother has breached a contract between them. What is your opinion? Support same with the use of relevant cases.
3. Seba offers $150 to anyone who will do his shopping at the green grocers every week. He likes to have fruits and vegetables but simply cannot find the time to do his own shopping. The following people comply with the terms of his offer:

(a) his wife, Carole
(b) his ex-wife, Kathy
(c) his mistress, Ashley
(d) his son, Boxill
(e) his nephew Collin, whom he has never seen before
(f) his god-child, Slabo
(g) his next door neighbor, Ricky
(h) his gardener whom he knows only as "Dread"

Advise Seba whether or not, in these circumstances, any legally enforceable contracts have been concluded. Support your answer with cases.

Chapter 4

CONSIDERATION

McKendrick has described consideration as the "badge of enforceability" because the mere fact of agreement alone does not make a contract. (2015, p.61) There has to be a mutual exchange between the contracting parties in order to enforce the contract. In other words, each party has to do or exchange something in order to satisfy the contract. However, where a contract is made by deed, then consideration is not needed.

Also, Lush J. in **Currie v Misa (1875) LR 10 Exch 153** defines consideration as "consisting of a detriment to the promisee or a benefit to the promisor ... some right, interest, profit or benefit accruing to one party, or some forbearance, detriment, loss or responsibility given, suffered or undertaken by the other."

TYPES OF CONSIDERATION

Consideration can either be executory or executed:

1. EXECUTORY CONSIDERATION

Executory consideration is a promise being exchanged for another where one person promises to do something and the other party promising to pay in the future. For example, calling the plumber to repair a pipe and he promises to come in two days to carry out the repairs.

2. EXECUTED CONSIDERATION

If on the promise of one party the other party acts, this is an executed consideration. Take a look again at unilateral contracts where a reward is offered for the return of a lost item. The party who returns the lost item has executed consideration.

RULES GOVERNING CONSIDERATION

1. "PAST CONSIDERATION IS NOT GOOD CONSIDERATION"

If one party takes it upon himself to complete a task that was not assigned to him, and the other party then makes a promise, the consideration for the promise is said to be in the past. The general rule is that past consideration is not good consideration, so it is not valid. For example, A paints B's house. On reaching his house B promises to give A $5000 for the good job he did. A cannot enforce this promise as his consideration of painting B's house, is past.

Re McArdle [1951] 1 All ER 905 - A wife and her three grown-up children lived together in a house. The wife of one of the children effected significant home improvement to the property and the children later promised to pay her £488 signing a document to this effect. She was never paid for the home improvement done and she sued.
It was held that the promise was unenforceable as all the work had been done before the promise was made and was therefore past consideration.

EXCEPTIONS TO THIS RULE:

(a) PREVIOUS REQUEST

Where, upon a previous request by the promisor, the promisee was asked to provide goods and services then the past consideration doctrine could not apply.

Lampleigh v Braithwait (1615) Hob 105 - Braithwait killed someone and then asked Lampleigh to get him a pardon. Lampleigh got the pardon and gave it to Braithwait who promised to pay Lampleigh £100 for his trouble.

It was held that although Lampleigh's consideration was past as he had secured the pardon before being paid, Braithwaite's promise to pay could be linked to Braithwait's earlier request and treated as one agreement, so it could be implied at the time of the request that Lampleigh would be paid.

(b) BUSINESS SITUATIONS

Past consideration will not be valid in a business context. In this context, there is usually the understanding that the goods or service will be paid for.

Re Casey's Patents [1892] 1 Ch 104 - A and B owned a patent and C was the manager who had worked on it for two years. A and B then promised C a one-third share in the invention for his help in developing it. The patents were transferred to C but A and B then claimed their return. It was held that C could rely on the agreement. Even though C's consideration was in the past, it had been done in a business situation, at the request of A and B and it was understood by both sides that C would be paid and the subsequent promise to pay merely fixed the amount.

Note: The principles in **Lampleigh v Braithwait** as interpreted in **Re Casey's Patents** were applied by the Privy Council in:

Pao On v Lau Yiu Long [1980] AC 614 where Lord Scarman said:

> *"An act done before the giving of a promise to make a payment or to confer some other benefit can sometimes be consideration for the promise. The act must have been done at the promisor's request: the parties must have understood that the act was to be remunerated either by a payment or the conferment of some other benefit: and payment, or the conferment of a benefit, must have been legally enforceable had it been promised in advance."*

(c) CHEQUES or BILLS OF EXCHANGE

When work is carried out by the promisee who is either paid later by way of a cheque or a bill of exchange, then the promisee's work, though it would have been past, is valid consideration.

2. "CONSIDERATION MUST BE SUFFICIENT BUT NEED NOT BE ADEQUATE"

The law is not particularly concerned about the adequacy of consideration. It is mainly concerned about the existence of value. The courts will not investigate contracts where there is no evidence of undue influence or duress. Providing that both parties are happy, the court will not interfere.

Chappell & Co Ltd v Nestle Co Ltd [1959] 2 All ER 701 - Nestle was running a special offer whereby members of the public could obtain a music record by sending off three wrappers from Nestlé's chocolate bars plus some money. The copyright to the records was owned by Chappell, who claimed that there had been breaches of their copyright. The case turned on whether the three wrappers were part of the consideration. It was held that they were, even though they were then thrown away when received.

3. CONSIDERATION MUST MOVE FROM THE PROMISEE

The onus is on the person who wishes to enforce an agreement to show that he provided consideration. Consideration does not have to move from the promisor. This is particularly true where the issue of past consideration is in issue. If there are three parties involved, problems may arise.

Price v Easton (1833) 4 B & Ad 433 - Easton made a contract with X that in return for X doing work for him, Easton would pay Mr. Price the sum of £19. X did the work but Easton did not pay, so Mr. Price sued. As Mr. Price provided no consideration it was held that his claim must fail.

4. FOREBEARANCE TO SUE

Where a person has a valid claim against another but decides to refrain from bringing a legal battle, that is sufficient consideration where the other party has made a promise to settle the claim.

Alliance Bank v Broom (1864) 2 Dr & Sm 289 - The defendant owed an unsecured debt to the plaintiffs. When the plaintiffs asked for some security, the defendant promised to provide some goods but never produced them. When the plaintiffs tried to enforce the agreement for the security, the defendant argued that the plaintiffs had not provided any consideration.

It was held that normally in such a case, the bank would promise not to enforce the debt, but this was not done here. By not suing, however, the bank had shown forbearance and this was valid consideration, so the agreement to provide security was binding.

5. EXISTING PUBLIC DUTY

An individual that is already obligated by way of a public duty will not be providing sufficient consideration for agreeing to do that task that he is already being compensated to do.

Collins v Godefroy (1831) 1 B & Ad 950 - Godefroy promised to pay Collins if Collins would attend court and give evidence for Godefroy. Collins had been served with a subpoena (i.e., a court order telling someone they must attend). Collins sued for payment. It was held that as Collins was under a legal duty to attend court he had not provided consideration. His action therefore failed.

If someone goes beyond the scope of their public duty, then this may be valid consideration. **Glassbrooke Bros v Glamorgan County Council [1925] AC 270** - The police were under a duty to protect a coal mine during a strike, and proposed mobile units. The mine owner promised to pay for police to be stationed on the premises. The police complied with this request but when they claimed the money, the mine owner refused to pay saying that the police had simply carried out their public duty.

It was held that although the police were bound to provide protection, they had a discretion as to the form it should take. As they believed mobile police were sufficient, they had acted over their normal duties. The extra protection was good consideration for the promise by the mine owner to pay for it and so the police were entitled to payment.

6. EXISTING CONTRACTUAL DUTY

If someone is already bound under a contract to do something, then promising to do that which they are already bound to do is no valid consideration.

Stilk v Myrick (1809) 2 Camp 317 - Two out of eleven sailors deserted a ship. The captain promised to pay the remaining crew extra money if they sailed the ship back, but later refused to pay.

It was held that as the sailors were already bound by their contract to sail back and to meet such emergencies of the voyage, promising to sail back was not valid consideration. Thus the captain did not have to pay the extra money.

Hartley v Ponsonby (1857) 7 E & B 872- When nineteen out of thirty-six crew of a ship deserted, the captain promised to pay the remaining crew extra money to sail back, but later refused to pay saying that they were only doing their normal jobs. In this case, however, unlike the circumstances in **Stilk v Myrick**, the ship was so seriously undermanned that the rest of the journey had become extremely hazardous. Additionally, most of the remaining crew lacked the experience of those who had deserted the ship.

It was held that sailing the ship back in such dangerous conditions was over and above their normal duties. It discharged the sailors from their existing contract and left them free to enter into a new contract for the rest of the voyage. They were therefore entitled to the money.

Where the performance of an existing contractual obligation confers a "practical benefit" on the other party, this can constitute valid consideration.

Williams v Roffey Bros Ltd [1990] 1 All ER 512 - Roffey had a contract to refurbish a block of flats and had sub-contracted the carpentry work to Williams. After the work had begun, it became apparent that Williams had underestimated the cost of the work and was in financial difficulties. Roffey, concerned that the work would not be completed on time and that as a result they would fall foul of a penalty clause in their main contract with the owner, agreed to pay Williams an extra payment per flat. Williams completed the work on more flats but did not receive full payment. He stopped work and brought an action for damages. In the Court of Appeal, Roffey argued that Williams was only doing what he was contractually bound to do and so had not provided consideration.

It was held that where a party to an existing contract later agrees to pay an extra "bonus" in order to ensure that the other party performs his obligations under the contract, then that agreement is binding if the party agreeing to pay the bonus has thereby obtained some new practical advantage or avoided a disadvantage. In the present case there were benefits to Roffey including (a) making sure Williams continued his work, (b) avoiding payment under a damages clause of the main contract if Williams was late, and (c) avoiding the expense and trouble of getting someone else. Therefore, Williams was entitled to payment.

7. EXISTING CONTRACTUAL DUTY OWED TO A THIRD PARTY

If a party promises to do something for a second party although bound by a contract to do this for a third party, this is good consideration.

Scotson v Pegg (1861) 6 H & N 295 - Scotson contracted to deliver coal to X, or to X's order. X sold the coal to Pegg and ordered Scotson to deliver the coal to Pegg. Then Pegg promised Scotson that he would unload it at a fixed rate. In an action by Scotson to enforce Pegg's promise, Pegg argued that the promise was not binding because Scotson had not provided consideration as Scotson was bound by his contract with X (a third party) to deliver the coal. It was held that Scotson's delivery of coal (the performance of an existing contractual duty to a third party, X) was a benefit to Pegg and was valid consideration. It could also be seen as a detriment to Scotson, as they could have broken their contract with X and paid damages.

8. PART PAYMENT OF A DEBT

THE GENERAL RULE

The rule in **Pinnel's case** purports that if someone owes money, he cannot pay only a portion of this debt in full settlement of the debt. This is the general position and so when the debtor cannot pay in full there is nothing to prevent the creditor from requesting the difference in the future. The facts of this case are that Cole owed Pinnel some money which was due in November. At Pinnel's request, Cole paid some of the money in October, which Pinnel acknowledged to be full settlement of the debt. After a period of time, Pinnel sued Cole for the amount owed. It was held that part-payment in itself was not consideration. However, it was held that the agreement to accept part-payment would be binding if the debtor, at the creditor's request, provided some fresh consideration. Consideration might be provided if the creditor agrees to accept:

(a) Part-payment on a date other than the agreed date.
(b) Chattel instead of money (a car, a generator, etc); or
(c) Part-payment in a branch or payment via a different mode such as online payment versus a visit to the bank than that originally specified.

In **Foakes v Beer (1884) 9 App, Cas 605** Mrs. Beers obtained an order against Dr. Foakes for money owing to her. Dr. Foakes asked for time to pay the debt owing. Mrs. Beer agreed that she would take no further action in the matter provided that Foakes paid £500 immediately and the rest by half-yearly installments of £150. Dr Foakes paid his debt as agreed. Mrs. Foakes later sued him for interest that accrued as a result of part payment arrangement made. The House of Lords held that Mrs. Beer was entitled to the £360 interest which had accrued. Foakes had not provided any consideration and so Mrs. Beer was able to successfully claim the payment of the interest from Dr. Foakes.

In **Re Selectmove [1995] 2 All ER 531**, Selectmove owed arrears of tax to the Inland Revenue. There was a meeting at which Selectmove proposed to pay all future taxes. Selectmove was advised that the proposal had to be approved by supervisors who would get back to them. The Inland Revenue proceeded to liquidate Selectmove as they were unable to pay their debts. Selectmove sought to rely upon the agreement made at the meeting held earlier.

The Court of Appeal dismissed the defence on the grounds that (i) it is not good consideration to make a promise to pay a sum which the debtor was already bound to pay; (ii) any promise made by the agents of the Collector of Taxes was made without the relevant authority as the agents are not the final decision makers.

EXCEPTIONS TO THE RULE

Pinnel's case have already provided some exceptions. However there are others at common law and in equity.

(a) PART-PAYMENT OF THE DEBT BY A THIRD PARTY

Where the part-payment is made by a third party on condition that the debtor is released from the obligation to pay the full amount, a promise by the creditor to accept a smaller sum in full satisfaction will be binding on a creditor.

Hirachand Punamchand v Temple [1911] 2 KB 330 - A money lender accepted in full settlement, a smaller sum paid by a father for a debt owed by his son. Later the money lender sued for the balance. It was held that the part-payment was valid consideration, and that to allow the moneylender's claim would be a fraud on the father.

(b) COMPOSITION AGREEMENTS

This is an agreement between several creditors and a debtor in which creditors agree to accept a reduced sum in full and final settlement of an obligation. In instances like these, the creditor is forbidden by the court to renege on his agreement despite the absence of consideration and to pursue the debtor for the difference in payment. In **Wood v Robarts (1818)** it was determined that to allow individual creditor to claim the balance would amount to a fraud on the other creditors who had all agreed to take a percentage of debt owing. In other words, having entered and agreed to a composite agreement, a creditor is estopped from suing a debtor for his outstanding sum.

(c) PROMISSORY ESTOPPEL

Promissory estoppel is an instrument used by the court to prevent persons going back on their promises to an individual promisee who may not have provided consideration. It operates to prevent hardship that could be encountered where there is reliance on the rule in Pinnel's Case.

The operation of the doctrine can be seen in the cases outlined below:
(a) Hughes Case (1877) – A tenant was given notice by the landlord to effect repairs on a property and forfeiture would ensue where the tenant fails to do the necessary repairs. The landlord and tenant simultaneously entered into negotiations for the purchase of the property. The negotiation was unsuccessful. During the period of negotiations however, the tenant did not conduct the repairs as they believed the property would ultimately be theirs. The Landlord gave the tenant notice to quit for failure to carry out the repairs. The court held that the notice to repair was suspended during the period of negotiation.

(b) Central London Properties v High Trees (1947) - The plaintiffs granted a long term lease on a block of apartments at an annual rate of £2500. The 1939 war erupted and the defendants could not get enough tenants. In 1940 the plaintiffs agreed in writing to reduce the rent to £1250. When the war ended in 1945 all the flats were occupied and the Plaintiffs sued to recover the arrears of rent.

Denning J held that they were entitled to recover money as at the end of the war as their promise to accept only half was intended to apply during war conditions. The Ps were restricted from going back on their promise and could not claim the full rent on the original contract for 1940-45. Notwithstanding the fact that the Ds did not provide consideration for the Ps' promise to accept half rent, this promise was intended to be binding and was acted on by the Ds. He indicated that had the Ps sued for the arrears from 1940-45, the 1940 agreement would have caused their claim to fail.

(c) Tool Metal Manufacturing v Tungsten [1955] 1 WLR 761 - Tungsten had been in breach of a patent right held by TMM. When TMM heard of this they agreed that all infringements be waived and royalty and compensation was agreed. The payments were onerous for Tungsten and during war times a further agreement was reached to waive the 'compensation' payments. TMM later insisted on these compensation payments. It was held by the court that the compensation agreement was payable when the war ended. Equity prevented TMM from going back on their promise.

It should be obvious by now that promissory estoppel generally places a pause on legal rights rather than extinguish them. However, because the doctrine is applied at the discretion of the court, where periodic payments have been reduced because of extenuating circumstances promissory estoppel can be used to extinguish legal rights.

What should also be seen in the abovementioned cases is that if a person assures another that he will not insist on his legal entitlement under a contract and the assurance is acted upon the authorities indicate that the law will require the assurance to be honoured although consideration was not supplied.

REQUIREMENTS FOR PROMISSORY ESTOPPEL

There are some elements that must be in place for this doctrine to take effect:

(a) EXISTING CONTRACTUAL RELATIONSHIP

An existing contractual or a pre existing legal relationship is one of the circumstance that will be relied on by the court in making a decision for the use of promissory estoppel. In **Combe v Combe** a husband promised to make maintenance payments to his estranged wife but failed to do so. The wife brought an action to enforce the promise invoking promissory estoppel and it was held that her action has to fail as there was no pre-existing agreement which was later modified by a promise. The wife sought to use promissory estoppel as sword and not a shield. Where for example, she had undertaken an expense for her husband and he understood that he has engaged in a legal relationship with her and make that same promise to pay her maintenance payment, he may have been bound and she could rely on promissory estoppel as a shield.

(b) PROMISE MADE BY PROMISOR

The promisor must be clear that his legal rights under a contract are suspended and will not be enforced.

(c) RELIANCE

The promisee must have relied on the promisor's undertaking not to go back on his promise. It is enough, according to the authorities that the promisee relied on a promise to his detriment or he altered his standing in life in some way which is not necessarily detrimental. The case of **Ajayi v Briscoe [1964] 1 WLR 1326**, and **Alan Co Ltd v El Nasr Export & Import Co [1972] 2 QB 189** are instructive.

(d) INEQUITABLE TO GO BACK ON PROMISE

The promisor is bound by the laws of equity and as such it may be unfair for the promisor to go back on his promise except where he was coerced or unduly influenced to make a decision. However if the promisor was forced to make a decision it will not be inequitable to go back on that promise.

D & C Builders v Rees [1965] 2 QB 617 – The plaintiff had completed some work for the defendant but was never paid despite making several requests. The defendants eventually made an offer to settle the debt by offering to pay a smaller amount. As the company was struggling financially, they were compelled to accept the lower sum in final settlement of the debt. They later sued for the remainder of the money owing. The Court of Appeal held that the company was entitled to succeed. Lord Denning was of the view that it was not inequitable for the creditors to go back on their word and claim the balance as the debtor had acted inequitably by exerting improper pressure.

(e) A SHIELD OR A SWORD?

The doctrine of promissory estoppel is an equitable one and thus can only be granted by the court. The doctrine generally can only be used "as a shield and not a sword". In other words, the doctrine could not be used to raise a cause of action and is used as a defence. The general position has been doubted by Templeman J in **Re Wyven Developments [1974] 1 WLR 1097** and Lord Denning in **Evenden v Guildford City AFC [1975] QB 917** who believed that the doctrine can be used as a right.

(f) SUSPENSION OF RIGHTS

The doctrine generally operates to suspend rights previously agreed to in a contract or consequent on a legal relationship but which can be reinstated by giving reasonable notice or by changes in conditions.

In order to decide whether an agreement is suspensive or not, the context of the decision has to be looked at. If it was intended to be permanent, then equity will intervene to ensure that what ought to be done is done and prevent the promisor from going back on his word. If it is intended to be temporary, then the act of reasonable notice should see the promisor enjoying his strict legal or common law rights under the agreement.

ACTIVITY PAGE

1. With reference to at least one decided case explain 'consideration'
2. Collin asks David, his brother, to start his truck each morning while he is away in Japan sourcing another truck and some parts. He is also to wash the truck every day. Collin tells David that he will compensate him when he gets back. Collin returns but refuses to pay David the money promised.

With reference to at least one decided case, advise David whether he is entitled to the money from Collin.

3. Terry is Norman's tenant. Terry undertakes repair of his flat, fixing the windows and painting the verandah. Terry later sends Norman a bill for $12,000. Norman writes IOU on the bill and gives it back to Terry. He then refuses to pay, telling Terry that his lawyer advises him that he is not liable for past consideration.

(a) Explain what is meant by the term "past consideration"
(b) Discuss whether Terry can insist upon payment of the $12,000

4. Explain the doctrine of "promissory estoppel" and its relevance in contractual relations.

Chapter 5

CAPACITY

Contractual capacity is that legal ability to enter into a contract. The general rule is that any person is competent to be bound to any contract that he enters into with the intention to be bound as providing there was no force or coercion. There are exceptions to this rule in the case of minors and the mentally incompetent as well as Corporations.

Minors

Minors are generally persons under the age of 18. The general principle is that where there is a contract between a minor and an adult, the minor will not be bound. The minor, however, may, after attaining his majority, ratify the contract by an act confirming the promise he made while he was a minor. The act of ratification requires no consideration.

There are three exceptions to the above mentioned general position:

(1) Food, clothing, lodging, education or training in a trade and essential services are classified as "necessaries" and are things without which a minor cannot reasonably exist. A minor is bound to pay for these necessaries supplied to him under a contract. What is regarded as necessary for the minor residing in a stately home may be unnecessary for the resident of a council flat. This type of identification of where the minor lives or what he is used to is known as his condition in life. In other words, the "condition of life" of the minor means his social status and his wealth.

Whatever the minor's status, the goods must be suitable to his actual requirements and so where he already has enough fancy waistcoats, more of the same cannot be necessary: **Nash v. Inman [1908] 2 KB 1, CA**.

If goods are not yet delivered the minor is not bound. However, where necessaries are sold and delivered to a minor he must pay a reasonable price. The 'necessaries' must be goods suitable to the 'condition of life' of such minor and to his actual requirements at the time of sale and delivery. It therefore means that the seller or adult contracting with a minor should ensure that the item of sale is a "necessary" at the time of sale and delivery.

A contract found to be one for necessaries may still be struck down as being too onerous on the minor. **Fawcett v. Smethurst (1914) 84 LJKB 473**, (Atkin J).

(2) Beneficial contracts of service. A minor benefits from being able to obtain employment. To obtain such employment would be difficult where he cannot enter into a binding agreement. Again, the contract cannot be too onerous on the minor. Also, contracts enabling a minor to pursue a career as a "professional boxer" and as "an author" have been held to be binding as being for their benefit.

(3) Entering into permanent obligations with periodic payments attached. When a minor enters into a contract for a lease or purchase of shares in a company, with the exception of a loan, for example, he is bound by these transactions. However, he may repudiate the contract at any time during his minor years or during a reasonable time after he reaches majority. Where he does not repudiate during a reasonable time, the transaction may be affirmed and the minor bound. The minor may not be able to recover money which he has already paid unless there has been a total failure of consideration, that is, he did not derive any benefit from the transaction. **Steinberg v. Scala Ltd [1923] 2 Ch 452, CA.**

Restitution by a minor

Where a minor secures property by way of a contract which is later found to be unenforceable against him, the adult may suffer an injustice. This is so as the adult can neither sue for the price nor get the property back even where the minor has lied about his age. No action in tort can be brought against the minor as this would be enabling the contract to be enforced against him albeit via another route. The court allows a limited measure of remedy to the adult plaintiff.

(1) Where a contract is found to be unenforceable against a defendant because he was a minor when it was made, the court may, exercise its discretion and to the extent that it is just and equitable to do so, require the defendant minor to transfer to the plaintiff any property acquired by the defendant under the contract or any property representing it.

This may help the plaintiff where the property is identifiable but where the plaintiff has loaned the money it will usually not be. (This point confirms the fact that minors may not be able to access loans). As it relates to a loan, the plaintiff will only be able to recover in equity if he is able to prove that he loaned the money for the express purpose of enabling the minor to buy necessaries. **Lewis v Alleyne (1888) 4 TLR 560.**

(2) A guarantee of a minor's contract is not unenforceable against the guarantor merely because the contract made by the minor is unenforceable against him on the ground that he is a minor. So that where a minor accesses a loan with the help of a guarantor, the guarantor may be liable. Where there is any misrepresentation on the part of the minor in inducing the guarantor, the guarantor may not be bound.

CAPACITY AND THE INSANE PERSON

A contract while binding on the other party to the contract will only be voidable at the instance of the mentally ill where his property is subject to the control of the court. The explanation for this rule is evident. If the court has control of the property, then the court's permission will be needed to dispose of or deal with the property.

Mental incapacity is not a ground for the setting aside of a contract or for the return of benefits conferred under a contract, unless the incapacity is known to the other party to the contract where the property is not subject to the control of the court. Where the other party to the contract does not know of the incapacity of his contracting party, the contract cannot be set aside, unless the contract is of such a nature as to attract the equitable jurisdiction to relieve against unconscionable bargains between two persons of sound mind.

The requirement that the other party be aware of the incapacity of a mental or insane person should be contrasted with the case of minors, where there is no such requirement that the other party be aware of the minority and, indeed, the minor may be relieved even when he has misrepresented his age.

Note: drunkenness is treated in the same way as mental incapacity, so that the contract may only be set aside by the drunken party where the drunkenness prevented him from understanding the transaction and the other party to the contract knew of his capacity.

ACTIVITY PAGE

Javon, a boy aged 15, is a well-known footballer. He and his father, Alton, regularly visit Gypsie Sports and Gym to purchase football shoes. Javon goes by himself to Gypsie's and takes two pairs of football shoes, on credit. He later refuses to pay, arguing that the contract is unenforceable against him because he is a minor.

(a) Explain the importance of capacity in the formation of a contract
(b) Can Gypsie's Sports and Gym enforce the contract against Javon? Give reasons for your answer.
(c) Javon accepts a scholarship from Inter Sports and agrees that he will appear in their advertisement for two years. He abandons the agreement when the sponsor of the Annual School competition offers him a better scholarship. Inter Sports wishes to enforce the contract but Javon argues that it is unenforceable because he is a minor. Can Inter Sports enforce the contract against Javon? Give reasons for your answer.

Chapter 6

PRIVITY OF CONTRACT

Privity is a doctrine in contract law which provides that a contract cannot confer rights or obligations on a person who is not a party to the contract. The principle is that only parties to contracts should be able to sue to enforce their rights or claim damages under a contract. However, the doctrine has consistently imposed hardship on third parties for whose benefit a contract was made. In **Dunlop v Selfridge [1915] AC 847** - the plaintiffs sold tyres to Dew & Co, wholesale distributors, on terms that Dew would obtain an undertaking from retailers that they should not sell below the plaintiff's list price. Dew sold some of the tyres to the defendants, who retailed them below the list price. The plaintiffs sought an injunction and damages. The action failed because although there was a contract between the defendants and Dew, the plaintiffs were not a party to it and "only a person who is a party to a contract can sue on it" (per Lord Haldane).

History

Prior to 1833 there existed decisions in English Law allowing provisions of a contract to be enforced by persons not party to it, usually relatives of a promisee. The doctrine of privity emerged alongside the doctrine of consideration, the rules of which state that consideration must move from the promisee. That is to say that if nothing is given for the promise of something to be given in return, that promise is not legally binding unless promised as a deed. 1833 saw the case of **Price v. Easton**, where a contract was made for work to be done in exchange for payment to a third party.

When the third party attempted to sue for the payment, he was held to be not privy to the contract, and so his claim failed. This was fully linked to the doctrine of consideration, and established as such, with the more famous case of **Tweddle v. Atkinson**. In this case the plaintiff was unable to sue the executor of his father-in-law, who had promised to the plaintiff's father to make payment to the plaintiff, because he had not provided any consideration to the contract.

Privity of Contract played a key role in the development of negligence as well. In the first case of **Winterbottom v. Wright (1842),** Winterbottom, sued the manufacturer of a faulty wagon for injuries he sustained as a postman. The courts however decided that there was no privity of contract between manufacturer and consumer. **Donoghue v Stevenson** appears to be the alternative course of remedy in these circumstances. This alternative relieve only became available in 1932 when this case was decided.

Exceptions:

Common law exceptions

There are exceptions to the general rule, allowing rights to third parties and some impositions of obligations. These are:

i. Where there is a separate or collateral contract between the third party and one of the contracting parties. An example of this situation can be seen in the case of **Shanklin Pier Ltd v Detel Products Ltd [1951] 2KB 854.** Paint manufactured by the defendants was purchased by the contractors on the instructions of the claimant.

The contract to purchase the paint was actually made between the contractors and the defendants but a representation was made by the defendant to the claimants that the paint would last for seven years. The paint only lasted three months. It was held that the claimants were entitled to bring an action for breach of contract against the defendants on the ground that there was a collateral contract between them to the effect that the paint would last for seven years, the consideration for which was the instruction given by the claimants to their contractors to order the paint from the defendants.

ii. The beneficiary of a trust may sue the trustee to carry out the contract
iii. Restrictive covenants on land are imposed upon subsequent purchasers if the covenant benefits neighbouring land as these covenants run with the land.
iv. Where assignments under an agency arrangement is permitted a third party enjoys a benefit.
v. A third party may claim under an insurance policy made for their benefit, even though that party did not pay the premiums.

Statutory exceptions

The Contracts (Rights of Third Parties) Act 1999 although not a Caribbean legislation gives a good idea of how statute treats with the issue of third party rights. The Act states:

(1) *Subject to the provisions of this Act, a person who is not a party to a contract (a "third party") may in his own right enforce a term of the contract if*

(a) *the contract expressly provides that he may, or*
(b) *subject to subsection (2), the term purports to confer a benefit on him.*

(2) *Subsection (1)(b) does not apply if on a proper construction of the contract it appears that the parties did not intend the term to be enforceable by the third party.*

The point being made in the Act is that a person who is named as a third party in the contract as a person entitled to enforce the contract or a person receiving a benefit from the contract may enforce the contract unless it appears that the parties to the contract intended otherwise.

The Act ensures that the intentions of the contracting parties be observed. This is illustrated in **Beswick v Beswick** where the only reason why Mr.

Beswick and his nephew contracted was for the benefit of Mrs. Beswick. Under the Act Mrs. Beswick would be able to enforce the performance of the contract in her own right. Therefore, the Act obeyed the intentions of the parties.

ACTIVITY SHEET

1. How does the Contracts (Rights of Third Parties) Act 1999 confer benefits on a third party? How can this legislation be used to provide guidance on improving this area of law in your jurisdiction?
2. Explain the relationship between the doctrine of privity and the rule that consideration must move from the promisee.
3. Nadine and Erica go out for a meal at The Food Stop restaurant. Nadine pays for the meal. Erica's meal is inedible. What remedies are available to Nadine? If Nadine refuses to sue, could Erica sue?
4. When can the contracting parties deprive the third party of his right to enforce the terms of the contract?
5. Have a look at **Price v Easton (1833) 4 B & Ad 433** and explain how you think it would have been decided in light of the Contracts (Rights of Third Parties) Act, 1999.

Chapter 7

TERMS OF CONTRACT

What the parties said or wrote in the establishing of a contract will assist in determining the terms of a contract. The remedy which a plaintiff seeks when there is the issue of a breach or discrepancy in the contractual experience will hinge on whether a statement made during negotiations is a representation or a term.

A representation is a statement of fact made by one party which induces the other to enter into the contract. If it turns out to be incorrect the innocent party may sue for misrepresentation.

A term is a provision that forms part of a contract. It creates obligations and breach of a term of the contract entitles the injured party to claim damages and repudiate the contract in instances where what was bargained for is significantly different.

Note however that where a statement is not a term of the principal contract, it is possible that it may be enforced as a collateral contract. A collateral contract (side contract) can be in writing or oral between the original parties or between a third party and an original party, before or at the same time the main contract is made.

Intention is the guide that the courts utilize in determining whether a statement is a term or a representation. **Heilbut, Symons & Co v Buckleton [1913] AC 30**. There are four factors that the courts will rely on in order to find intention and make a determination on a statement as a term or representation:

(a) TIMING

There has to be a nexus between the making of the statement and the conclusion of the contract. It therefore means that the shorter the interval between these two events, the more likely will the statement be construed as a term of the contract.

Routledge v McKay [1954] 1 WLR 615 -The plaintiff negotiated with the defendant for the sale of a motorcycle which the defendant represented to be a 1942 model. This motor cycle was in fact an older model. The contract was executed approximately one week later with no further mention of the model of the motorcycle. The court considered the time frame between the negotiation and the contract and determined that the year of the vehicle was a representation and not a contractual term as it was never brought up during signing.

Schawel v Reade [1913] 2 IR 64 – The plaintiff entered into an agreement to purchase a horse for stud purposes. The defendant indicated that the horse was perfectly sound for the purpose and gave the plaintiff a guarantee that he would disclose whether anything was awry with the horse. The price was negotiated and agreed and the plaintiff bought the horse. The horse in fact had a hereditary eye disease and could not be used as a stud. The statement made by the defendant that the horse was "perfectly sound" was held to be a term of the contract. The defendant owner of the horse also had special knowledge and could therefore be easily seen as misrepresenting the facts.

(b) IMPORTANCE OF THE STATEMENT

Where it can be proven that the injured party would not have entered the contract but for the statement in issue, the court may determine the statement to be a term of the contract.

Bannerman v White (1861) CB (NS) 844 - Before purchasing hops and during the negotiations, the buyer asked whether sulphur had been used in its cultivation. He made this inquiry because where sulphur was used, he would not proceed with the purchase. On the assurance of the seller that there was no sulphur involved, the buyer proceeded. This assurance was of such importance that without it, the buyer would not have contracted and the court determined that it was a condition of the contract.

Couchman v Hill [1947] 1 All ER 103 - "All lots must be taken subject to all faults or errors of description (if any), and no compensation will be paid for the same." By No 3 of the conditions of sale: "The lots are sold with all faults, imperfections, and errors of description, the auctioneers not being responsible for the correct description, genuineness, or authenticity of, or any fault or defect in, any lot, and giving no warranty whatever." The plaintiff bought "a red and white heifer" at an auction sale belonging to the defendant on the basis of the aforementioned description in a catalogue. The catalogue further described the heifer as "unserved". The plaintiff visited the ring where the heifer was kept before the sale and at that point asked whether the heifers were "unserved". He was told they were unserved.

After the purchase the heifer was found to be with calf which obviously meant she was "served". It died after a few weeks from a miscarriage as it was too young for carrying a calf. The plaintiff brought an action for breach of a warranty and it was held that the conditions of sale mentioned in the catalogue protected the defendant as well as the auctioneer in respect of misstatements and misdescriptions in the catalogue. However, the court determined that representations made before the sale assisted in the formation of a contract and therefore information relevant to the heifer being "unserved" was in fact a condition which, on its breach, the plaintiff was entitled to treat as a warranty and recover the damages claimed.

(c) REDUCTION OF TERMS TO WRITING

Where a statement was made but was not incorporated in a later written contract, the inference to be drawn is that the parties did not intend the statement to be a contractual term. Remember that the court will consider the importance of the statement to the formation of the contract. See the facts of **Routledge v McKay [1954] 1 WLR 615** already mentioned above where it was held on the point of whether the discussions was a representation or a term, that what the parties intended to agree on was recorded in the written agreement, and that it would be inconsistent with the written agreement to hold that there was an intention to make the prior statement a contractual term.

Birch v Paramount Estates (1956) 167 - The Court of Appeal regarded a statement as a term that formed the basis of the contract when the defendants with special knowledge made a statement about the quality of a house and the contract, when reduced to writing, made no reference to the statement. The defendants were liable.

(d) SPECIAL KNOWLEDGE/SKILLS

If the maker of the statement has superior knowledge, the court will construe statements made by him to be a term of the contract.

Harling v Eddy [1951] 2 KB 739 - A causal factor that led the Court of Appeal to decide whether a statement was a term of the contract was that the vendors were in a special position to know of the heifer's condition where the vendors of a heifer represented that there was nothing wrong with the animal but, in fact, it had tuberculosis from which it died within three months of the sale.

Oscar Chess v Williams [1957] 1 All ER 325 - A 1948 second hand Morris car was purchased and owned by Mrs Williams. 1948 was reflected on the documents for the car. Her son, one year later traded in the car for credit on a brand new Hillman Minx he was purchasing from Oscar Chess. The son relied on the documents for the car that his mother had.

Oscar Chess consequently gave him £290 credit towards his purchase. Some months later Oscar Chess Ltd contacted the manufacturer and discovered that the Morris was in fact a 1939 model and so the value was worth less. An action was brought against Williams for breach of a fundamental term of a contract claiming damages. The court held that the statement relevant to the age of the car was a mere representation as Mrs Williams was inexperienced on the topics of age and model of vehicles and therefore could not be held to an expert standard.

The facts and principle of **Dick Bentley Productions v Harold Smith Motors [1965] 2 All ER 65** are also instructive - Dick Bentley asked the defendant to search for a very good car in the high end market. The defendant identified a Bentley and recommended it to the claimant representing that the car had been owned by a German elitist and has been reconditioned with a replacement engine and gearbox and had only done 20,000 miles since the replacement. Mr Bentley Purchased the car on the basis of the defendant's recommendation and which later developed faults. Although the defendant had done some repair to the car under the warranty, the faults persisted and it was discovered that the car had clocked over 100,000 miles after the repairs and servicing of the vehicle.

The question for the court was whether the statement amounted to a term in which case damages would be payable for breach of contract, or whether the statement was a representation, in which case no damages would be payable since it was an innocent misrepresentation and the claimant has also lost his right to rescind due to lapse of time. The court held that the statement was a term of the contractual agreement and that Mr Smith as a car dealer had greater expertise and as such the claimant relied upon that expertise and was entitled to damages.

CONDITIONS AND WARRANTIES

Terms are usually divided into two categories: conditions and warranties.

(a) CONDITIONS

A condition is a very important term of the contract. It is often said to go to the core of the contract. It is the essence on which the contract hinges and without which the contract could not have survived. The injured party will be entitled to repudiate the contract and claim damages if a contract is breached. The injured party may also choose to affirm the contract. That is, he may choose to continue the performance of the terms of the contract despite the breach, and recover damages instead.

Poussard v Spiers (1876) 1 QBD 410 – The plaintiff Poussard fell ill after being engaged in a three months contract to make an appearance at an operetta in London. As a result of the plaintiff's illness which was brief, the producers had to recruit another singer. They refused to take the plaintiff back after she felt better.

As there was no certainty about when the plaintiff, being seriously ill would get better, it was determined by the court that there would be no liability to the defendant as it would be unreasonable to reschedule the opening night as that was a condition of the contract. Poussard's contract was therefore rescinded.

(b) WARRANTIES

A warranty is a less significant term and does not go to the core of the contract. It is not the basis on which the contract is built unlike a condition. A breach of warranty will only give the injured party the right to claim damages, he cannot repudiate the contract because it has not been severely compromised and can therefore survive a breach.

Bettini v Gye (1876) 1 QBD 183 – After entering into a six month contract to perform at an opera house Bettini fell very ill. His illness was not of a serious nature and had taken place during the rehearsal period before the contract was due to start. His contract was terminated and another singer hired. It was held by the court that being sick during rehearsals was a breach of warranty and therefore the contract should not have been terminated.

(c) INTERMEDIATE TERMS

Sometimes it is only after looking at the consequences of the breach that a term can truly be labeled as a condition or a warranty. So that, if the consequence of a breach is that the contract is crippled, then the intermediate term is labeled a condition. However, where the breach involves minor loss, the injured party's remedies will be restricted to damages and so will be aptly labeled warranty. These intermediate terms which must wait to be determined by the court are known as innominate terms.

Hong Kong Fir Shipping Co v Kawasaki Kisen Kaisha [1962] 1 All ER 474 – The defendants hired a ship for a two year period under the condition that it would be seaworthy for the period. In fact, the engine developed trouble for a period of 20 weeks. The defendants terminated the contract and the claimants brought an action against them for wrongful termination claiming that seaworthiness was not a condition but was in fact a warranty. The court introduced the concept of innominate or intermediate term approach where it sought to look at the effect of the breach and where it is substantial, it would be a condition. Since the mechanical issues lasted 20 weeks out of a two year contractual arrangement, it was not substantial and thus was not a condition.

Have a look also at **Mihalis Angelos [1971] 1 QB 164** and **Hansa Nord [1976] QB 44**

IMPLIED TERMS

Most contracts make provisions by way of express terms. However, there may be circumstances where terms will have to be implied by the courts to give business efficacy to a contract or simply to make the contract fair and workable.

(a) TERMS IMPLIED BY CUSTOM

Customs or traditions may have determined what terms are negotiated or rather, not negotiated. The parties may have taken it for granted that the particular term is covered by customs or tradition.

Hutton v Warren (1836) 1 M&W 466 – A landlord gave a tenant six months to quit the land while insisting that the tenant continue to plant on the land during the notice period as per the customs of the times. The tenant was able to sue successfully relying on the same rules of custom that entitled him to a fair allowance for the seeds and labour he used on the land.

(b) TERMS IMPLIED BY THE COURT

(i) Intention of the Parties

The court will supply a term in the interests of 'business efficacy' so that the contract makes commercial sense. The courts will do this by looking at the intentions of the parties to the contract. The intentions of the parties may have been overlooked or they may not have been clearly stated.

The Moorcock (1889) 14 PD 64 - The owner of a wharf was found to be in breach when he negligently allowed The Moorcock to run aground at his wharf. The court held that there was an implied undertaking on the part of the wharf owner that the place was reasonably safe and that undertaking was breached.

The 'officious bystander' test was discussed in the **Shirlaw v Southern Foundries [1940] AC 701** in which it was explained that if while the parties were making their contract, an officious bystander were to suggest some express provision, they would both reply, "oh, of course." So that in the Moorcock case if the owner of the ship had asked the owner of the wharf if the area is safe in the presence of an officious bystander, the latter would have heard "of course" in response to the question.

Wilson v Best Travel [1993] 1 All ER 353 - Glass which conforms to Greek safety standard but not British standard injured the claimant while on vacation in Greece when he fell through a patio door. The claimant brought an action against the travel agent asking for a term to be implied as a matter of law, that all accommodation offered by the defendant should conform to British safety standards. It was held that the court could not imply a term as whilst this was a contract of a defined type, it was not reasonable for the travel agency to ensure that all accommodation offered, no matter where in the world, conformed with British safety standards.

(ii) Relationship between the parties/Terms Implied by Law

In certain relationships and contracts the law seeks to impose a model or standardised set of terms as a form of regulation. Such terms arising from the relationship between the parties will be implied as of law.

Liverpool City Council v Irwin [1976] 2 All ER 39 - The defendant was a tenant in a set of housing owned by the Liverpool City Council. The common areas had fallen into disrepair and the tenants decided to withhold rent and the council sought to evict the tenants for non payment of rent. The defendant counter sued for failing to execute repairs on the property. The lease did not expressly compel the council to effect repairs and so the tenant sought the court's assistance in implying a term into the contract regarding repair to the common areas. The court granted the defendant's request outlining in ratio that the landlord has an obligation to take reasonable care in ensuring repairs are done to the common areas of the units.

(c) TERMS IMPLIED BY STATUTE

It is now clear that while a contract is made on the basis of express terms there are instances when terms have to be implied in order to ensure the contract is fair and even effective. Legislations are relied on to give contracts business efficacy as well. The following are just some pieces of statute that you will encounter throughout your studies.

- Sections 12, 13, 14 and 15 of the Sale of Goods Act 1979;
- Sections 13, 14 and 15 of the Supply of Goods and Services Act 1982; and
- the relevant provisions of the Sale and Supply of Goods Act 1994.

EXCLUSION CLAUSES

Exclusion clauses are clauses which are usually written down and which outline that one party to the contract will not be responsible for certain happenings or that liability will be limited. For example, if you go to a theme park, it is common for the contract to say that the theme park owner will not be responsible if you are injured while taking part in the various activities. If you arrange to park your car at the airport for a fee, the management will often seek to include in the contract a provision that they will not be responsible for damage to your vehicle, or theft of goods from it, while it is in the car park.

However, the party may only rely on such a clause if:

(a) It has been included into the contract
(b) The loss in question was foreseeable
(c) Its validity can be tested under the Unfair Contract Terms Act 1977 and the Unfair Terms in Consumer Contracts Regulations 1999

(a) INCORPORATION

An exclusion clause can be incorporated in the contract by signature, by notice, or by a course of dealing. However, the person wishing to rely on the exclusion clause must show that it was incorporated into the contract as one of its terms.

> ✓ *Now it is time to review your notes on privity of contract.*

(i) SIGNED DOCUMENTS

We own our signatures and when we sign a document of contract that contains an exclusion clause we are bound by it. This is the case whether or not we read or understood what we signed.

L'Estrange v Graucob [1934] 2 KB 394 – L'Estrange signed an order form for the purchase of a cigarette vending machine in her shop. Included in the contract is the following clause *'Any express or implied, condition, statement of warranty, statutory or otherwise is expressly excluded'*. The machine malfunctioned within a very short period and the claimant sought to repudiate her contract with the defendant under the Sale of Goods Act for not being of merchantable quality. By signing the document she was obliged to observe the contract whether she red same or not and as such her claim was unsuccessful. However, the document though signed may become voidable where there is coercion, fraud or undue influence. The following case illustrates the point:

Curtis v Chemical Cleaning Co [1951] 1 KB 805 - After being told that the cleaners are exempt from liability for damage to "beads and sequins", the plaintiff signed a piece of paper that represented a receipt and deposited her wedding dress. When she returned, her dress was damaged extensively and discovered that the cleaners, according to the receipt she signed, were not liable for "any damage howsoever caused". As the extent of the cleaner's liability was misrepresented by the defendant's assistant, the defendant was not able to relay on the exemption clause.

(ii) UNSIGNED DOCUMENTS

Frequently we purchase tickets that have exclusion clauses contained in them. There may also be notices seen when we enter a factory or even a hotel. On these occasions, reasonable notice of the existence of the exclusion clause should be given. For this requirement to be satisfied:

(A) The clause must be contained in a contractual document that the reasonable person would assume to contain contractual terms, and not in a document which merely acknowledges payment such as a receipt.

Parker v SE Railway Co (1877) 2 CPD 416 – The plaintiff's bag went missing from a storage area at a train station. He was given a ticket for the use of the said area which instructed him to "see back". On the back of the ticket was the following clause "The company will not be responsible for any package exceeding the value of £10." The plaintiff claimed £24 10s as the value of his bag, and the company pleaded the limitation clause on the back of the ticket in defence. Mellish LJ in the Court of Appeal gave the following opinion:

a. If the plaintiff had no way of seeing or knowing that there were any terms or writings on the ticket he is not bound;
b. If the plaintiff knew or has reason to believe that the ticket had conditions on it then he is bound by the conditions;
c. If the plaintiff did not know that the writings on the back of the ticket included conditions he will be bound;
d. if the delivering of the ticket to him in such a manner that he could see there was writing upon it, was reasonable notice that the writing contained conditions.

Chapelton v Barry UDC [1940] – The plaintiff leased chairs from the defendants. The chairs were stored and members of the public who wished to use them had to get tickets and retain them for inspection. Members of the public were able to access and use the chairs and await the inspector to collect the relevant fees which could be an hour later. On the back of these tickets were printed words purporting to exempt the council from liability but this was not previously read by the plaintiff before the chair was used. He was later injured when his deck chair collapsed. It was held by the court that the ticket was merely for the purpose of inspection, to prove that the chairs were paid for and as such the clause was ineffective.

(B) The existence of the exclusion clause should not be a secret and must be brought to the attention of the other party before or at the time the contract is entered into.

Olley v Marlborough Court [1949] 1 KB 532 - Strangers entered the hotel room of the plaintiff and stole her mink coat. The hotel sought to rely on a notice on the back of the room door that reads *"the proprietors will not hold themselves responsible for articles lost or stolen unless handed to the manageress for safe custody."* As the contract was executed in the lobby of the hotel and before the plaintiff had gone to the room and before being given an opportunity to see the notice the Court of Appeal held that the notice was not incorporated in the contract between the proprietors and the guest.

(C) Actual notice is not a requirement, however, reasonable notice of the clause is a very important requirement.

Thompson v LMS Railway [1930] 1 KB 41 – The plaintiff was not successful in a suit she brought against the defendant when, not being able to read, she gave her niece money to purchase an excursion ticket. On the face of the ticket was printed "Excursion, For Conditions see back"; and on the back, "Issued subject to the conditions and regulations in the company's time-tables and notices and excursion and other bills." Lord Hanworth MR in the Court of Appeal said that anyone who took the ticket was conscious that there were some conditions and as such, it was irrelevant that the plaintiff could not read.

(iii) INCORPORATION THROUGH PREVIOUS DEALINGS

An exclusion clause may be incorporated where there has been a previous consistent course of dealing between the parties on the same terms, even where there has been insufficient notice.

McCutcheon v MacBrayne [1964] 1 WLR 125 - Exclusion clause was held not to be incorporated as they were contained in paragraphs of small print inside and outside a ferry booking office and in a 'risk note' which passengers sometimes signed. There was no consistency in dealing with passengers and so the clauses could not be relied on.

Hollier v Rambler Motors [1972] 2 AB 71 - The defendant sought to rely on an exclusion clause which excluded them from liability for damage caused by fire. Their clients rarely received notice of this clause. The plaintiff in this instance visited the garage at least annually over a five year period and notice was also infrequently given. On this occasion nothing was signed and the plaintiff's car was badly damaged in a fire. It was held that there was no regular course of dealing, therefore the defendants were liable. The court referred to **Hardwick Game Farm v Suffolk Agricultural Poultry Producers Association (1969)** where no course of dealing could be established when only one hundred notices were given over a three year period.

An exclusion clause may still become part of the contract through trade usage or custom, even if there is no course of dealing.

British Crane Hire v Ipswich Plant Hire [1974] QB 303 - By way of an oral contract that was arranged without discussing terms and conditions, the plaintiff delivered a crane on lease to the defendant. Before the defendants could sign a contract sent to them, the crane sank in water logged soil. The conditions in the said contract were standard ones used by the industry and which compels the hirer to pay all expenses relevant to the use of the crane. The court held that the terms became a part the contract because there was a common understanding between the parties and relying on industry practices was not relevant and so the defendants had to be liable

(iv) USING PRIVITY OF CONTRACT TO INCORPORATE A CLAUSE

Even where an exclusion clause purports to extend to a third party, the doctrine of privity does not allow third party to benefit. This is so as the third party was not a party to the contract. However, if the contract is made for the benefit of the third party or for the third party to benefit, then he may be able to sue.

Scruttons v Midland Silicones [1962] AC 446 - A contract to ship drums of chemicals between the shipping company/Carriers and the plaintiffs included a limitation clause in favour of the carrier of £179 per package. Through the negligence of the defendant stevedores the drum was damaged. The Stevedores were hired by the carriers for the purpose of unloading the ship. The plaintiffs brought a claim against the defendants in tort for the damage to the drum, which amounted to £593. The defendant stevedores claimed the protection of the limitation clause. The House of Lords held in favour of the plaintiffs. The defendants were not parties to the contract of carriage and so they could not take advantage of the limitation clause.

(v) COLLATERAL CONTRACTS

An exclusion having been incorporated in the main contract may not have been incorporated in a collateral contract.

Andrews v Hopkinson [1957] 1 QB 229 - "It's a good little bus. I would stake my life on it". This was the defendant's description of a car he had for sale in his garage. The plaintiff agreed to take it on hire-purchase and the defendant sold it to a finance company that made an agreement with the plaintiff. The plaintiff signed his delivery note having been satisfied with the condition of the car. He later had an accident because of the defectiveness of the vehicle but was prevented from suing the hire purchase company. He sued the defendant successfully as it was held that there was a collateral contract with the defendant on the basis of his statement that the car was in good condition.

(vi) THE BATTLE OF THE FORMS

Where contracts are made using standard forms that may also have terms incorporated in them, it is the last form that is exchanged that will stand, ie the terms of the last form will be binding on the parties. By way of example, if one party sends a form with terms of a potential contract and the second party accepts by sending a form with their own set of terms, then the contract is made on the second sets of terms.

b. FORESEEABILITY AND INTERPRETATION

Where a contract is breached and it has an exclusion clause that is incorporated, then the contract will have to be interpreted to determine whether the breach in question is covered by the clause. In order to exclude liability, the words have to be clear. There can be no ambiguity. The clause has to be constructed as per the rules outlined below:

CONTRA PROFERENTEM RULE

Where there is uncertainty as it relates to an exclusion clause, the court will interpret same in favour of the injured party to the contract. Further in order to exclude liability in the tort of negligence, the words of the clause must be unambiguous.

Baldry v Marshall [1925] 1 KB 260 - The plaintiff requested a car from the defendant for touring purposes. The plaintiff bought a Bugatti on the recommendation of the defendants. The contract which supported the sale incorporated an exclusion clause which excluded the defendant's liability for any "*guarantee or warranty, statutory or otherwise*". The plaintiff returned the car as it was unsuitable for touring and sued to recover the monies paid. The Court of Appeal held that the plaintiff made it clear that he needed a car for touring and that request being incorporated into the contract is a condition. Since the clause did not exclude liability for breach of a condition, the plaintiff was not bound by it.

White v John Warwick [1953] 1 WLR 1285 - The plaintiff entered into a contract for the hire of a bicycle subject to the exclusion clause which read "Nothing in this agreement shall render the owners liable for any personal injury". The plaintiff was injured when the saddle shifted and tilted forward. The Court of Appeal held that the ambiguous wording of the exclusion clause would effectively protect the defendants from their strict contractual liability, but it would not exempt them from liability in negligence.

THE MAIN PURPOSE RULE

This rule allows the court to strike out an exclusion clause where it offends the main purpose of the contract.

Glynn v Margetson [1893] AC 351 - The defendant Carriers entered into a contract to take oranges from Malaga to Liverpool under a contract which allowed the ship to call at any port in Europe or Africa. The ship went off the agreed route by approximately 350 miles to pick up additional cargo, a decision that caused the oranges to decompose. The House of Lords held, as the defendants attempted to rely on an exclusion clause that the main purpose of the contract was to deliver oranges in a good state to Liverpool. The carriers were held liable as the wide words of the clause could be disregarded and the ship could only make calls at ports along the way from Malaga to Liverpool.

Evans Ltd v Andrea Merzario Ltd [1976] 1 WLR 1078 – The defendant gave an oral guarantee that goods would be carried below deck so they would not be lost at sea. They were in fact placed above deck and were consequently washed overboard during a storm. The Court of Appeal held that there was a breach of the oral assurance that goods would be carried inside the ship and was a part of the contract. The exclusion clause could not be relied on.

THE DOCTRINE OF FUNDAMENTAL BREACH

In the past a fundamental breach could not be excluded or restricted in any circumstances as this would amount to giving with one hand and taking with the other. This became elevated to a rule of law.

However, the rule of law approach was rejected in **UGS Finance v National Mortgage Bank of Greece [1964] 1 Lloyd's Rep 446,** on the basis that it conflicted with freedom of contract and the intention of the parties. The question of whether a clause could exclude liability for a fundamental breach was held to be a question of construction.

The UGS case was unanimously approved by the House of Lords in the **Suisse Atlantique** case [1967] 1 AC 361, and **Photo Production Ltd v Securicor Transport [1980] AC 827.**

THE COURT'S INTERVENTION

The court tries to assist litigating parties by relying on the extent to which a particular term or clause is reasonable in excluding liability in negligence or contract. The court will also seek to restrict the extent to which liability

in a contract can be excluded by imposing specific prohibition on the reliance on the clause.
In determining whether the clause is a reasonable one, regard shall be had to s. 11 of the Unfair Contracts Terms Act, 1977 which reads as follows:

i. The term is required to be a fair and reasonable one to include in the contract.
ii. The burden is on the party seeking to enforce the term to show that it was fair and reasonable
iii. This is judged by all the circumstance which were known, or ought to have been known or in the contemplation of the parties
iv. Where the term is restricting rather than excluding liability regard is to be had to the resources of the party seeking to rely on the term and the availability of insurance.
v. The fairness and reasonableness is decided at the time the contract is entered - not with hindsight knowing of the events which in fact occurred

Subsection (3) of Section 11 in the Act declares that in relation to a notice (not being a notice having contractual effect), the requirement of reasonableness under this Act is that it should be fair and reasonable to allow reliance on it, having regard to all the circumstances obtaining when the liability arose or (but for the notice) would have arisen.

Subsection (4) states that where by reference to a contract term or notice a person seeks to restrict liability to a specified sum of money, and the question arises (under this or any other Act) whether the term or notice satisfies the requirement of reasonableness, regard shall be had in particular (but without prejudice to subsection (2) above in the case of contract terms) to:

(a) the resources which he could expect to be available to him for the purpose of meeting the liability should it arise; and
(b) how far it was open to him to cover himself by insurance.

ACTIVITY SHEET

1. Howard is an activist for consumers. He is unhappy about the numerous complaints he has been receiving from consumers about defective products they have purchased and unscrupulous workmen who provide sub-standard work. Many of these consumers find that when they seek redress the defendants rely on the "fine print" of exemption clauses in contracts signed to or accepted by the consumers.

Advise Howard on the effect of exemption or exclusion clauses on such contracts

2(a). Some terms cannot be classified as being "conditions" or "warranties". Using at least one relevant case to support your answer, discuss the court's approach in dealing with this issue.

2(b). Using relevant examples, explain the difference between a "term of a contract" and a "mere representation".

2(c). Distinguish between conditions and warranties and the impact on contract.

3. With reference to decided cases:

(a) Discuss the inclusion of exclusion clauses into contracts.

(b) Discuss how the courts make a determination on whether an exclusion clause covers a breach.

Chapter 8

MISREPRESENTATION

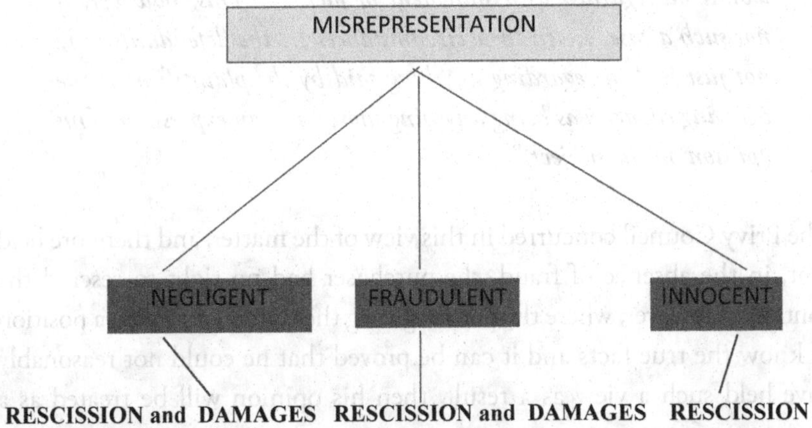

According to McKendrick "a misrepresentation is an unambiguous, false statement of fact (or possibly law) which is addressed to the party misled, which is material and which induces the contract". (2000, p. 267)

Where misrepresentation is found, the contract is generally voidable at the instance of the innocent party who then has the option to rescind and or claim damages.

FALSE STATEMENT OF FACT

In order to make out an action in misrepresentation, the statement that induced the contract must be a false statement and cannot be an opinion, statement of intention or law.

(a) STATEMENTS OF OPINION

Merely stating an opinion, though false, is not a misrepresentation.

Bisset v Wilkinson [1927] AC 177 - The plaintiff acquired land from the defendant based on representations that 2000 sheep could be contained on the land. The defendant had in fact not reared sheep before and had no experience in what capacity the land had. Both parties being inexperienced were unaware of this fact. In an action for misrepresentation, the trial judge said:

> *"In ordinary circumstances, any statement made by an owner who has been occupying his own farm as to its carrying capacity would be regarded as a statement of fact. ... This, however, is not such a case. ... In these circumstances ... the defendants were not justified in regarding anything said by the plaintiff as to the carrying capacity as being anything more than an expression of his opinion on the subject."*

The Privy Council concurred in this view of the matter, and therefore held that, in the absence of fraud, the purchaser had no right to rescind the contract. However, where the person giving the statement was in a position to know the true facts and it can be proved that he could not reasonably have held such a view as a result, then his opinion will be treated as a statement of fact.

Smith v Land & House Property Corp. (1884) 28 Ch D 7 - The plaintiff described his tenant who was a bankrupt as "a most desirable tenant" in order to sell his hotel. The defendant agreed to purchase the property on the basis of the statement but later changed his mind and was sued by the plaintiff for specific performance as they refused to complete the execution of the contract. It was held by the court that the plaintiff's statement was a statement of fact and not an opinion.

Some expressions of opinion are baseless talk. Thus, in **Dimmock v Hallet (1866) 2 Ch App 21**, it was held that unless one party was making statements in an expert capacity, the description of land as 'fertile and improvable' was held not to constitute a representation.

(b) STATEMENTS AS TO INTENTION

Unless the statement is incorporated into a contract, a statement though false made by a person as to what he intends to do in the future will generally not be found to be misrepresentation and thus will not be binding on the maker of the statement.

However, where a person induces another to contract on a promise that he, the maker of the promise, has no intentions of carrying out, then he will be liable.

Edgington v Fitzmaurice – The defendant company represented in its Prospectus that money was being raised through an invitation to purchase share in the business was going to be used as investment or expansion. The proceeds from purchase of the shares were in fact used to pay down debt. The court held that the statement of intention was an actionable misrepresentation as the defendant had no intention of using the money to expand the company.

Esso Petroleum v Mardon [1976] QB 801 – In negotiating a lease agreement for a petrol station with Esso Petroleum Mr Mardon was told, based on the assessment of the experts at Esso that the new location has a capacity for 200000 gallons of petrol. The estimate was based on town planning information which later changed and diverted traffic away from the new gas station. Esso made no amendments to the estimate given to Mardon even when they became aware of the changes. The rent for the property was also incorrectly calculated based on the same inaccurate information. Mr Mardon failed in his effort to run the petrol station profitably and sold only 78,000 gallons in the first year and made a loss of £5,800. On the basis of **Hedley Byrne v Heller**, the Court of Appeal held that although the information from the experts was not misrepresentation, the claimant was entitled to damages based on either negligent misstatement at common law or breach of warranty of a collateral contract.

(c) STATEMENTS OF THE LAW

"Ignorance of the law is no excuse" and so misrepresentation cannot generally be made out on information in this regard. Have a look at the following case and try to make the distinction between fact and law.

Solle v Butcher [1950] 1 KB 671 - The defendant converted a house into a block of flats. Rent was originally charged at £140 per flat per year. The defendant eventually gave a lease of the property for a long duration with a promise to correct bomb damage and modify the structure significantly. It was only after the work was effected on the flats that the parties discussed rent to be charged. The plaintiff agreed to pay and did pay £250 for a while but later brought a suit on the basis that he was being charged greater than the control rent. The defendant contended that as a result of the extensive modification, the flat had changed character and therefore not subject to monitoring by the Rent Restriction Act. That statement was held to be a statement of fact.

(d) SILENCE

Generally, in a purchase and sale scenario, for example, the seller has no obligation to disclose. The burden is on the purchaser to ensure that he gets a good bargain and therefore, silence generally cannot be said to be misrepresentation.

Smith v Hughes (1871) LR 6 QB 597 - The Claimant wanted to purchase horse feed and so ordered what he believed to be old oats based on a sample he was shown by the defendant. The oats were in fact new (green) oats and could not be used for feeding the horses. The vendor was aware of the mistake but said nothing. An action was brought on the grounds of misrepresentation and mistake. It was held by the court that the action in misrepresentation had to fail as silence is generally not misrepresentation. Mistake also failed as the mistake was relevant to quality and not a fundamental term of the contract.

The following exceptions are to be noted:

(i) HALF TRUTHS

A contracting party may intentionally make statements that only reveal a portion of the truth. So that where this half-truth induces a contract, it may be a misrepresentation. **Nottingham Brick & Tile Co. v Butler (1889) 16 QBD 778** – A solicitor negligently told the purchaser of a lot of land that he was not aware of the existence of Restrictive covenants on the land. The solicitor had not reviewed the document for such an encumbrance which in fact existed. The court held that the contract could be rescinded as even though the statement was literally true it was a misrepresentation.

(ii) STATEMENTS WHICH BECOME FALSE

A statement may be true when made but subsequently becomes false before the contract is executed, there is a duty to reveal the truth. For example, where you entered into negotiations with a bank to get a loan while you are employed but before the contract is signed or the loan disbursed, you become unemployed, this information is to be disclosed.

With v O'Flanagan [1936] Ch 575 – A doctor, the vendor of a medical practice negotiated to sell his property and represented that it is valued at £2000. This was a good estimate at the time of the representation but the doctor became ill and the value depreciated and no update given to the purchaser. This was held by the court to be misrepresentation. Lord Wright MR quoted: "So again, if a statement has been made which is true at the time, but which during the course of negotiations becomes untrue, then the person who knows that it has become untrue is under an obligation to disclose to the other the change of circumstances."

(iii) CONTRACTS UBERRIMAE FIDEI

Where one party is in a superior position of knowledge, he is obligated to disclose all important facts on which a contractual decision relies. Important facts are things that will convince an individual to enter into a contract relationship. These are known as contracts of good faith and so where information is not disclosed then the contract may be avoided. Insurance contracts are the most popular category of utmost good faith arrangements. All pertinent information must be disclosed.

Lambert v Co-Operative Insurance Society [1975] 2 Lloyd's Rep 485 – Mrs Lambert entered into a contractual relationship with the insurance company to insure her husband's jewellery. She did not disclose that he was previously convicted and fined for receiving stolen goods. She later renewed the policy and yet again, did not disclose the fact that her husband was convicted of more offences and was even imprisoned. Some time after the renewal and in April 1972 some items worth £311 were lost or stolen and the Co-op refused to indemnify Mrs Lambert on the grounds of non disclosure. Mrs Lambert's claim was dismissed by the Lower Court and the decision was upheld by the Court of Appeal on the reasoning that the information should have been disclosed in order to give the insurers the opportunity to evaluate their risk.

(e) OTHER REPRESENTATIONS

One should always safeguard against a literal interpretation of the term 'statement' as a statement could extend to an action or even an event that is used to convey a message that is not necessarily true. So that:

(a) In **Gordon v Selico Ltd (1986) 278 EG 53**, paint applied to a rotten wooden structure being negotiated for sale was held to be fraudulent misrepresentation.

(b) In **St Marylebone Property v Payne (1994) 45 EG 156**, the use of a photograph taken from the air, printed with arrows (misleadingly) indicating the extent of land boundaries, was held to convey a statement of fact and therefore a misrepresentation.

THE MISREPRESENTATION MUST HAVE INDUCED THE CONTRACT

The injured party must have been persuaded to enter into the contract as a result of the false statement. He must be able to show that the misrepresentation was material and that it was at least one of the factors relied on.

(a) MATERIALITY

The misrepresentation must be of substance or such great importance so that it would have persuaded a reasonable person or the "officious bystander" to execute the contract. The case of **Museprime** also indicated that if the officious bystander would have been induced then the representee would be so induced. This case is instructive on the basis that it applies an objective and a subjective test.

According to dicta in the case, "If the misrepresentation would have induced a reasonable person to enter into the contract, then the court will presume that the representee was so induced, and the onus will be on the representor to show that the representee did not rely on the misrepresentation either wholly or in part. If, however, the misrepresentation would not have induced a reasonable person to contract, the onus will be on the misrepresentee to show that the misrepresentation induced him to act as he did".

Museprime Properties v Adhill Properties [1990] 36 EG 114 – The plaintiff commenced an action for misrepresentation when it was discovered that properties that he successfully bidded on were subject to rent reviews. This encumbrance would limit the extent to which rent on the properties can be increased. The defendant company countered the application for rescission with the defense that the misrepresentations were not such as to induce any reasonable person to enter into the contract.

The judges held that any misrepresentation is grounds for rescission and therefore the plaintiffs would be awarded the return of their deposit, damages in respect of lost conveyancing expenses and interest. If the plaintiffs knew the truth they would not have entered into the contract to convey the properties and as such the misrepresentation had in fact induced the contract.

(b) RELIANCE

There has to be reliance by the representee on the misrepresentation. It is a frequent saying "what you don't know, won't kill you". The saying holds true for misrepresentation. If the misrepresentee does not know about the misrepresentation, then there could not have been reliance on it.

Horsfall v Thomas [1862] 1 H&C 90 - The gun being purchased had a defect which was hidden by the sellers. The buyer unfortunately could not rely on misrepresentation as he did not inspect the item before he purchased same. The misrepresentation did not induce the contract as he was unaware of its existence. The buyer's suit thus failed.

Reliance will be established if the representee relies on his own judgment and or carry out his own investigations.

Attwood v Small (1838) 6 CI & F 232 - The vendors in the sale of a mine misrepresented the earning capacity of the venture when they exaggerate the figures. The Purchasers secured the services of an independent expert agent who erroneously affirmed the inflated figures. Six months after the sale was complete the plaintiffs discovered that the defendant's statement had been inaccurate and they sought to rescind on the ground of misrepresentation. As the purchasers had sought to verify the figures themselves through an independent expert agent, the House of Lords held that there was no misrepresentation.

The decision would not have been the same where as in **Pearson v Dublin Corp [1907] AC 351** the misrepresentee was given an opportunity to discover the truth but did not take the offer up. The misrepresentation was considered an inducement.

Redgrave v Hurd (1881) 20 Ch D 1 - A solicitor acquired a share in the partnership in another solicitors' firm. He was informed that the partnership had an approximate income of between £300 and £500 per annum and was given several sheets of papers with information that the partner indicated would prove his representation. He declined the offer to check the accounts and took them at their word. The income per annum was in fact £200.

The Court of Appeal gave judgment in favour of the defendant and he was entitled to rescind the contract as he relied on the Solicitor's statement. Although Redgrave had declined to check the books the court was of the view that, that reinforced Redgrave's reliance.
Lord Jessel MR in his judgment commented thus:

> *"If a man is induced to enter into a contract by a false representation it is not a sufficient answer to him to say, "If you had used due diligence you would have found out that the statement was untrue. You had a means afforded to you of discovering its falsity, and did not choose to avail yourself of them." I take it to be a settled doctrine of equity, not only as regards specific performance but also as regards rescission that this is not an answer unless there is such*

delay as constitutes a defence under the Statute of Limitations. That, of course, is quite a different thing."

There will be reliance even if the misrepresentation was not the only inducement for the representee to enter into the contract. Remember that misrepresentation must be at least one of the factors that induced a contract.

Edgington v Fitzmaurice - The plaintiff was induced to lend money to a company by (a) the statement of intent, and (b) his mistaken belief that he would have a charge on the assets of the company. He was able to claim damages for deceit even though he admitted that he would not have lent the money, had he not held this mistaken belief.

TYPES OF MISREPRESENTATION

The classification of misrepresentation is vital as it informs the remedies available for each type. Fraudulent, negligent and wholly innocent are three main types of misrepresentation.

(a) FRAUDULENT MISREPRESENTATION

Lord Herschell in **Derry v Peek (1889)** described fraudulent misrepresentation as a false statement that is "made (i) knowingly, or (ii) without belief in its truth, or (iii) recklessly, careless as to whether it be true or false."

Derry v Peek (1889) 14 App Cas 337 – the defendant stated in their prospectus that they had the right to use steam powered trams. This was a right that had to be secured by a Board of Trade which was empowered by a Special Statute. The company did not receive the approval of the Board and had to be wound up. The claimant had purchased shares in the company in reliance on the statement made in the prospectus and brought a claim on the grounds of the fraudulent representation of the defendant.

It was held that the statement was not fraudulent but made in the honest belief that approval was forthcoming. Lord Herschell defined fraudulent misrepresentation as a statement which is made either:

i) knowing it to be false,
ii) without belief in its truth, or
iii) recklessly, careless as to whether it be true or false.

The burden of proof is on the plaintiff - he who asserts fraud must prove it. Tactically, it may be difficult to prove fraud, in the light of Lord Herschell's requirements.

The remedy is rescission and damages in the tort of deceit.

(b) NEGLIGENT MISREPRESENTATION
This is a false statement made by a person who had no reasonable grounds for believing it to be true. Maker of the statement and the person relying on it are in a special relationship giving rise to a duty of care. There are two possible ways to claim: either under common law or statute.

(i) NEGLIGENT MISSTATEMENT AT COMMON LAW
The House of Lords have held that in certain circumstances damages may be recoverable in tort for negligent misstatement causing financial loss:

Hedley Byrne v Heller [1964] AC 465 - Hedley Byrne was an advertising firm. They intended to enter into an advertising contract with Easypower Limited. Before proceeding into the contract they contacted their bank, The National Provincial Bank, in order to secure background information on Easypower which would give reliable information on their creditworthiness. The National Provincial got in touch with Easypower's bankers, Heller & Partners. Heller told the National Provincial, "in confidence and without responsibility on our part," that Easypower were good for £100,000 per annum on advertising contracts. Hedley Byrne relied on this statement and entered into a contract with Easypower and lost more than £17,000 when Easypower was wound up. They sought to recover this loss as damages.

Lord Pearce in the House of Lords stated that a man giving information or advice may be vested with a special duty of care. This duty of care in a special relationship will arise based on the circumstances, and or where the person giving the advice does not absolve himself of liability by indicating, as National Provincial Bank did, that the statement is being given without liability. A special relationship will also arise where in a business or commercial relationship one party presents himself as having superior knowledge and the other party relies on it or it is reasonable to assume that one party will rely on the information be presented.

(ii) NEGLIGENT MISREPRESENTATION

NEGLIGENT MISREPRESENTATION UNDER STATUTE

Section 2(1) of the **Misrepresentation Act 1967** provides:
"Where a person has entered into a contract after a misrepresentation has been made to him by another party thereto and as a result thereof he has suffered loss, then, if the person making the misrepresentation would be liable to damages in respect thereof had the misrepresentation been made fraudulently, that person shall be so liable notwithstanding that the misrepresentation was not made fraudulently unless he proves that he had reasonable ground to believe and did believe up to the time the contract was made that the facts represented were true."

This provision does not require the representee to establish a duty of care and reverses the burden of proof. Once a party has proved that there has been a misrepresentation which induced him to enter into the contract, the person making the misrepresentation will be liable in damages unless he proves he had reasonable grounds to believe and did believe that the facts represented were true.

This burden may be difficult to discharge as shown in:

Howard Marine v Ogden **[1978] QB 574** – The claimant, Ogden was engaged with Northumbrian Water Authority to do excavation work. They entered into a contract with the defendant to lease two dredging barges for £1800 weekly in order to complete the work. Ogden asked HM about the capacity of the barges in order to make a concise estimate for tender of the completed work. Lloyd's Register was checked by HM. HM then told Ogden that the capacity was 1600 tonnes. The entry in Lloyd's Register was incorrect, and the correct tonnage was 1195. Ogden, the claimant brought an action for negligent misrepresentation. The defendant argued that they had a reasonable basis for believing the statement to be true as they checked Lloyd's register. The court, held that the burden of proof was not discharged by the defendant, as demonstrating that they had a reasonable basis for believing Lloyd's documents were accurate when the registration documents were the source on which they should rely.

Recent case law has shown that the remedies available for negligent misrepresentation are as those available in fraudulent misrepresentation unless the representor discharges the burden of proof. In particular, damages will be based in the tort of deceit rather than the tort of negligence.

(c) INNOCENT MISREPRESENTATION

This type of misrepresentation is neither fraudulent nor negligent but is a statement which the person makes honestly believing it to be true which turns out to be false.

The remedy is either:

a. rescission with an indemnity, or
b. damages in lieu of rescission under the court's discretion in s2(2) Misrepresentation Act 1967.

REMEDIES FOR MISREPRESENTATION

Where it has been determined that a misrepresentation exist, the next step is to identify remedies that are available for the type of misrepresentation identified.

(A) RESCISSION

Rescission allows the parties to be put back in a position as if the contract had not been made. It is the setting aside of the contract and is an equitable remedy that is awarded at the discretion of the court. The contract can be set aside by giving the representor notice of the intention to set aside, notifying the authorities or by performance of any act that will indicate the representee's intention to proceed with the contractual arrangement.

Car & Universal Finance v Caldwell [1965] 1 QB 525 - The defendant, Caldwell sold his car to Norris. The next day, when the cheque was presented it was referred to drawer for insufficient funds. The fraudulent transaction was immediately communicated to the Automobile Association and the police by Caldwell. Norris, subsequently, sold the car to X who sold it to Y who sold it to Z who sold it to the plaintiffs. One of the issues to be tried was whether all that the defendant did to prevent title to the car from passing to Norris, amounted to a rescission of the sale. The contract was held to be voidable as the original owner had done everything he could in the circumstances to avoid the contract which was in fact made on the basis of fraudulent misrepresentation. As good title was not passed to Norris, X, Y or Z, the original owner could reclaim the car.

BARS TO RESCISSION

Rescission may not be available to the injured party in the following instances:

(i) AFFIRMATION OF THE CONTRACT

The contract can be affirmed expressly or by an act of the injured party. The injured party, despite the knowledge of the misrepresentation can continue with the contract. Also, the injured party may behave in such a way that affirmation may be implied.

Long v Lloyd [1958] 1 WLR 753 –A lorry was purchased by the plaintiff, and, two days later, on a short run, faults developed and the plaintiff noticed that it did only about 5 miles to the gallon. The problems with the car contradicted the defendant's representations that the car was in 'exceptional condition' and that it did 11 miles to the gallon. The claimant reported further faults to the defendant and the plaintiff accepted the defendant's offer to pay for some of the repairs. The next day the lorry broke down as it set out on a longer journey. A letter was written to the defendant by the plaintiff, asking for the return of his money. The lorry was not in an exceptional condition, but the defendant's representations concerning it had been honestly made.

It was held that Long was not entitled to a rescission of the contract as he had finally accepted the lorry before he had purported to rescind and that affirmation of the contract was evidenced in the second journey. Contrast the decision in **Peyman v Lanjani [1985] Ch 457** in which the Court of Appeal held that the plaintiff could rescind the contract as he did not know he had such right and since he did not know he had such right, he could not be said to have elected to affirm the contract.

(ii) LAPSE OF TIME

The option to rescind may not be available if the injured party does not act in a reasonable period of time.

In order to determine reasonable time, different rules apply based on the type of misrepresentation in issue. Fraudulent misrepresentation will see time running from the time when fraud was discovered. While for misrepresentations that are not fraudulent, time will start running from the date of the contract.

Leaf v International Galleries [1950] 2 KB 86 –The plaintiff purchased what he believed was a 'J. Constable' based on an innocent misrepresentation by the defendants. The inaccurate representation was only discovered five years after the purchase. Time had eroded the claimant's right to rescind and his only recourse was damages which was not an order that he asked the court for.

(iii) RESTITUTION IN INTEGRUM IMPOSSIBLE

Exact restoration is not required when claiming restitution. Consequently, if it is impossible for the injured party to be reasonably restored to his original position, then rescission may not be available. In **Vigers v Pike (1842) 8 CI&F 562** a lease of a mine which had been entered into as a result of a misrepresentation could not be rescinded as there had been considerable extraction of minerals since the date of the contract.

Precise restoration is not required and the remedy is still available if substantial restoration is possible. Thus, deterioration in the value or condition of property is not a bar to rescission.

Armstrong v Jackson [1917] 2 KB 822 - A broker who was commissioned to purchase shares for a client, sold the client his personal shares instead. Sometime later, the value of the shares fell substantially and it was held that the client could rescind on account of the broker's breach of duty. The client still had the identical shares and was able to return them, together with the dividends he had received. McCardie J. in arriving at a decision said

> *"It is only ... where the plaintiff has sustained loss by the inferiority of the subject-matter or a substantial fall in its value that he will desire to exert his power of rescission ... If mere deterioration of the subject-matter negatived the right to rescind, the doctrine of rescission would become a vain thing."*

(iv) THIRD PARTY ACQUIRES RIGHTS

The injured party will lose his right to rescind where a bonafide third party acquires rights in property, in good faith and for value. Thus, if Norma obtains goods from Val by misrepresentation and sells them to Sam, who takes in good faith, Val cannot later rescind when he discovers the misrepresentation in order to recover the goods from Sam because Sam is a bonafide purchaser. Have a look at **Phillips v Brooks [1919] 2 KB 243.**

It is important to note that the right to rescission, an equitable remedy, will be lost if the court decides that damages is an appropriate remedy.

(B) INDEMNITY

Indemnity may be ordered by the court where the injured party incurred expenses in honoring the obligations of the contract. An indemnity can be ordered simultaneously with an order for rescission.

Whittington v Seale-Hayne (1900) 82 LT 49 - The plaintiff who were poultry farmers entered into a simple oral contract with the defendants. The obligations of the plaintiffs under the lease included payment of rent to the defendants, payment of rates to the local authority and they were also obliged to undertake repairs as well. The defendants in order to induce a contract represented that the property was sanitary for rearing poultry.

The property was not sanitary as the water supply was contaminated causing the poultry to be killed and the property manager became ill.

Following the decision in **Newbigging v Adam (1886) 34 Ch D 582,** Farwell J rescinded the lease, and, following the judgment of Bowen LJ who posited that the plaintiffs could recover the rents, rates and repairs under the covenants in the lease but nothing more. They could not recover removal expenses and consequential loss (i.e., loss of profits, value of lost stock and medical expenses) as these did not arise from obligations imposed by the lease (the contract did not require the farm to be used as a poultry farm). Had they been awarded, they would have amounted to an award of damages (i.e., expenses resulting from the running of the poultry farm).

Notwithstanding the reasoning observed in both cases a remedy could be found in the law of tort.

(c) DAMAGES:

Damages assist the injured party, as far as money can do so, to be restored to his pre-contract state. The injured party may claim damages for fraudulent misrepresentation in the tort of deceit. Consequently, the injured party may recover for all the direct loss incurred as a result of the fraudulent misrepresentation, regardless of Foreseeability.

Doyle v Olby (Ironmongers) Ltd [1969] 2 QB 158 - The plaintiff was awarded damages for fraudulent misrepresentation when the contract to purchase an iron-mongering business into which he was induced turned out to be very dissimilar from that which the vendors had led the plaintiff to believe. Lord Denning MR was concerned mostly about the measure of damages and said that: "The defendant is bound to make reparation for all the actual damage directly flowing from the fraudulent inducement ... It does not lie in the mouth of the fraudulent person to say that they could not have been reasonably foreseen."

East v Maurer [1991] 2 All ER 733 - The plaintiffs were induced to purchase one of the defendant's two beauty salons after they represented there would be no competition between them as the defendant intended to work only where there was an emergency. The defendant continued to operate his remaining business and his clients followed him. Consequently, the plaintiffs suffered a huge loss and were forced to resell the venture for a significantly reduced price. The court at first instance found that the defendant's representations were false. The defendant appealed on the assessment of the award of damages.

The correct approach according to the Court of Appeal was to assess the profit the plaintiff might have made had the defendant not made the representation(s). 'Reparation for all actual damage' as indicated by Lord Denning in **Doyle v Olby** would include loss of profits. The assessment of profits was however, to be on a tortuous basis, that is, placing the plaintiff in the same position he would have been in, had the wrong not been committed as far as money can do so.

Royscott Trust Ltd v Rogerson [1991] 3 WLR 57

A car dealer misrepresented to the finance company the amount of deposit paid by a customer thus inducing them to enter into a hire purchase agreement. The customer subsequently reneged on his obligation to pay and sold the car to a third party. The finance company sued the car dealer for innocent misrepresentation and claimed damages under s2 (1).

As the Misrepresentation Act s2 (1) prescribes that the court is able to rely on evidence of deceit, the Court of Appeal held that the dealer was liable to the finance company for the outstanding balance under the agreement plus interest. Under this rule the dealer was liable for all the losses suffered by the finance company even if those losses were unforeseeable, provided that they were not otherwise too remote.

EXCLUDING LIABILITY FOR MISREPRESENTATION

Any term of a contract which excludes liability for misrepresentation or restricts the remedy available is subject to the test of reasonableness.

ACTIVITY PAGE

1. Maurice is a professional property development officer. He encourages Dane to buy a lot in a development in the hills overlooking the sea, assuring Dane that within weeks he will get the subdivision approval, as he had been told by the chairman of the local council that the application was "a mere formality". Dane intends to build a guest house for local and foreign visitors who are interested in "faith based tourism". The administration of the local council changes and Maurice's application is rejected. Dane seeks your advice about filing a suit against Maurice for misrepresentation. Will Dane be successful?

   (a) Explain the three types of misrepresentation and say which one, if any, Dane will rely on.
   (b) Suggest the nature of Maurice's misrepresentation and its effect on the transaction

2. Explain the impact of each of the following on a contract:

   (a) Fraudulent misrepresentation
   (b) Negligent misrepresentation

3. With reference to at least one decided case, explain each of the following:

   (a) Fraudulent misrepresentation
   (b) Negligent misrepresentation
   (c) Rosetta tells Keisha that she intends to open another branch of her beauty salon and wants Keisha to be her partner. She takes Keisha to a town where she saw a store which appeared to be a beauty salon. Rosetta told Keisha that she has secured a lease on the property and that the men at the location a workers that she hired for renovation. Keisha gives Rosetta $15,000 to assist in the opening of the store after she was told that the property is able to her. Four months has passed and Rosetta has not opened the

new store. Keisha then discovers that Rosetta has never rented the shop.

With reference to at least one decided case, advise Keisha whether she can recover her money.

Chapter 9

ILLEGALITY

TYPES OF ILLEGALITY

COMMON LAW ILLEGALITY ⟺ STATUTORY ILLEGALITY

There are many different types of illegality. These will be explored in this chapter along with their effect on a contract. According to MacKendrick, "illegal contracts come in different shapes and sizes. Some involve gross immorality or a calculated attempt to break the law, while others involve innocent infringement of regulatory legislation. A contract to rob a bank has little in common with a contract which is performed by one of the parties in such a way that a statutory instrument is innocently infringed" (2015, p.270).

Types of illegality

A contract to commit murder is an example of a common law illegality, while a statutory illegality includes, for example, a situation where the operator of a business venture who requires a license to operate, conducts his business without securing said license. This latter group includes anyone bound by the law to practice under regulated guidelines such as doctors, pharmacists, restaurant operators, and hairdressers.

Illegal contracts are also classified as contracts that are determined to be illegal in their formation and contracts that are illegal in the way they are executed. For instance, a contract can be illegal because of its formation such as one formed to engage in prostitution or murder. On the other hand, a contract, while legal in its formation, can become illegal because of how it is executed. A contract to take passengers in a taxi that is licensed to operate in that way can become illegal in its performance if the driver chooses to speed during the charter.

Contracts that are illegal in its formation

This type of contract may be void ab initio. That is, it is illegal as formed and the illegality exists from the beginning of the contract.

A primary or even a secondary legislation may expressly prohibit a certain type of contract as can be seen in **Re Mahmoud & Ispahani (1921)** in which a contract was made to sell linseed oil at a time when it was an offence to buy and sell this item without a license. The seller was only licensed to sell to buyers who themselves also have a license. One buyer induced the seller to enter into a contract and unknowing to the seller he had no license. The buyer refused to complete the transaction and it was held that the seller could not claim damages for non acceptance even where his lack of mens rea would prove his innocence. It would appear that the legislation that governs the sale and purchase of linseed created a strict liability offence.

However in **Mohamed v. Alaga & Co (A Firm) (2000)** the Court of Appeal found that while it is illegal to accommodate refugees according to immigration and border control legislations, it might be possible to recover on a *quantum meruit* basis for translation services that were provided in relation to the refugees in the instant case. Translation services were not contemplated by the legislation as one of the services that should be extended to refugees but public policy would not be offended by allowing such a recovery.

In the instances illustrated immediately above, where the contract is void thought has to directed at whether or not a party who is innocent of wrong doing can recover a benefit conferred by the contract. The result is that sometimes the benefit can be recovered, whilst in other cases it cannot.

Both Statutory and common law illegality can be found to be illegal it their formation and thus will be void ab initio.

Contracts that are illegal as performed

The birth of a contract may be legal, that is, legal in its formation but illegal as to how it is performed. An example of this can be seen in **St. John's Shipping Corporation v. Joseph Rank Ltd. (1957)** where a contract for the carrying of goods by sea was lawful in its formation but was performed illegally when the ship's owner exceeded the recommended capacity of the vessel in carrying the goods. Exceeding capacity was a statutory offence and the master of the ship was prosecuted and fined for this offence.

In this instance, the court held that the ship's owner was entitled to the recover the monies owed for the freight and therefore a contract of this nature would not be deemed void ab initio.

Common Law Illegality

Common law illegality concerns cases involved in the commission of a legal wrong. These include for example, the contract to commit murder **(Alexander v Rayson)** and **(Beresford v Royal Exchange Assurance)**. There are also cases that involve contracts contrary to public policy **(Pearce v Brooks)**. It is always difficult to define public policy because of its shifting nature. As a result, it is often difficult to determine whether or not a contract offends it. It therefore means that older precedents must be treated with great care as they may not provide proper guidance consistently.

The contract in **Pearce v Brooks (1866)** involved the hire of a carriage to the defendant that would assist her in her trade as a prostitute. This case may now be seen as a difficult decision since public policy is somewhat divided on the feelings towards prostitution. The principle established in **Pearce v Brooks** most certainly remains in place in jurisdictions such as Jamaica that recognize prostitution as an illegal activity.

Courts have found that public policy can be offended in such a way as to make the contract illegal in a number of different areas. Thus, a contract which is contrary to good public morals may be illegal. At one point in time, contracts between cohabiting couples who were not married were contrary to public policy. The attitude of society has now changed since even legislation has now accommodated decisions of unmarried, cohabiting couples.

Franco v Bolton involved payment by a man to a woman to become his mistress, a contract which was found to be illegal. Contracts to promote sexual immorality are now less likely to be found to be illegal due to the changing public views of immorality.

Contracts which are found to be damaging to the general welfare of the family are affected by illegality **(Lowe v Peers)** and **(Hermann v Charlesworth)**. Thus contracts in which there was an agreement to restrain the freedom to marry, or some agreements to separate a family are illegal. In addition, Courts are particularly suspicious of agreement to oust the jurisdiction or authority of the court.

Contracts which tend to injure the State in its relations with other States have been deemed to offended public morals. A contract with an alien enemy is illegal in time of war and contracts which contemplate hostile action to a friendly foreign country are also illegal.

The effects of illegality on a contract

A contract may have both legal and illegal terms. Where this exists and it is possible to remove an illegal term or an illegal part of a term, the court will do so and leave the remainder of the contract binding.

While the court will generally not enforce an illegal contract, it may be able to provide an injured party with a remedy in some other manner. As seen in **Strongman v. Sincock (1955)** a plaintiff may sometimes be able to get redress on the basis of a breach of a collateral warranty. In **Shelley v. Paddock** the injured innocent party was allowed damages for a fraudulent misrepresentation.

There is also the issue of whether a party can be permitted to recover a benefit conferred upon the other party to an illegal contract. Again, the general rule is that courts will not permit recovery under an illegal contract **(Holman v Johnson)** but there are cases which illustrate methods by which recovery may be allowed. For example, where the parties are equally guilty, the public policy considerations in preventing illegal contracts may be outweighed by the desire to prevent the other party from retaining a benefit which constitutes an unjust enrichment. Thus in **Kiriri Cottons v. Dewani** the innocent party to an illegal contract was able to recover the money paid pursuant to the illegal contract. The party was innocent in the sense that he was unaware that the contract was illegal.

There is also the possibility that the innocent party could be allowed to recover a benefit when he withdraws from the contract before the illegality has been committed. This is illustrated in any of the following authorities: **Taylor v Bowers (1876), Kearley v. Thomson (1890) and Tribe v. Tribe (1996).**

ACTIVITY SHEET

1. Carol and Donna are known prostitutes in the capital of your parish. They frequently rent venues from Donat, to put on functions that facilitate them in the pursuit of their trade. Donat is a frequent client of both women. They both agree that they will give Donat complimentary passes to the functions instead of paying him their hard earned cash for rent. Donna and Carol are now frustrated with Donat turning up at every single function and they now refuse to renew his complimentary pass. Donat threatens to sue for the rent. Both women declare that any contract between them and Donat is illegal. Advise Donat

2. Outline, using decided cases, the different classifications of illegality.

3. In groups of four explain how a taxi operator may be found guilty of illegality in carrying out his job on a daily basis. Choose creative ways of presenting your responses while examining his legal role, obligations, and breaches.

Chapter 10

DISCHARGE OF CONTRACT

There are several ways in which a contract may be discharged or brought to an end. We will however be concentrating on the following four ways:

1. Performance
2. Agreement
3. Breach
4. Frustration

1. PERFORMANCE

Performance of a contract is the means by which the contracting parties are relieved of their obligations under an agreement. They do so by executing the terms precisely as agreed and in some instances, performing only substantially. The importance and hardships created by performance is illustrated in the case of **Cutter v Powell (1795) 6 Term Rep 320** where a widow unsuccessfully attempted to recover wages owed to her deceased husband after he died only a few days before his ship came into port and the end of his contractual period. The law has since been modified but the case certainly has made the point that performance of contractual terms is the essence of a contract.

Circumventing the general rule of contractual performance

The position as to performance seen in **Cutter v Powell (1795)** has been modified using the many rules outlined below.

(a) DIVISIBLE CONTRACTS

The modification of the general rule has allowed a contract to be identified as, entire or divisible contract. Where there is an entire contract, complete performance by one party is a condition precedent. This concept refers to what has to take place before contractual liability can be imposed on the other contracting party. With a divisible contract, part of the consideration of one party is set off against part of the performance of the other. Have a look at the following contrasting cases:

Sumpter v Hedges [1898] 1 QB 673 - The court in this case determined that having agreed to erect two houses on the defendant's property and stables for £565, the plaintiff had abandoned the contract and therefore could not recover £333 on his outstanding fees.

Roberts v Havelock (1832) 3 B. & Ad. 404 - A shipwright agreed to repair a ship. The contract did not expressly state when payment was to be made. He chose not to go on with the work. It was held that the shipwright was not bound to complete the repairs before claiming some payment.

G. H. Treitel, (2011, p.702) posits that in such cases the question whether a particular obligation is entire or severable is one of construction; and where a party agrees to do work under a contract, the courts are reluctant to construe the contract so as to require complete performance before any payment becomes due. "Contracts may be so made; but they require plain words to show that such a bargain was really intended": **Button v Thompson (1869) LR 4 CP.**

(b) ACCEPTANCE OF PARTIAL PERFORMANCE

Where a party receives a promise of performance and receives the benefit of partial performance but had the option to have accepted or rejected the work but he chooses to accept, then he is obligated to pay a reasonable price for the partial performance or benefit received. A variation of the agreement that payment for goods and or services is to be made must be understood.

Christy v Row (1808) 1 Taunt 300 - A cargo ship originally bound for Hamburg was diverted because of a 'restraint of princes' to another port on the instructions of the Consignees where the goods were then accepted. The consignees were held liable upon an implied contract to pay for freight at the contract rate for the proportion of the voyage originally undertaken which was actually accomplished. An implied contract was formed when they directed the cargo to an alternative port.

(c) COMPLETION OF PERFORMANCE PREVENTED BY THE PROMISEE

Where a promisee prevents a party to an entire contract from performing, the party can recover a reasonable price for what he has in fact done on a quantum meruit (what one has earned or reasonable value of service) basis in an action in quasi-contract.

Planche v Colburn (1831) 8 Bing 14 - The plaintiff entered into a contract to write a book. The research for the book had been conducted when the contract was eventually discontinued by the publishers. The court held that the plaintiff was able to receive payment on a quantum meruit basis and was therefore entitled to £50.00

(d) SUBSTANTIAL PERFORMANCE

Where a person fully performs the contract, but the performance is somewhat deficient but it can still be said that he has substantially performed, it is regarded as far more just to allow him to recover the contract price reduced by the extent to which his breach of contract lessened the value of what was done, than to leave him with no right of recovery at all. In other words, pay the person because he has substantially performed but deduct an amount that is reasonable to correct the relevant defect.

Dakin v Lee [1916] 1 KB 566 - The Court of Appeal held that the contract price was recoverable by the builders less an amount that would be allowed in respect of the items found to be defective after the defendants built a house contrary to agreed specifications.

(e) TENDER OF PERFORMANCE

Tender of performance is an offer or attempt to execute what is required under a contract. It is equivalent to performance in the situation where party (a) cannot complete performance without the assistance of party (b) and party (a) makes an offer to perform which party (b) refuses. This is illustrated in **Startup v M'Donald (1843) 6 M&G 593** in which the court held that a tender was equivalent to performance and the plaintiffs were entitled to recover damages for non-acceptance where in a contract the plaintiffs agreed to sell oil to the defendant and to deliver it to him during the last two weeks in March, payment to be in cash at the end of that period. The delivery of the oil was tendered during the night on the final day of March and the defendant refused to accept or pay for the goods because of the odd hour of delivery.

(f) STIPULATIONS AS TO TIME OF PERFORMANCE

At common law, in the absence of contrary intention, time was regarded as being of the essence. Thus if a party did not perform on time he could not enforce the contract against the other party. Where time is not of the essence, then a reasonable time will be inferred, damages may accrue but the contract cannot be terminated.

In equity, time was not regarded as being of the essence, except in three circumstances:

(a) time is of the essence is a term of the contract.
(b) reasonable notice given to make time of the essence after the contract was entered into.
(c) the context within which the contract was made suggested that time was of the essence.

2. AGREEMENT

The contracting parties can agree that they do not want to be further bound under the contract. This has to be done in writing and supported by consideration. Where the agreement for discharge is not under seal, the legal position varies according to whether the discharge is bilateral or unilateral:

(i) BILATERAL DISCHARGE

Bilateral discharge is the termination of an unfulfilled agreement. Non-performance or part performance by either or both parties to the contract is a reason for its occurrence. This kind of discharge is frequently practiced for the following reasons:

(a) Accord and satisfaction

The release from the agreement may be all the parties intend. This mutual agreement is known as an accord and satisfaction.

(b) Rescission and substitution

The parties may express accord and satisfaction on the original agreement and may want to substitute a new agreement.

(c) Variation

Circumstances of contract may have changed since entering into the agreement and the parties may want to modify or alter the terms to secure (enure) a practical benefit.

(d) Waiver

One party may decide, on the request of another to forbear his entitlement under a contract. He may also, on his own initiative, decided to waive his rights under the contract.

(ii) UNILATERAL DISCHARGE

One party's right to surrender is a unilateral discharge. A party is under no obligation where he has performed entirely but, he has right to insist on the performance by the other contracting party. For unilateral discharge, there has to be accord and satisfaction. Consideration must be given unless the agreement is under seal.

3. BREACH

A breach is a failure to perform according to the terms of the contract. A serious breach resulting in a discharge can occur in one of two ways:

i. It can be anticipatory. This is where either party may show by express words or by implications from his conduct at some time before performance is due that he does not intend to observe his obligations under the contract; or
ii. Nonobservance of a term of the contract that is identified as a condition

In cases of anticipatory breaches it is important, as a first step, to establish whether the innocent party knows of the breach and whether or not it was accepted. The innocent party may immediately treat the contract as being discharged and proceed to sue for damages. He is not under an obligation to wait until the contract was expected to begin.

Hochster v De La Tour (1853) 2 E&B 678 - The court held that an employee was entitled to sue for damages immediately when an employer breached his contract before he (employee) who was employed as a courier started performance.

The contract remains open for the benefit and risk of both parties if the innocent party does not indicate his acceptance of the other party's repudiation within a reasonable time so that the contract is discharged. The breach was not accepted in:

Avery v Bowden (1855) 5 E&B 714 - A charter party agreed to retrieve cargo from the charterer's agent in Odessa. The vessel arrived in Odessa but the agent did not supply the cargo. The ship's master insisted on getting the goods for which he was sent. Subsequently, a war broke out. The charterer sued. The court held, inter alia, that if the agent's conduct amounted to an anticipatory repudiation of the contract, the master had elected to keep the contract alive until it was discharged by frustration on the outbreak of war.

Where the contract remains operative at the benefit and risk of both parties, damages may be obtained even where the innocent party did not mitigate his losses.

White & Carter v McGregor [1962] AC 413 – The plaintiff advertising contractors entered into a three year contract with the defendant garage to display advertisements for the garage. The contract was instantly cancelled by the defendants who no longer wanted to be parties to the contract but the plaintiff refused and insisted on its performance. The plaintiffs ultimately displayed the advertisements for 156 weeks and then claimed the contract price of £196 and 4s. The plaintiffs were held to be entitled to enforce the contract and claim the amount agreed in the contract. They were not bound to accept the repudiation and sue for lost profit on the contract as their damages.

If in the first instance the innocent party treats the contract as operative, he is said to have affirmed it. This affirmation is a type of waiver and having waived his rights he may be estopped from changing his mind.

Panchaud Freres SA v Establissments General Grain Co [1970] 1 Lloyd's Rep 53 - Purchasers of maize rejected it on a ground which was subsequently found to be insufficient. Three years afterward, they discovered that the grain had not been shipped within the period agreed in the contract. They, therefore, sought to validate their dismissal on this ground. The Court of Appeal held that they were not at liberty to do so. Lord Denning MR stated that the buyers were prevented by their conduct from setting up late delivery as a ground for dismissal because they had led the sellers to believe they would not do so.

An innocent party is not excused from honouring the terms and obligations under the contract where he has waived his rights in light of an anticipatory breach. As a result, the repudiating party could escape liability if the affirming party was subsequently in breach of the contract. It is tantamount to "having your rights and losing it".

The circumstances of the particular case will dictate if the anticipatory breach amounts to a repudiation. Lord Selborne stated thus in **Mersey Steel v Naylor Benzon (1884) 9 App Cas 434**: "you must examine what (the) conduct is to see whether it amounts to a renunciation, to an absolute refusal to perform the contract and whether the other party may accept it as a reason for not performing his part."

The conduct which amounts to a repudiation is often difficult to determine. **Federal Commerce & Navigation v Molena Alpha [1979] AC 757** – the signing of the bills of lading on behalf of the masters of the ship that the cost of freight had been correctly paid was an implied term of the charter contract. The master of the ship was eventually instructed not to sign any such bills of laden as a dispute had arisen regarding deductions from a time charter hire payment by the charterers which the ship owners regarded as unjustified. The charterers were put in an impossible position commercially and the charterers treated the owner's actions as a repudiation of the charter. The House of Lords agreed and held that although the term broken was not a condition, the breach was of sufficient importance in the contract and would deprive the charterers of virtually the whole benefit of the contract because the issue of such bills was essential to the charterers' trade.

Woodar Investment v Wimpey Construction [1980] 1 WLR 277 - Wimpey entered into a contract to purchase property for an agreed sum and agreed to make further payments to Transworld Trade Ltd, a third party. The contract made provision for the purchaser to rescind the contract if before completion a statutory authority 'shall have commenced' to acquire the property by compulsory purchase. Both parties knew that a draft compulsory purchase order had been made as at the commencement of the contract. Wimpey sought to terminate the contract in reliance on this provision. Woodar sought damages in their own right and on behalf of the third party alleging that any repudiation would amount to a wrongful repudiation. The House of Lords decided in favour of Woodar.

4. FRUSTRATION

A frustrated contract occurs when unforeseen events occur after the contract has been concluded which make performance of the contract impossible, illegal, void of its commercial purpose or radically different from that which the parties contemplated. The automatic discharge of a contract by way of frustration will occur despite the wishes of the parties.

TESTS FOR FRUSTRATION

There are two alternative tests for frustration:

(i) The implied term theory test, as in **Taylor v Caldwell (1863) 3 B&S 826** in which Blackburn J stated: "The principle seems to us to be that, in contracts in which the performance depends on the continued existence of a given person or thing, a condition is implied that the impossibility of performance arising from the perishing of the person or thing shall excuse the performance."

Lord Loreburn explained in **FA Tamplin v Anglo-Mexican Petroleum [1916] 2 AC 397**, that the court:

> *'... can infer from the nature of the contract and the surrounding circumstances that a condition which was not expressed was a foundation on which the parties contracted ... Were the altered conditions such that, had they thought of them, the parties would have taken their chance of them, or such that as sensible men they would have said "if that happens of course, it is all over between us".'*

(ii) The radical change in the obligation test. This can be seen in the House of Lords' case of **Davis Contractors v Fareham UDC [1956] AC 696** where the plaintiff entered into a contractual agreement to build several houses in an eight months period. As a result of bad weather, and labour shortages, the work was protracted for approximately 22 months and cost £17,000 more than was agreed or expected. Consequently, the plaintiffs held that the contract was frustrated amd filed a suit to recover £17,000 by way of a quantum meruit. The House of Lords held that the contract was not frustrated on the basis of onerous unforeseen events.

Lords Reid and Radcliffe stated that the 'radical change in the obligation' test required the court to:

(1) Construe the contractual terms in the light of the contract and surrounding circumstances at the time of its creation.

(2) Examine the new circumstances and decide what would happen if the existing terms are applied to it.

(3) Compare the two contractual obligations and see if there is a radical or fundamental change.

Have a look at **National Carriers v Panalpina [1981] AC 675** in which Lord Wilberforce was reluctant to choose between the theories. He took the view that they merged one into the other and that the choice depends upon "what is most appropriate to the particular contract under consideration".

EXAMPLES OF FRUSTRATION

(a) DESTRUCTION OF THE SUBJECT MATTER ESSENTIAL FOR PERFORMANCE OF THE CONTRACT

Where the subject matter that is essential for performance is destroyed, this will frustrate a contract.

Taylor v Caldwell (1863) – Caldwell and Taylor entered into a lease agreement to use a music hall for hosting a concert. Unfortunately before the scheduled date for the concert, the hall was destroyed by a fire. Taylor sued for damages on the grounds that Caldwell failed to make the hall available for the concert. As the fire was not caused by any of the contracting parties the court held that the claim for breach of contract could not succeed since it had become impossible to fulfill.

(b) PERSONAL INCAPACITY

A contract may be frustrated where there is personal incapacity of a personality or skill set of one of the parties is unavailable.

Condor v The Baron Knights [1966] 1 WLR 87 – The drummer in a pop group was contracted to work seven nights per week but became ill and was medically certified to work only four nights thereafter. The court held that the drummer's contract of employment had suffered from commercial frustration as it would have been impractical to engage a substitute drummer for the three nights a week when Condor could not work as it would have been financially onerous to facilitate two sets of rehearsals for the four concerts arranged.

Phillips v Alhambra Palace Co [1901] 1 QB 59 - One partner in a firm of music hall proprietors died after contracting with a troupe of performers. The court decided that the contract was not personal in nature and could be executed by the existing partners and as such the contract was not frustrated.

Graves v Cohen (1929) 46 TLR 121 - The court held that the death of a racehorse owner frustrated the contract with his employee, a jockey, because the contract created a relationship of mutual confidence.

(c) THE NON-OCCURENCE OF A SPECIFIED EVENT

Where the occurrence of a specified event is the core of a contract, the non-occurrence of a specified event may frustrate the contract. Compare the following leading cases:

Krell v Henry [1903] 2 KB 740 - Henry entered a contract with Krell to use a room for two days for the viewing of the king's procession. The purpose for taking the rooms was not communicated. The king became ill and so Henry would no longer need the room for the purpose. The court held that the contract was frustrated as both parties would have understood that rental of rooms during that time period would have been for the sole purpose of viewing the procession. The procession being cancelled because of the king's ill health released both parties from any obligation. Henry therefore did not have to pay for the room.

Herne Bay Steamboat Co v Hutton [1903] 2 KB 683 - A contract was held not to be frustrated when the Naval Review on Edward VII's coronation was cancelled. The circumstances of the contract were twofold (1) that Herne Bay agreed to hire a steamboat to Hutton for a period of two days for the purpose of taking passengers to cruise around the fleet at Spithead and (2) see the naval review on the occasion of Edward VII's coronation. As the holding of the naval review was not the only event upon which the contract hinged, the other object of cruising around the fleet remained capable of being performed.

(d) INTERFERENCE BY THE GOVERNMENT

An action by the government may frustrate a contract. This can be seen in **Metropolitan Water Board v Dick Kerr [1918] AC 119** – where a six year contract became frustrated by a wartime statute that demanded that work on the reservoir be ceased and the plant sold.

(e) SUPERVENING ILLEGALITY

Illegality may frustrate a contract.

In **Denny, Mott & Dickinson v James Fraser [1944] AC 265** a contract for the sale and purchase of timber contained an option to purchase a timber yard. However, trading under the agreement became illegal because of a wartime control order. It was held that the order had frustrated the contract so the option could not be exercised.

Re Shipton, Anderson and Harrison Brothers [1915] 3 KB 676 – Wheat which was stored in a warehouse was purchased but never delivered and ownership was never passed to the purchaser based on the terms of the contract. A war time rule that was made to control the supply of food permitted the government to be in control of all distribution of foods. The seller was excused from further performance of the contract as it was frustrated by the government regulation.

(f) DELAY

Excessive and unexpected delay may frustrate a contract. The circumstances of the contract or the nature of the contract will have to be considered.

Jackson v Union Marine Insurance (1873) LR 10 CP 125 - Jackson chartered a ship in November 1871 to proceed with all possible dispatch, danger and accidents of navigation excepted, from Liverpool to Newport where a cargo of iron rails was to be loaded for carriage to The United States. The vessel left port on January 02 and ran aground on January 03 and was eventually taken back to Liverpool on February 18th. Repairs lasted approximately 6 months but Jackson had repudiated the contract from February 15th.

The court held that such a time was so long to put an end in a commercial sense to the commercial speculation entered upon by the shipowner and the charterers. The express exceptions were not intended to cover an accident causing such extensive damage. The contract was to be considered frustrated.

LIMITATIONS OF THE DOCTRINE

Viscount Simmonds in **Tsakiroglou [1961]** stated that frustration must be confined and Lord Roskill in **Pioneer Shipping v BTP Tioxide [1982] AC 724** said that the doctrine of frustration should not be used frivolously to relieve contracting parties of bad business decisions.

(a) EXPRESS PROVISION FOR FRUSTRATION

Express contractual provision for the occurrence of a frustrating event cannot be overridden by the doctrine of frustration.

(b) MERE INCREASE IN EXPENSE OR LOSS OF PROFIT

Frustration cannot be relied on where there is a mere increase in expense or loss of profit.

Davis Contractors v Fareham UDC [1956] AC 696 - The House of Lords held that a contract was not frustrated when the plaintiff contracted to build 78 houses in eight months but due to bad weather, and labour shortages, the work was completed several months later and at a cost £17,000 above budget. Events that were unforeseen and which made a contract more onerous than was anticipated did not frustrate the contract.

(c) FRUSTRATION MUST NOT BE SELF-INDUCED

Frustration brings a contract to an end by an operation of law despite the wishes of the parties.

Maritime National Fish v Ocean Trawlers [1935] AC 524 - The claimant chartered one of his five shipping vessels to the defendants. New legislation was introduced requiring licenses to be held by ships using otter trawl nets. The claimant applied for five licenses as the fishing vessels were all fitted with otter trawler nets. Only three license were granted and the ship's name had to be noted on the license. The claimant's vessel was named and excluded the vessel which the defendant charterer was using. The defendant was therefore unable to use the vessel for fishing. The claimant sued the defendant for the price of hire. The defendant counterclaimed in his defence stated the claimant had committed a breach in not providing a license. The claimant argued there was no breach as the failure to provide a license was a frustrating event in that the decision to grant licenses rested with the secretary of state. It was held by the court that the contract was not frustrated as the claimant had chosen to apply the three licenses for himself rather than using one to fulfill his contractual obligation. He had therefore induced the frustrating event and was therefore in breach of contract.

(d) FORESEEABILITY OF THE FRUSTRATING EVENT

A party cannot rely on an event which was, or should have been, foreseen by him but not by the other party as can be seen in **Walton Harvey Ltd v Walker & Homfrays Ltd [1931] 1 Ch 274** - The defendants entered into an arrangement with the plaintiffs to display an advertising sign on the defendant's hotel for seven years. The hotel was acquired by the government during the period of the right and was demolished by the local authority. The court held that the right was not frustrated but was in fact breached as the defendant knew or had an idea that the place would have be acquired.

EFFECTS OF FRUSTRATION

The **Law Reform (Frustrated Contracts) Act 1968** was passed to provide for the recovery of money and a just apportionment of losses where a contract is discharged by frustration.

(a) RECOVERY OF MONEY PAID

Section 3(2) provides three rules:

1. Money paid before the frustrating event is recoverable, and
2. Money payable before the frustrating event ceases to be payable, whether or not there has been a total failure of consideration.
3. If, however, the party to whom such sums are paid/payable incurred expenses before discharge in performance of the contract, the court may

award him such expenses up to the limit of the money paid/payable before the frustrating event.

For an example of how funds are treated in the event of frustration have a look at the following authority:

Gamerco v ICM/Fair Warning (Agency) Ltd [1995] 1 WLR 1226 - The plaintiffs, pop concert promoters, agreed to promote a concert to be held by the defendant group at a stadium in Spain. A deposit of $412,500 was paid to the defendants. The stadium was held by authorities and experts to be unsafe and its use was banned. The plaintiff's permit to hold the concert was therefore revoked and the concert cancelled as there was no suitable alternative site available. The plaintiffs sought to recover the deposit made under s1(2) Law reform (Frustrated Contracts) Act 1943 (British legislation), and the defendants counterclaimed for breach of contract by the plaintiffs….

The court held that using section 1 of the 1943 Act, the plaintiffs were entitled to recover their deposit and that although the court had a discretion to allow the defendants to offset their losses against this amount, in all the circumstances of the present case the court felt that no deduction should be made in favour of the defendants and their counterclaim should be dismissed.

(b) VALUABLE BENEFIT

Section 3 (3) provides:

> *If one party has, by reason of anything done by the other party in performance of the contract, obtained a valuable benefit (other than money) before the frustrating event, he may be ordered to pay a sum in respect of it, if the court considers it just, having regard to all the circumstances of the case.*

ACTIVITY SHEET

1. Lorane rents a ballroom for her annual holiday bash. She also engages caterers to prepare meals for 500 persons. The ballroom is damaged by fire the night before the concert and Lorane has to use a room which can accommodate only 250 persons, as all the other rooms are booked. Many of the guests have to be turned away. She refuses to pay for more than 250 meals, arguing that her contract with the caterer is frustrated.

Explain each of the following:

(a) The doctrine of frustration
(b) Whether or not Lorane can rely on the doctrine of frustration

2. Using appropriate illustrations, explain the relationship between anticipatory breach and mitigation of damages.

3. he plaintiffs, pop concert promoters, agreed to promote a concert to be held by the defendant group at a stadium in Spain. However, the stadium was found by engineers to be unsafe and the authorities banned its use and revoked the plaintiffs' permit to hold the concert. No alternative site was at that time available and the concert was cancelled. Both parties had incurred expenses in preparation for the concert; in particular the plaintiffs had paid the defendants $412,500 on account.

The plaintiffs sought to recover the advance payment under s.3(2) Law reform (Frustrated Contracts) Act 1968, and the defendants counterclaimed for breach of contract by the plaintiffs in failing to secure the permit for the concert. Discuss how the principles of Frustration are relevant in the above case

REAL PROPERTY

Chapter 11

BACKGROUND TO LAND LAW IN COMMONWEALTH CARIBBEAN COUNTRIES

William the Conqueror used the Battle of Hastings to invade England and defeat its king Harold in the year 1066. This invasion paved the way for an elaborate land grab that was not previously known to England. William secured all lands for himself, the church and selected persons of his choosing such as soldiers, nobles and barons. These people held a tenurial (i.e. tenancy) relationship (discussed below) which gave the tenant's rights over the land, but never ownership. These rights included the right to enjoy an income from the agricultural production of the land and were accompanied by certain obligations to the king.

The concept of "tenure" is itself closely associated with the seminal Act of 1066. As J.G. Riddall puts it… "tenure….was the foundation of the feudal structure of land holding and this structure was, in turn, the foundation on which England land law has been built". (1979, p.1).

The word "tenure" means "occupying or holding", its essence being that the "tenant" holds the property at the instance of a superior lord. When the King made a grant or gave a tenure he would receive service from the grantee in a manner determined by him. The "tenant" could himself make a grant to someone else on terms determined by him, or so on down the line. When a tenant dies the tenure or holding passes to his heir. There are several types of tenure discussed below:

(1) **Socage Tenures** historically is a type of tenure where the tenant held certain lands in exchange for his performance of certain inferior services of nonmilitary nature for the lord of the land. For instance, in the King's household, one might perform tasks such as "carrying his letters, or feeding his hounds or hawks" (Riddall p.5) or perform largely any ancilliary tasks for which payment to the King could be in the form of agricultural produce or money or "quit rents". The tenant paying the rent thereby being quit of his services and is able to continue occupying the land.

(2) **Spiritual Tenures** is granted in return for spiritual services or other religious services such as the saying of prayers for the soul of the grantor or the making of special monetary gifts to a specified person or group. So, a church for instance could be built on the property in return for the spiritual services provided to the King.

(3) **Tenures in chivalry** was practiced where a knight would provide the knight services in the form of armed horsemen and even delayed payments. Tenures in chivalry was also called Grand Sergeant who would provide honorable state office to the lord or king.

(4) **Villein Tenure** is comparatively of least importance and which involves a duty on the part of the tenant to carry out jobs on the lord's land for a specific number of days. The tenant would not know ahead of time what the exact nature of the job would be. But he would be instructed by the lord's bailiff who was usually the overseer.

The Conquest ultimately brought with it a sharp distinction between land and chattels. Chattels are things that can be owned and as it were, land could not be owned, except by the monarch. The Commonwealth Caribbean received the abovementioned land practices and the phenomenon that we do not "own" land but rather, that we hold an "interest" in land, or have "tenure" of it.

A summary of the history of ownership of land in the Commonwealth Caribbean

With the capture of our territories by the English, we received their legal systems and traditions. Like England, land was vested in the Crown and large swathes (areas) were granted to the nobility in return for their loyalty and service as seen above in the discussion on Tenures.

The need for labor in the various territories was filled by the introduction of slavery by the relevant European power at the time but eventually, the slaves were freed and so, with the purchase of freedom by some slaves, land was acquired by them, sometimes in large tracts as well.

Free villages were established by the churches and that in itself saw the rise of free peasantry in the early years after slavery was abolished. In other cases, ex-slaves themselves purchased land and a new period in land possession had begun. Many former slaves remained as workers on the plantations because they could not afford to purchase property. Some were simply afraid to go out on their own. However, they were able to live in rented properties as a part of their service.

WHAT IS REAL PROPERTY?

Land is frequently referred to as "real property". "Ownership" of real property gives a right against the world, that is, a right in rem. A right in rem suggests that the "owner" has a right to take action against anyone who violates his interest for example, by trespassing on the land. Real property is different from "personal property" which refers to "things", such as machines, trailers and "choses in action", such as stocks and copyrights.

Common Law and the Classification of Property

(a) Corporeal and Incorporeal property

Corporeal property such as stove, truck and land and its attachments are physical objects which can be touched and seen.

Rights over land such as restrictive covenants, easements, rent charges and choses in action that have no physical existence but are recognized in law are referred to as incorporeal property.

(b) Immovable and movable Property

Civil law makes the distinction between immovable and movable property.

Immovable property

Immovable property refers to land, anything underneath the land and things attached to the land. This includes the earth's surface and all the ground beneath and to the center of the earth. It also includes minerals under the earth's surface, the airspace above, natural vegetation, trees and the fruits and fixtures. So, when we speak of a definition of land, we are therefore talking about much more than the dirt we can physically see.

Movable property

Movable property is not permanently attached to the land and can be destroyed. It includes items on the land such as a generator and other chattels.

The distinction between personalty and realty

Property is divided into two main categories: real property and personal property or realty and personalty. Real property consists of all the estates and interests in land, with the exception of leases.

Personal property is divided into three categories: choses in possession, choses in action and chattels real (leases).

Choses in possession - tangible or touchable objects other than land which can be owned absolutely, such as cars and clothes.

Choses in action - these are intangible rights other than those relating to land and of which one cannot take physical possession and also depend for their existence on enforcement by the court. In this category you will find debts, copyright, patents, etc.

Chattels real - these are leases which are estates in land and classified as personal property. They are so called because a lease is a chattel but closely aligned to real property.

The distinction is not always easy but it is important to note that personalty can be absolutely owned while realty cannot. Remember that under common law we do not "own" land absolutely, we have an estate in land. All realty are essentially owned by the Crown or State.

FIXTURES AND CHATTELS

A fixture is any structure which is attached to the land, thereby becoming a part of the land. Additionally, it can be a piece of equipment or furniture that is fixed in position in a building or vehicle and is considered legally part of it so that they normally remain in place when an owner moves. It is important to know the distinction because it will determine what a tenant, for example takes when the tenancy is determined.

A chattel on the other hand is a structure which does not form part of the land and can be removed where necessary or relocated. When it is removed it should not transform or damage the character of the land.

Examples of fixtures

(a) fireplaces
(b) water heaters
(c) light fixtures
(d) some appliances such as stoves and dishwashers, for example, are commonly considered fixtures by virtue of being built into a kitchen.

The general idea is that if the items when removed will cause the property to change, then they are fixtures.

Examples of Chattels

(a) Machines standing unattached on a floor
(b) Power supplies that are connected by electrical wires to a building.

(c) Greenhouses that are movable.
(d) Stone wall unattached by cement
(e) A zinc shed or store room, bolted to a concrete floor

Removal of these items after a period of time will not generally destroy the land.

Development of the law on fixtures and chattels

Whether a structure is a fixture or a chattel becomes very significant in matters relating to the effect its removal would have on the person who stands to benefit from its determination as a fixture for example a landlord, a beneficiary of an estate or a mortgagee. The law of fixtures is grounded in the maxim "quicquid plantatur solo solo cedit", a Latin phrase which translates to mean that whatever is affixed to the land becomes a part of it and therefore belongs to the owner of the soil.

It therefore means that if anyone wants to dispute or rebut that general position, that person must satisfy the relevant tests as follows:

(1) Whether the chattel has become so attached that it can be classified as a fixture.
(2) Whether or not the law would allow the owner of the chattel to remove what could otherwise be considered a fixture (discretionary)

Mitchell v Cowie [1964] 7 WIR 118 addressed the effect of the two tests. Wooding C.J states that:

> *"…It is essential not to confuse what are really two separate and wholly independent issues: the first, whether the thing in question is a chattel or a fixture: if it is a chattel….its owner may dispose of it without let or hindrance whenever he pleases: but if it is a fixture, then and only then, the second issue may be raised - whether it is subject to any right of removal."*

He advanced six criteria which will determine whether a chattel has or has not become a fixture:

(1) *"A house may be a chattel or a fixture depending upon whether it was intended to form part of the land on which it stands. But the intention is to be determined objectively rather than subjectively, that is to say, according to the circumstances as they appear and by application of rules as set out hereunder.*

(2) *To distinguish chattel from fixture, a primary consideration is whether or not the house is affixed to the land*

(3) *If the house is not affixed to the land but simply rests by its own weight thereon, it will generally be held to be a chattel unless it be made to appear from the relevant facts and circumstances that it was intended to form part of the land, the onus for doing so being on him who alleges that it is not a chattel.*

(4) *If the house is affixed to the land, be it however slightly, it will generally be held to form part of the land unless it be made from the relevant facts and circumstances that it was intended to be or continue as a chattel, the onus for so doing being upon him who alleges that it is a chattel.*

(5) *Specifically as regards a house affixed to land by a tenant thereof, a circumstance of primary importance is the object or purpose of the annexation.*

(6) *To ascertain the object or purpose of the annexation, regard must be had to whether the affixation of the house to the land is temporary and for use as a chattel, or is permanent and intended to be for the better enjoyment of the land. But for this purpose it must at all times be bone in mind that the intention or right of the tenant to remove the house from the land on the cesser of his interest as tenant with the result that no improvements will accrue to the landlord's reversionary interest does not make the annexation temporary. The critical consideration therefore is whether the tenant in affixing his house to the land has manifested a purpose to attach it thereto so that it becomes and remains a part thereof co-terminously with his interest as tenant."*

As a basis for these tests Wooding C.J. reflected an earlier view, that of Blackburn, J. in **Holland v Hodgson [1872] L.R. 7 C.P. 328 and 335**, where His Lordship said:

> *"perhaps the true rule is, that articles not otherwise attached to the land than by their own weight are not to be considered as part of the land, unless the circumstances are such as to show that they were intended to be part of the land, the onus of showing that they were so intended lying on those who assessed that they have ceased to be chattels, and that, on the contrary, an article which is affixed to the land, even slightly is to be considered as part of the land, unless the circumstances are such as to show that it was intended all along to continue as chattel, the onus lying on those who contend that it is a chattel."*

Intention is very important in determining if a chattel or fixture exists. In order to establish intention, annexation has to be discussed. The following five points are usually considered:

(a) Degree and mode of annexation
(b) Purpose of annexation
(c) Who makes the annexation and in what relationship to the land
(d) Whether or not the land and the chattel would be damaged upon removal
(e) Custom and usage

Degree and Mode of Annexation

Annexation, a nexus or joining is an activity in which two things are joined together, usually with a lesser thing being attached to a greater thing.

In **Burke v Bernard [1930]**, the removal of the upper wooden floor from lower concrete floor was not permissible as its removal would render the lower floor roofless contrary to the intention of the owner. The court examined the intention of the owner of the land and concluded that the upper floor could not be regarded as a chattel.

As indicated earlier, the degree and mode of annexation are among the criteria set for determining whether or not a structure is or was intended to a fixture. Thus, the Courts have taken into consideration such factors as the extent to which, or if at all, the superstructure would be destroyed, if removed. Wooding C.J. discussed this factor at great length in **Mitchell v Cowie** and cited some interesting cases in which the principle is also implied.

In **Eva Fields v Rosie Modeste and Jrine Joseph [1966-69] LR 251**, the house in question was built of tapis (tapestry or beautifully decorated cloth used for hanging as decoration), plastered with concrete noggin (marl and clay) and resting on wooden pillars. It was covered with galvanized iron roofing, or zinc. The Court of Appeal in Trinidad and Tobago found that the house was a chattel as it could be removed without being damaged. This finding was based to a great extent on the material out of which the house was made.

Even though the disintegration of a structure, were it to be removed, is likely to lead to the conclusion that it is a fixture, the proposition is not always conclusive. Again, in **Burke v. Bernard** when the Court's common sense approach was based not so much on how the top floor was affixed, but rather on the fact that the top floor was an integral part of the entire building, its removal having the effect of making the bottom floor roofless.

It was held in the case of **Matthew v Bruno [1954] 14 Trin LR 95**, that "whatever the character of the house may be, although chattel houses are moveable their removal necessarily involves disintegration of the house on its site, and reconstruction elsewhere."

The court gives regard to the legal principles and the justice of the cases that it is faced with, the intention of the parties is of great importance also, as well as the nature of the economic loss which would be suffered by the claimant in order to make a determination as whether an item is a chattel or fixture.

Purpose of Annexation

The main purpose of annexations is that it helps to determine whether a chattel has been fixed with the intention that it shall remain in position 'permanently or for an indefinite or substantial period', or only for some temporary purpose. In addition, Cheshire and Burns indicates that the purpose of annexation "is to ascertain whether the chattel has been affixed for its more convenient use as a chattel, or for the more convenient use of the land or building."

Thus in **Leigh v Taylor [1902] AC 157**, the House of Lords found that the purpose of the annexation of tapestry which was affixed to a wall by tacks on a wooden framework, remained a chattel, as it was placed for its more convenient use.

Decades later, a similarly view was taken in **Burkeley v. Poulett [1976] 120 S.J.836**, where pictures were fixed to the paneling of two rooms, a heavy marble statue of a Greek athlete was attached to the plinth and a sundial were placed for the better enjoyment of the defendant who removed them when the property changed hands.

On the other hand, In **D'Eyncourt v. Gregory [1872] L.R.C.P. 328**, statues, stone seats and ornamental vases were held to form part of an integral architectural design of the property and therefore was held to be a fixture.

Opposing views have been taken in Caribbean cases, namely **Mitchell v. Cowie** and **O'Brien v. Missick** as to when a chattel house became a fixture. Compare the following two findings:-

1) Wooding C.J. in **Mitchell v. Cowie [1964] 7 WIR 118** held by saying that,

> *"In like manner, in my view if a house is affixed to land by a tenant who took the tenancy for the purpose of building or maintaining the house thereon and who intends to retain the house there so long as tenancy subsists, he does so for the better enjoyment of the land of which he is the tenant and of which while it remains thereto affixed the house forms part; the house is so far permanent that it is intended to remain on the land at least until the determination*

of the tenancy: and its affixation thereto is not for its better use as a chattel but rather for the accommodation which the letting of the land was meant to provide and which it would be impracticable for it to provide if it remained bare."

2. Georges, J.A. in **O'Brien v. Missick.**

"In many parts of the West Indies persons become the yearly tenant of plots of land on which they build houses. In a sense the purpose for which the house is built is always the proper enjoyment of the plot of land but even though there may be some minimal attachment which will make the house less liable to damage from stormy weather, there is no intention to benefit the landlord by adding value to the land. In a sense the conclusion that the tenant did not intend to benefit the landlord can be said to be subjective but in sense objectively be determined from the nature of the tenancy and the method of construction which aims to make the annexation minimal".

Adaptation

If the articles are not intended to be part of the land, but are adapted for its better use, and enjoyment, they will remain chattels. Farming implements and domestic animals would fall under this head. However, where a structure is placed on land for the purpose of making it a part of the land, it is regarded as a fixture. For example, especially cut stone on an incomplete building would be fixtures, once they were intended to be part of the building.

Custom and Usage

Custom and usage are often indicators of the very important distinction between chattel and fixture. It is therefore common practice that an employer/landowner would provide land for the workers to build a home during the period of employment. This is important to note since a house built on property belonging to a landowner would generally become the landowner's

RIGHTS THAT "RUN WITH THE LAND"

Restrictive covenants and easements are examples of rights that "run with the land". Because these right run with the land, a landholder may take action to protect himself against their removal or modification.

Riparian Rights

Ownership of the bed of a river or the bed of a lake is referred to as riparian rights. This is the case when land is covered with water, such as a river or lake. The holder of the fee simple through which the river passes or on which the lake is located owns the bed of that river or lake. Where the lake or river divides two properties then both owners will enjoy rights up to the middle of the lake or river. This position is true of all non-tidal water. The state or crown on the other hand, owns the bed of all tidal waters. Tidal water refers to the sea.

Although a riparian owner has exclusive fishing and navigational rights over the water on his land, he may be restricted in its use or enjoyment by way of law of the land, for example when government grants the right of use to the public. The public may even restrict the owner's use through the practices of customs.

Legislation often guides the extent of the use of the river. This is so as the interest of the general public has to be served and landowners at the river's lower course also need to be protected.

Wild animals

While a landowner has rights over water that passes through or on his land, subject to restrictions by government, a landowner does not own wild animals on his land as such animals are incapable of being owned. He may hunt those animals and, when captured or killed, they become his. The same rules apply to wild birds.

Minerals and natural gas

The State owns all minerals and other natural resources beneath the soil. These do not belong to the landowner, but to the Crown or State. However, the government may grant rights to persons for the extraction of such natural resources and is obligated to compensate the landowner as prescribed by the Constitution. The landowner is sometimes relocated.

TYPES OF LANDHOLDING OR "OWNERSHIP"

1. Fee simple or freehold
2. Fee tail
3. Life estate
4. Leasehold

The Fee simple or Freehold

This is the closest one will get to "owning land". Remember that all lands are owned by the state. However, the owner has the latitude to dispose of his interest by sale or otherwise, conferring on his successor, similar rights as those previously held by him, subject only to such encumbrances which run with the land, such as easements and restrictive covenants.

The Fee Tail

A concept that is only of historical interest and value in our jurisdiction, the fee tail was a form of freehold transferable for the lifetime of the grantee's heirs.

The Life estate

A life estate is conferred on a "life tenant" or "tenant for life". It is an interest that is granted for the duration of the life of the life tenant. It is generally used by a spouse, husband or wife who has children or grandchildren that they want to benefit from a property in land. It usually reads:

(a) To Melrose for life and thereafter to Kalfani and Zoeie or
(b) To Kalfani during the life of Melrose and thereafter to Zoeie

Upon Melrose's death, the life estate ends and the property passes to Kalfani and Zoeie (remaindermen) who will own the fee simple. The Life tenant, as Melrose is known, can enjoy the property fully, benefitting from the rents and profits and may even sell the property, at which point the proceeds of sale are to be held in trust for Kalfani and Zoeie, with Melrose benefitting from the interest until her death.

Leasehold

A leasehold is held at the pleasure of the fee simple owner or another leaseholder. Where a leaseholder grants a lease, this is known as a sub-lease. The parties to a lease are called respectively, lessor (owner or someone with a longer lease) and lessee (the tenant). A lease is not held indefinitely, it is held for what is called a term which is usually months or years. The lessee is entitled to certain rights and these include the right to have the property properly maintained and the right to quiet enjoyment.

WHAT ARE MY RIGHTS AND HOW ARE THEY AFFECTED?

(a) Constitutional Protection

The right of every citizen is enshrined in the Constitutions of the different jurisdictions to ensure that these rights are protected against government's compulsory acquisition without adequate compensation. The interest of nation generally, and public policy can dictate that the right is removed.

Section 18(1) of the Jamaican Constitution makes the following provisions:

No property of any description shall be compulsorily taken possession of and no interest in or right over property of any description shall be compulsorily acquired except by or under the provisions of a law that:

- Prescribes the principles on which and the manner in which compensation thereof is to be determined and given; and
- Secures to any person claiming an interest in or right over such property a right of
- access to a court for the purpose of:

(i) Establishing such interest or right (if any);
(ii) Determining the amount of such compensation (if any) to which he is entitled; and
(iii) Enforcing his right to any such compensation

Section19 (1) protects one against unlawful search on entry upon one's property. It provides, inter alia as follows:
Except with his own consent, no person shall be subject to the search of his property or the entry by others on his premises.

(b) Restrictions
Some of the restrictions on the landowner's rights include: leases and licenses, the law of nuisance, restrictive covenants and easements, mortgages, town and country planning regulations such as those related to zoning and subdivision provisions, regulations as to the use of beaches, national parks and buildings.

A landholder's right may also be restricted by the nature of his holding e.g. the doctrine of waste, which relates to a life tenant and a lessee. In addition, the express and implied covenants of a leasehold such as in the case of a residential lease where the property is to be kept in tenantable repair is also a restriction and in the case of an agricultural lease where the leaseholder is able to reap such crops as are bearing at the expiration of the lease, but may not destroy the crops.

WHAT IS WASTE?

The "doctrine of waste" is applicable to:

(a) A tenant for life
(b) A leaseholder

It has to do with the upkeep, or lack thereof, of the property by the tenant for life or lessee and the extent to which the character of the property has been altered. The property may be altered and the value is reduced or increased as a result of waste. There are four (4) types of waste, namely

(i) Permissive
(ii) Ameliorating
(iii) Voluntary
(iv) Equitable

Permissive waste
This is a failure on the part of the tenant to maintain the quality of the estate whether physically or financially. It is causing the property to fall into disrepair, for example, by the life tenant's failing to maintain ordinary repairs on property such as not fixing leaks, minor repairs to fencing etc.

Ameliorating waste
Ameliorative waste is an improvement to an estate that changes its character that generally increases the land's value. An injunction will rarely be granted in these instances. However, the tenant for life or lessee may find that they have to pay monetary compensation to a landlord for having changed the character of the property.

Voluntary waste
This is any structural change made to the estate that intentionally or negligently causes harm to the estate or depletes its resources, unless this depletion is a continuation of a pre-existing use. In this instance, the life tenant alters the land to its detriment e.g. felling of specially protected trees and the opening and exploitation of a mine or quarry that causes the land to move away. The mining of sand on a leased property is an example of voluntary waste.

Equitable waste
This refers to acts of unjustifiable destruction such as the cutting down of trees intended to prevent slippage of land, pulling down of a house in anger, removing zinc from a roof rendering the property uninhabitable. There are a number of possible remedies that can be awarded or ordered by the court. These are:

(1) The court may award sufficient money damages to compensate the injured party for the loss resulting from the waste.

(2) The court may directly require the party responsible for the waste to restore the property to its original condition.

(3) The court may accelerate the passage of title in the land, divesting a tenant or life estate holder of the property and vesting it in the landlord or remainderman.

ACTIVITY SHEET – INTRODUCTION

(1) There are two major classifications of items found on land - "chattel" and "fixtures".

(a) Define the term "chattel"
(b) State TWO tests that may be used to determine whether a structure is a fixture or a chattel
(c) In Mitchell v Cowie, Wooding C.J. advanced six criteria for determining whether a chattel had become a fixture or not. Explain any two of these criteria.

(2) You will agree that "waste" can add or take away from the value of land.

(a) Name two types of waste
(b) Melane is a life tenant of property given to her by her late husband, with remainder to their children. She falls upon hard times and cuts a large number of trees for sale. Her son Harry accuses her of wantonly destroying the trees.

Explain to Melane her obligations as a life tenant to protect the property against waste.

(3) "A house may be a chattel or a fixture depending upon whether it was intended to form part of the land on which it stands." Discuss

Chapter 12

CONCURRENT INTEREST IN LAND

An interest in land can be owned by several persons at the same time. We will discuss two of the most recognized interest in this chapter:

(1) Joint tenancy
(2) Tenancy-in-common

What is "tenancy?"
"Tenancy" in this context does not refer to the landlord and tenant relationship. Instead, it refers to the manner in which more than one person enjoys an interest in land simultaneously.

Joint Tenancy

This is a very popular means of tenancy. Joint tenants possess a right of survivorship, that is, the interest of a deceased joint tenant passes to the surviving joint tenant(s). This means that a joint tenant does not have an interest in the land that can be passed to another through a will unless they become a sole owner because the other joint tenants have predeceased him or her. Dixon J in **Wright v. Gibbon** states that

> *"In contemplation of law joint tenants are jointly seised for the whole estate they take in land and not one of them has a distinct or separate title, interest or possession."*

It has also been said in **Panton v. Roulstone [1976] 24 WIR 462 at 465** by Watkins J.A. that "in beneficial joint tenancy, each joint tenant holds nothing by himself but holds the whole together with his fellows". However, a joint tenant cannot benefit from his wrong and so where one joint tenant is killed by the other, the surviving joint tenant cannot benefit from the interest.

Three essential features of a joint tenancy are:

(i) There is a right of survivorship or ***Jus Accrescendi***
(ii) The four unities MUST be present
(iii) There are no words of severance to suggest anything having to do with proportions such as "in equal shares", "share and share alike", "divided between" and "equally".

***Jus Accrescendi*-The Right of Survivorship**
It was said in **Panton v. Roulstone** that:

> *"As against third parties (they) are in a position of a single owner, but as against each other, each has equal rights. Each has an equal interest in the land. And the interest of each is severable, should he care to do so in his lifetime. It is only if he dies without having in his lifetime severed that interest that his interest is extinguished and accrues to the survivor."*

Jus Accrescendi demonstrates the maxim that the parties own everything, yet owning nothing i.e. *"totum tenet et nihil tenet"*. It refers to the situation that states that the last survivor takes everything. Where there is severance before the death of a joint tenant, then *jus accrescendi* does not apply.

At common law where the deaths can be determined in time, the property passes to the younger or youngest, as the case may be. However, in the event of death of joint tenants in circumstances where it is difficult to determine who died first, the common law conceives that there can be no survivorship and the property could pass to the heirs of the joint tenants with the same interest. This is an exception to the rule that a joint tenant cannot leave an interest held as such by way of a will.

The Barbados Succession Act (s.105) provides that where the deaths of joint tenants occur at the same time, the younger is deemed to survive last. A similar provision is contained in the Trinidad and Tobago Succession Act (s.2 (2)). In both situations, this is so unless a court rules otherwise. Where beneficiaries are not one and the same for both parties *Jus Accrescendi* frequently creates hardship. When they are, as in the children of a couple, it can be beneficial in saving estate duties.

Jus accrescendi is not applicable where there is a tenancy in common. So that if joint tenancy has been severed or partitioned, the parties can bequeath their share of the property because they have a tenancy in common.

A joint tenancy is recognized by what are referred to as "the four unities".

The Four Unities

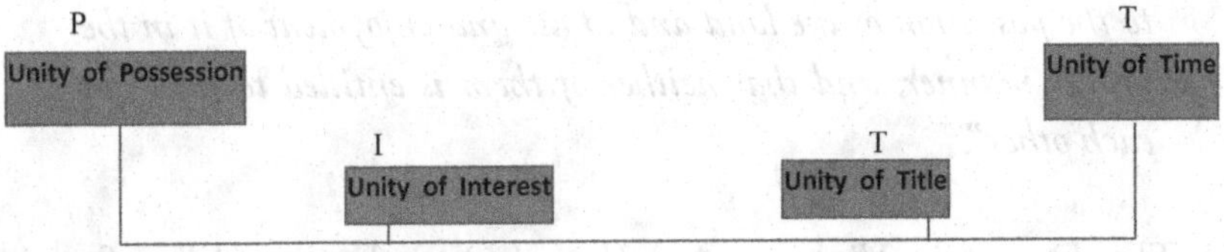

JOINT TENANCY

Possession

One co-owner cannot oust another as all parties are entitled to possession of the whole of the land, and may not exclude each other as co-owners. This indicates that each co-tenant holds no separate or undivided share in the property; each occupies it "in common", and possesses the interest simultaneously.

Some consequences of the unity of possession are:

(1) A co-tenant who is out of possession cannot bring an action in trespass against co-tenant.

(2) A co-tenant does not have to pay rent to the co-tenant who is out of possession. However, in matrimonial cases where the interests are being determined, rent may be payable.
(3) A co-tenant who is in possession is not obliged to keep the property idle for fear that he might have to pay rent to his co-tenants.
(4) A co-tenant cannot evict another co-tenant. In **Forbes v. Bonnick [1968] 11 JLR 67,** the facts are that Forbes and Bonnick both purchased a house and lived together. Forbes was given notice to quit by Bonnick, but Forbes remained on the property and was sued for recovery of possession. The lower court granted an order in favour of Bonnick for Forbes to quit possession of property. Forbes successfully appealed to the Court of Appeal (J.) who relied on Lord Denning's dictum in **Bull v. Bull [1955] 1 AII ER 253**, as follows:

> *"......when there are two equitable tenants in common, then until the place is sold each of them is entitled concurrently with the other to the possession of the land and to use and enjoyment of it in the proper manner; and that neither of them is entitled to turn out each other".*

(5) The Domestic Violence Act (Jamaica) makes provision for the ouster of a co-tenant. This statute may be relied on where co-tenants cannot mutually continue to coexist on the same property. These circumstances are generally dealt with on a case by case basis as the court will not lightly oust someone from his or her property.
(6) In **Jones v. Jones [1977] 1 WLR 438**, it was held that a tenant in possession who is not guilty of ouster is not liable at common law to account to other co-tenants for rent received. This may appear to be contrary to **Bull v Bull**. However, the circumstances of the lease has to be examined and the extent to which the property is to be maintained may be in issue as the co-owner who is not in possession may not be contributing to the upkeep of the property and as such would quite likely not be entitled to a benefit from rent collection.
(7) Where there is an agreement that rent will be collected by one co-tenant, this co-tenant must account to the others.

(8) Where the co-tenancy is being severed and the claimant who is also in occupation is seeking compensation for any expenditure on the property, he must account for the benefits of his occupation as well. In other words, the benefits may very well outweigh the expenses and the claimant may not be entitled.

(9) Where a co-tenant farms the land for example and derives a profit from doing so, this profit does not have to be shared with the remaining co-tenant. This was illustrated in the case of **Henderson v. Eason [1851] 17Q.B70.** This reasoning may however change where minerals are contained on the property and exploited by one co-tenant, the remaining co-tenant will be entitled to a share of the benefit of such exploitation.

(10) A co-tenant who is in possession must keep the property maintained and may not seek a contribution from other co-tenants. In **Leigh v. Dickerson [1844-85] 15Q.B.D. 60** it was held that a co-tenant is not entitled to recover expenses for voluntary improving property, but may recover where there was an agreement with other co-tenants for such improvements, whether such agreement be implied or express.

Unity of interest

Each joint tenant holds an interest with his fellow joint tenants, equal in extent, nature and duration. A remainderman and a life tenant does not have unity of interest. A person who has a lease does not have the same interest as the person who has the fee simple to the same property. No unity of interest exists.

In **Singh v. Mortimer [1967] 10 WI.R. 65** the unity of interest is evident where **A** contracted to purchase property from **B** who is also co-owner with **C.** Unknown to the purchaser and **B, C** had died. As the contract for the sale of the land was not executed by both co-owners, The Court of Appeal of Guyana held that the contract was not enforceable as the intention was to convey the whole estate and there was no consensus on the transaction.

Joseph v. Joseph [1961] 3 W.I.R. 78 - The appellant and the respondent, were joint owners of a property that they purchased. The property was registered in the appellant's name only. He sought to transfer the premises and the respondent opposed the conveyance by applying for an injunction. She further sought an order declaring that her grounds for restricting the transfer were legal, just and equitable.

The trial judge declared that she had an equitable interest in the property. The amount she was entitled to was not determined in that hearing and was to be decided at a later hearing.

Stanley Johnson v. R. Terrier & Anor [1974] 22 W.I.R. 441- The appellant was interested in purchasing a piece of land and so he made contact with RT, real estate dealer. RT coincidentally owned a piece of land jointly with his wife and offered it to Stanley. RT retrieved the Certificate of Title from his wife having spoken to her on the phone in order to show Stanley same. Stanley examined it and was satisfied that he could proceed with his purchase. He later inspected the land and entered into the contract for the purchase of the said land for £900.

A receipt for £300, being the amount he was required to pay, and did pay, by way of deposit in pursuance of the agreement was issued. This receipt was signed by RT and his secretary on behalf of RT's wife and contained all the relevant particulars of the agreement. The following day the appellant received a telegram and a letter that the land was £9,000 and not £900, and that the contract should be regarded as having been cancelled. The said letter was signed by RT who signed on behalf of his wife.

In an action by the appellant claiming specific performance against RT and BT the resident magistrate found that although the receipt constituted an accurate record of the agreement concluded between RT and the appellant it "was not a sufficient memorandum in writing as it was not signed by (BT) or a lawful agent". Judgment was awarded in favour of RT and BT. On appeal it was held that:

(i) there was no evidence to support authority given by the wife.
(ii) the essential elements of agency by estoppel were:

(a) a representation by the principal by words or conduct that the agent had authority to act;
(b) a reliance on that representation by the person to whom it is made; and
(c) an alteration, in consequence of that reliance, in the position of the person by whom the representation is acted upon.

The appeal was therefore dismissed as there was no evidence that BT had given anyone authority to sign on her behalf.

Unity of title
All of the co-owners must receive their interest in land under the same document or instrument. All interest must have been given under the same will for example.

Unity of time
Each joint tenant's title must vest at the same time. A life tenant and a remainderman could not therefore be a joint tenant in respect of the same property because the remainderman would get possession later in time.

Note however, that it has been the Writer's experience in practice that a property purchased by an individual who later wants to add another person onto the title may indicate same by way of an application to the Registrar of Titles that the property be held as joint tenancy. This practice therefore disregards unity of time.

TENANCY-IN-COMMON

Tenancy in common allows each party to own a definable share (not an identifiable section) of the property which they may sell, mortgage, give away or leave to their estate by way of a will.

There are a few important distinctions between a joint tenancy and a tenancy in common:

(1) Right of survivorship does not apply to tenancy in common.

(2) All tenants in common hold an individual, undivided ownership interest in the property. This means that each party has the right to alienate, or transfer the ownership of interest.
(3) Unlike the unity of possession, the unities of time, title and interest need not be present under a tenancy in common.

Li v. Walker [1968] 12 W.I.R. 195 – Both parties owned undivided half share in the property in issue. The appellant having bought his portion from a third party and the respondent and her predecessors in title had occupied their portion at least between 1896 and 1909.

The respondent's mother had divided the property, intending them to be true halves in about 1909 by erecting a fence in the middle of the land. Half was sold and ultimately purchased by the appellant while the other half was retained by the mother. Upon the mother's demise, the respondent continued in occupation. A survey conducted in 1956 came up with a breach that showed a deviation of eleven inches from the original boundary line between the two properties. A subsequent survey in 1960 confirmed this.

On discovering the breach the appellant asserted that he was entitled to a half of the property as surveyed. The respondent argued that the remedy of partition as an equitable remedy was not available within the meaning of the Civil Law of British Guiana Ordinance and that time ran against the appellant.

It was held by the court that the remedy of partition was available as a doctrine of equity and the parties were each entitled to one-half division of the lot of land in question.

ACTIVITY SHEET – COOWNERSHIP

(1) Andrew receives an email that his father, Bob is seriously ill and that he should return home immediately. Unfortunately, Bob dies before Andrew reaches home. When Andrew arrived home he was surprised to see his stepmother, Martha, from whom his father is divorced, making herself homely. He was particularly annoyed because she has disappeared for years and his father had remarried. Andrew ordered her to leave.

Martha was adamant that she would not leave and would not be ordered around her own house, by a boy whom she changed diapers on not so long ago. She told Andrew that she was given a letter written by her father wanting her to transfer her share in this house to him. She told Andrew that she was not stupid and so the transfer was never done. She is angry and has instructed Andrew to get out of her house.

With reference to decided cases:

(a) Identify and explain Martha's basis for claiming that she is entitled to the property which she held as a joint tenant with Bob.

(b) Comment on the likelihood of Martha succeeding with her claim

(2) **(a)** Distinguish between a "joint tenancy" and a "tenancy in common".

(b) With the use of illustrations, describe the ways in which a joint tenancy can be severed.

(c) Enid aged 30 and Jim, aged 32, purchases a new home as joint tenants as soon as they left university and got a job. Unfortunately, Jim died in an accident after the purchase. Jim's father is claiming an entitlement to the property on the basis that he had given the couple the deposit for the purchase. Advise Jim's father.

Chapter 13

LEGAL AND EQUITABLE INTERESTS

It is important that the distinction between legal and equitable interests in land be understood because they impact one's possession of the land. As all equitable rights are enforceable only at the discretion of the court and legal interests may be enforced as of right, it is of significance that these interests be explored.

Legal Interests

Legal interests are binding on and protected as a right against the world. It is a *Right in Rem* and may exist in several forms. Some examples of legal right include registration of the owner's name on the duplicate certificate of title, Common law Conveyance, lease and mortgages. However, there are times when a legal owner's ability to deal with his land as he wishes may be encumbered by someone's equitable interest. This is the case when a legal owner holds land on behalf of beneficiaries. This restriction may have come about by virtue of the instructions in a Will.

Equitable Interests

A claimant may not have a *Right in Rem* as his name is not noted on a title or a mortgage for example. However, an equitable interest may exist. These rights are protected in the Court of Equity from dishonest or unconscionable legal owners. Examples of equity exist for example where a wife is registered as the sole owner on the title of a house. The husband may have contributed to the purchase of the said house but may have been abroad when the property was being acquired and so would not have been able to sign the relevant documents for his name to appear on the title. A Court of Equity will have regard to any detriment that the husband may suffer at the hands of a wife who may be claiming the entire property for herself. Equity will scrutinize the circumstances in order to determine each party's rights. The husband has a *right in personam*. The protection of such rights is not against the world (in rem) but would be protection against the person intent on carrying out dishonest or unconscionable behavior.

Weaknesses of equitable interests

(1) The onus is on the Claimant or person with an equitable interest to prove that the legal interest of the other party is to be shared.
(2) Only awarded at the discretion of the court.
(3) The holder of the legal interest can deal with the property (sell, mortgage) without the consent of the equitable holder. The latter will only be protected by tracing and tacking.
(4) In order to protect the equitable interest, the injured party will have to attend court which is time consuming.
(5) A bona fide purchaser for value without notice of the equitable interest is protected. It therefore means that property cannot be recovered from him. The injured party will have to settle for damages. This illustrates the fragile nature of equitable interests.

ACTIVITY SHEET - LEGAL AND EQUITABLE INTERESTS

1. A summons was taken out by a wife to determine what share, if any, she is entitled to in the following property:

   (a) A house given as a gift to her husband before marriage
   (b) A house purchased during the marriage
   (c) Undeveloped land in the country
   (d) a lease on a commercial building

All transactions above were entered into by the husband and all receipts were written in his name. What type of interest is held by each party? Give reasons for your answer.

2. Mark and Sheenal are married. They purchased a piece of property with Mark's name being the only one recorded on the Certificate of Title.

(a) What type of interest, if any, does Sheenal hold in this property? Mark?
(b) What, if any, are the disadvantages of holding this type of interest?

Chapter 14

PROTECTION BY LEGISLATION: THE RENT RESTRICTION ACT

Statutes in the various jurisdictions provide guidance with regard to leases of residential, commercial buildings and agricultural lands. They set out the rights and obligations of landlord and tenant. Premises that fall under the scrutiny of the relevant legislation are referred to as controlled premises.

The main points to be considered in relation to these rights and obligations are:

(a) Premises to which rent restriction legislation is applicable - "controlled premises"
(b) Provisions for recovery of possession

Controlled premises

The Rent Restriction Act in Jamaica dictates the rights and responsibilities of both landlord and tenant. Properties that fall under its scrutiny are known as controlled properties. A tenant who occupies controlled premises is a statutory tenant and is therefore expected to pay controlled rent.

The maximum permitted rent for controlled premises is known as standard rent. It is therefore a breach of the legislation to charge more than this amount. Where the landlord charges more than the standard rent, the tenant can take the matter to the Rent Assessment Board. However, if the landlord can show that rates and taxes have increased or that he has made significant improvement to the property he may apply for an increased rent. Where properties are controlled, unless the proprietor applies for an exemption, it is an offence for a landlord to claim or contract for more than the controlled rent. Notwithstanding, in practice, it is often a feature of the lease agreement that the parties agree on a percentage increase and the standard rent is rarely ever used.

Commercial properties can be exempt from this monitoring under the Act. However, this is not an automatic right and the proprietor of the property must apply for this exemption through the National Rent Board.

Grant v. Bennett [1959] 2 W1R, 140 - In 1941, Bennett leased Grant a portion of his lands to build a dwelling-house at a quarterly rental of 14s. Grant built a two bedroom "board-house" and lived in it for approximately two years. He later subletted the property to two separate sublessees and ceased to reside on the premises. He later improved the property and added more rooms to be used as a rental income. The landlord increased the rent. Grant then applied to the Rent Board and the Board assessed the rent on that property to be 30s per quarter. This figure was paid until around 1957 when the landlord served notice to quit on Grant. The defendant Grant refused to quit and proceedings for ejectment were commenced as the landlord argument was that the defendant was not protected by the Rent Restriction Law, Cap 341 [J], as he did not personally reside on the premises. The court ordered that the defendant vacate the property and the defendant Grant appealed and it was held that a tenant who leases a "building land" and erects buildings thereon, which he sublets, is entitled to the protection of the Rent Restriction Law as he is still a tenant for the purposes of the Act.

Crampad International Marketing Co. Ltd v. Thomas [1989] 1WLR 242 - It was held in this case, an appeal from Jamaica to the Judicial Committee of the Privy Council, that the tenant of commercial premises was protected under the Rent Restriction Act as all property fall under the scrutiny of the Act unless there is an application for exemption made and granted. Section 31 would therefore apply and the tenant has to be served notice to quit with all the grounds or reasons why the landlord needs the property clearly stated.

Recovery of Possession

Recovery of possession, as you are already aware by virtue of the **Crampad** decision, is dealt with by the Rent Restriction Act. The grounds for recovery of possession can be found in s.31 of the Act and which addresses the issue of notice to quit and has to be at least one of the following grounds:

(i) The landlord requires the premises for his own use and occupation.
(ii) The tenant has failed and/or refused to pay rent for 30 days or more
(iii) The tenant is in breach of a covenant.
(iv) The tenant or other person occupying the premises with him has premises in such a way as to commit a nuisance or annoyance to neighbors.
(v) The tenant has used the premises for immoral or illegal purposes, or has caused them to fall into disrepair or to become unsanitary through acts of waste or neglect.
(vi) The tenant has assigned possession or sub-let the premises without the landlord's permission.

It is submitted that point (i) above is one of the most difficult ground for a landlord to rely on. This is so as the legislation's original intent was to protect the tenant from a landlord's arbitrary behaviours. The landlord will have to prove that he needs the premises for his own use and occupation. The onus is therefore on the landlord to show that he genuinely needs the premises for a valid reason. The following cases will demonstrate the court's reluctance to remove the tenant from occupation and thus confirm what is submitted.

Quinlan v. Philip [1965] 9W1R 269 – D who had been a tenant in an apartment complex purchased a detached dwelling house with the intention to live in it with his wife and to accommodate his daughter in law's occasional visit. The new house purchased by D was occupied at the time of purchase by P and her husband, seven children and an old aunt. P was served with notice to quit the dwelling house and D offered the apartment he occupied to P as alternative accommodation. P refused to move into the apartment as she was sure that it could not accommodate her large family. The D brought a claim for ejectment which was unsuccessful at first instance and on appeal. The basis of his appeal was that The magistrate had confined his reasons to the question of hardship only.

The Court of Appeal in dismissing D's appeal held that:

1. an order for ejectment cannot be made unless two, and often three, conditions are satisfied, viz:

   (a) the landlord must establish one of the grounds specified in the Ordinance;
   (b) the court must consider it reasonable to do so; and
   (c) in the case of certain grounds which may be relied upon by a landlord, the court must be satisfied that less hardship would be caused by granting the order than by refusing it;

2. having regard to the wording of the Ordinance, the onus of showing that less hardship would be caused by granting an order than by refusing it is upon the landlord, so that if in the result the issue lies in medio, it must be resolved in favour of the tenant.

Williams v. Storey [1973], A landlord's genuine and present need appears to be the basis on which the landlord will be able to eject a tenant in Guyana.

The landlord's reason in **Ribera v. Fortune [1965]** that he needed the premises for his own use because it was "convenient" was upheld as the landlord himself was occupying another rented premises. This decision is in total contrast to Quinlan already illustrated above.

ACTIVITY SHEET - RENT RESTRICTION

1. Define the following terms:

   (a) Rent control
   (b) Controlled premises
   (c) Standard rent

2. What are the grounds for recovery of property? Support your response with appropriate cases.

3. Jerry owns a house in Norbrook. He leased half of it to Sabrina who has now refused to pay her rent because she lost her job. Jerry now wants her out of the house so that he can execute repairs and secure a new tenant that is working and is able to pay his rent. What are the grounds for recovery of property? Support your response with appropriate cases.

4. Jerry owns a house in Norbrook which is leased to a family who has occupied the property for a number of years, but he lives in an apartment complex in Barbican. He has recently indicated that he is now tired of apartment living and would like to live in his house in Norbrook where he has a scenic view of the city and a decent garden to tend. He has decided to serve notice to quit on his tenant. Discuss Jerry's likelihood of successfully evicting his longstanding tenant.

Chapter 15

LEASES AND LICENSES

What is a lease?

A lease is considered to be the grant of a right to exclusive possession of land for a determinate term less than that which the grantor or landlord holds. A lease gives a lessee or tenant a right in rem. This right is one that allows the tenant to take action against anyone who violates his interest. A lease is also referred to as a "demise" or "term of years absolute" and is distinct from a license which gives the user of land mere permission to use the land.

Distinctions between Leases and Licenses

(1) A lease when created can give a legal or equitable interest in land to the tenant. While a license does not create an interest. A license is usually personal to the licensee. As Lord Denning said in **Facchini v Bryson** "In all the cases where an occupier has been held to be a licensee there has been something in the circumstances, such as a family agreement, an act of friendship or generosity, or such like, to negative any intention to create a tenancy".

(2) The tenant can sell his interest, obtain a mortgage, dispose of it by way of a will and create a sublease. The licensee generally cannot do these things.

(3) The Lessee, unlike the Licensee has rights against a trespasser that can be enforced.

(4) A Lessee, unlike a Licensee can assign his interest in the property for a shorter period than his own lease.

(5) The Rent Restriction Act protects the lessee. The licensee has no such protection.

(6) A lease has to be agreed for a specified period of time. It is said to have certainty of duration while a license generally has no such requirement or feature.

(7) **Street v Mountford** has now settled the law that a lessee always has exclusive possession of the leased premises. A licensee does not.

Characteristics of Leases and Licenses

(1) Intention of the parties:
The "intention of the parties" was originally the basis upon which a lease or license was established. Kodilinye, (2000 p.8).

In **Isaac v. Hotel de Paris [1960] 1All ER 348,** intention of the parties is the test that was relied on in order to establish whether there is a lease or license. The facts of the case are that the respondent company leased a part of the building which it operated as a hotel in Port of Spain. The hotel allowed the appellant to operate a night club on the first floor. A sum of $250.00 was agreed by the parties after the appellant has been in business for approximately a year. Profits were also kept by the appellant who also had responsibility for managing the bar.

After operating for approximately three months the appellant was given notice to quit the property. He sued unsuccessfully in the high court where it was held that the appellant had a license and not a lease. He appealed further to the Judicial Committee of the Privy Council, where the decision was upheld on the basis that no tenancy was intended.

Intention was also the issue in **Marcroft Wagons v Smith [1951]2 KB 496,** where a controlled or protected property was occupied by a tenant, his wife and their daughter. He eventually died and the mother and daughter continued to occupy the property. When the widow became deceased, the daughter sought to have her name in the rent book. The landlords refused but continued to collect rent. Six months after the mother died, they brought recovery proceedings against the daughter which went as far as Court of Appeal where it was held that there was no intention on the part of the landlords to enter into a lease agreement with the daughter and as such there was no lease.

Intention as a criteria for determining whether or not a lease exists is now mainly of historical value. In **Street v. Mountford [1985] A11ER, 289, [1985] 2WLR, 877,** the "intention test" was demolished and has restricted the finding of a lease or license to "exclusive possession". It therefore means that, regardless of the intention of the parties to the arrangement, if there is exclusive possession, there is a lease.

The facts of **Street** are that by an agreement dated March 7, 1983 S granted M the right to occupy two rooms for £37 per week, subject to termination by 14 days' notice. Several terms were included in the document titled "license agreement" and which also had a clause which asked M to confirm that she understood that there was no tenancy giving her statutory protection as per the relevant statute. M and her husband moved into the rooms, having exclusive possession. In August 1983, S sought a declaration from the court whether the agreement was a license or a protected tenancy. At first instance it was held to be a tenancy. The Court of Appeal held that M occupied as a licensee. The House of Lords held that a tenancy had been created. Their Lordships said that where a residential accommodation had been created for a term at a rent with exclusive possession, the grantor providing neither attendance nor service, the legal consequence was the creation of a tenancy.

It is submitted that **Marcroft Wagons v Smith** would have been decided differently today.

Have a look at **Marchant v Charters [1977] 1WLR, 1181** which was decided prior to 1985 and in which seven rooms were occupied individually with each person having a handful of furniture, a sink, hot and cold water, gas ring, cooking utensils but they all shared the one bathroom. The rooms were kept clean by a housekeeper who was hired for the purpose

of cleaning up and, who lived on the property, and provided linen weekly to the occupants. The court was asked to determine whether one of these occupants was a tenant or a licensee. The Court of Appeal held that he was a licensee. Per Lord Denning, M.R.
1185:

> *"what is the test to see whether the occupier of one room in a house is a tenant or a licensee? It does not depend on whether he or she has exclusive possession or not. It does not depend on whether the occupation is permanent or temporary. It does not depend on the labels which the parties put on it. All these are factors which may influence the decision but none of them is conclusive. All the circumstances have to be worked out. Eventually the answer depends on the nature and quality of the occupancy. Was it intended that the occupier should have a stake in the room or did he have only permission for himself personally to occupy the room, whether under a contract or not, in which case he is a licensee?"*

How do you think this case would have been decided today?

(2) Exclusive Possession

Exclusive Possession is a right to exclude or keep out, all persons from the property, including the landlord. A landlord must indicate within the contract that he wishes to reserve a right to enter the property from time to time, and even so, he has to give reasonable notice of this intention to enter. Where a person is granted the right to use premises without the right to exclusive possession, the grant is a license and not a lease. It does not matter what the intention of the parties were at the time of making their arrangement.

As indicated earlier, the House of Lords' decision in **Street v Mountford [1985] 2 All ER 289** happily signaled a "come back" to the traditional test of whether exclusive possession has been granted. There, Lord Templeman stated that "the true test is whether the occupier has been granted exclusive possession for a fixed or periodic term at a stated rent". If these requirements exist, a tenancy will arise unless there are some special circumstances which negative a presumption (belief or assumption) of a tenancy. If there are special circumstances, then the intention of the parties may be of relevance.

The usual special circumstances that will arise are:

(i) Family and social relationships; **Romany v. Romany (1972) 21 WIR 491**

(ii) Employer/employee relationships; **Facchini v Bryson [1952] 1 TLR 1386.** In this case, an employer let a house to his employee, for a money that was to be paid weekly and a clause in the agreement stated that "nothing in this agreement shall be construed to create a tenancy". The court was of the view that the agreement should be read as a whole regardless of how the parties chose to label the transaction and as such a tenancy agreement was in place and not a license.

(iii) The authority of the party granting the tenancy has to be considered.

(3) Certainty of duration

The period of the lease must be clear and definite. It must be ascertainable. Occasionally, however, persons enter into unusual agreements which make the period of the tenancy uncertain, for example, a demise until "the river changes its course", or a demise until the war ends in the "Middle East". This kind of situation, however, should not be confused with the situation where a grant is made for a definite period but the grant may be terminated at an earlier time upon the occurrence of a specific event. For example, a demise for 90 years or if my employment contract is terminated earlier than planned. Once the maximum period is known then it is a valid lease. This will give effect, for example to the lessee's rights to sublet or assign. The lessee cannot sublet for a period longer than his prevailing lease. He therefore needs to know the length of his lease and so he can grant one that is for a shorter duration than his. A lease can be for a week or 999 years. The rules remain the same. Where the words creating the lease are uncertain, the lease will be held to be void for uncertainty.

The purpose for which the property is occupied has sometimes led the Courts to conclude that a license, and not a lease was intended. This is especially true of short occupancy. These include the hire of a concert hall for several days for public performances, permission given to view a race or to use part of a shop front to sell tickets to a night club which operated in the basement.

Can a lease be for less than a week? Black J in the Irish case **Boylan v. Mayor of Dublin [1949] I.R** asked a question and answered, "Why not?" There, a hall was hired for a charity event. A flag pole dislocated and fell on one of the patrons. Whether the arrangement is a lease or a licence had to be determined in order to vest the occupants in negligence for this incident. The learned judge found that a license existed and said, in passing "I doubt whether the shortness of the hiring matters. Can there be a tenancy for three days, and if so, why not for three hours?"

In **Marshall v. Berridge [1881] 19Ch.D.233,** Lush L.J. puts it thus: "It is essential to the validity of a lease that it shall appear in express terms or in reference to some writing which would make it certain on what day the term is to commence. There must be a certain beginning, and a certain ending, otherwise it is not a perfect lease...."

FORMALITIES OF A LEASE

A lease may be valid if created as follows:

(1) less than 3 years; unregistered land, it may be made orally or in writing or by deed.
(2) registered land; more than 1 year in the case of Barbados and Jamaica and 2 years in the case of the other jurisdictions, it must be in writing. See however, s.70 of the Registration of (Titles) Act of Jamaica.
(3) more than 3 years; unregistered land, it must be made by deed.
(4) more than 3 years; made orally and there is part performance, an equitable lease will arise.
(5) more than 3 years; sufficient memorandum in writing, an equitable lease will also arise.

(6) up to 4 or 5 years; tenant has been guilty of bad conduct or for some other reason which will affect the grant of specific performance, there will be no equitable lease. However, if the tenant enters into possession and pays rent, a periodic tenancy will arise.

(7) more than 3 years; neither sufficient memorandum nor part performance, specific performance will not be granted but if the tenant enters into possession and pays rent a periodic tenancy will arise.

Non-compliance with formalities

A lease will be void where it does not comply with the relevant formalities. Kodilinye makes the point:

> *"A lease which does not comply with the necessary formalities is void at law, but it has long been the rule that if the intended tenant goes in to possession with the landlord's consent, a tenancy at will arises, and if the tenant then pays rent which is accepted, he becomes a yearly or other periodic tenant depending on the period with reference to which rent is paid". (Kodilinye 2000 P.15)*

"An agreement for a lease is as good as a lease"

This is the situation in equity as illustrated in the case of **Walsh v. Lonsdale [1882] 21 Ch D9.** There it was agreed between the parties that they would enter into a lease of a mill, for the period of seven years. The lease would be by way of a deed, a term of which was that the tenant would pay a year's rent in advance. The deed was not executed, but the tenant was put in possession, paying rent in arrear; in law being a yearly tenant. The landlord demanded a year's rent and when it was not forthcoming, he distrained against the tenant, who brought an action for illegal distress and for an injunction to restrain the distress. It was held that the right and obligation of both parties were the same as if the deed had been executed. Equity would prevail, consistent with the principle that where there is conflict between law and equity, equity prevails. The Court found that there existed an equitable lease for 7 years.

In **Metcalfe and Eddy Ltd. V. Edgill [1961] 5 WIR 417**, the formalities of a lease were not complied with and which resulted in an equitable lease. Consequently, the tenant's purported vacation of the premises was a breach of contract. The Court of Appeal of Trinidad and Tobago applied the rule in **Walsh v. Lonsdale.**

Benefits of a Lease over an Agreement for a Lease

(1) The rights and obligations can be established by the court in a legal lease that has specific terms. The situation is not so clear where there is an equitable lease. This is so as the remedy for an agreement for a lease is discretionary. In order to seek and receive discretionary remedy, equitable principles and maxims such as "he who comes to equity must come with clean hands" or "Equity looks on as done that which ought to be done". It is important that the person who seeks equity, does equity.

(2) A lessee under a lease has more advantages or leverage against a third party than a lessee under an agreement for a lease. Two examples of the advantages available are listed:

   a. The bonafide purchaser for value has no notice of the lessee who simply has an agreement for a lease. This type of lessee you encountered earlier in your studies, has only equitable rights which is not a *right in rem.*

   b. The enforceability of covenants (whether positive or negative) between a landlord and his tenant under a lease, under the principle of "privity of estate". In an agreement for a lease where the principles of contract apply, only benefits, not burdens can be assigned.

TYPES OF TENANCIES

(1) *Leases for a fixed period*

These leases terminate automatically by effluxion of time (expiration of time), but may be renewed according to the wishes of the parties. Long leases are usually determined by effluxion of time. In this regard, the lessor does not have to serve a notice to quit. The tenant cannot deliver up the premises without the landlord's permission and the landlord is within his rights to refuse such a request and then take legal action to recover damage from the tenant should he unilaterally surrender the lease. Where either party wants to end the lease ahead of the stipulated time, for example, a one year lease, a six months' notice is required.

While the lease is running, either party may serve notice to exercise an option to purchase or an option to renew as per the terms of the contract.

(2) *Periodic tenancies*

This type may be for a week, month, or year. This type of tenancy is what most of us are familiar with. We speak frequently about living in a "rented house" or that "we have to pay rent every month". It is important to note that a periodic lease become frozen into a fixed period lease when notice to quit is served on the tenant. Remember that a notice to quit is generally for 30 days as per the Rent Restriction Act of Jamaica.

The periodic tenancy on the other hand, can arise where a fixed term lease expires and the tenant continues to be in occupation and the landlord collects rent. Kodilinye makes an important point:

> *"No such tenancy will be implied where the tenant remains in possession as a statutory tenant under the rent restriction legislation, or where there is evidence that the landlord wished to evict the tenant, or where he did not know the relevant facts, such as where the tenant had died, unknown to the landlord, and the landlord had accepted rent from the tenant's widow". (Kodilinye 2000 p.19)*

(3) Tenancy at will

This is a sort of leasehold such that either the landlord or the tenant may terminate the tenancy at any time by giving reasonable notice. Notice that it is of no specific duration and notice to quit does not have to be 30 days as per the Rent restriction Act. It usually occurs in the absence of a lease, or where the tenancy is not for consideration. Under the modern common law, tenancy at will can arise under the following circumstances:

i. the parties expressly agree that the tenancy is at will and not for rent.
ii. A family member is allowed to live at home without formal arrangement. A nominal consideration may be required.
iii. A tenant wishes to occupy the property urgently, but there was insufficient time negotiate and execute a lease. The tenancy at will terminates in this case as soon as a written lease is completed. If a lease fails to be realized, the tenant must vacate the property.

A tenancy at will terminates by operation of law, if:

a. the tenant commits waste against the property;
b. the tenant attempts to assign his tenancy;
c. the landlord transfers his interest in the property;
d. the landlord leases the property to another person;
e. the tenant or the landlord dies.

The landlord's permission is critical in these situations. In **Romany v.Romany (1972) 21 WIR, 491**, the matter for the Court of Appeal of Trinidad and Tobago was to decide whether a license or tenancy at will existed based on the facts. The Magistrate's decision was upheld on appeal when it was determined that a person who is let into exclusive possession of premises, prima facie becomes a tenant unless there are circumstances which support a contrary intention. Where there is exclusive possession granted to a new occupant, it is almost decisive of a tenancy and special circumstances or conduct must be shown to negative that tenancy into a license. The appellant, A had failed to show any such special circumstances or conduct and therefore a tenancy at will had to succeed. Where the parties offend the terms of the tenancy at will, it ceases and it is sometimes very difficult to distinguish a tenancy at will from a license.

In **Deen v Mahabir** a mother gave her son an old property that she owned for some time. He later occupied with his wife and subsequently a child. Sometime after occupation the mother requested that the son vacate the property on several occasions. He continued in occupation until his death in around 1952 but his wife continued to reside on the property.

Approximately ten years later, the mother conveyed the property to a third party who brought an action for eviction against wife/widow. The wife pleaded exclusive possession of the premises for over 30 years, relying on the Real Property Limitation Ordinance. The Trial judge held that time had run in favour of the wife and that the third party's appeal had to be dismissed. The court's reasoning was on the basis that generally in family relationships of this sort there is no intention to create legal relationships and so there is no tenancy at will, there was a mere license which was destroyed on each occasion the mother told the deceased son to leave the property. The wife had therefore acquired a good title that destroyed the third party's interest.

(4) Tenancy at sufferance

This misnomer comes into existence when a tenant remains in possession of property even after the end of the lease, until the landlord acts to eject the tenant. The occupant may legally be a trespasser or a squatter at this point. If the landlord collects rent, then a periodic tenancy may arise. The landlord may be able to evict such tenant at any time, without notice.

(5) Tenancy by estoppel

This is a tenancy that remains in effect despite the fact that its grantor had no legal right to grant it. This is for example the situation when a mortgagor in possession breaches the conditions of the mortgage and grants a lease. The lease will bind the tenant and, under the doctrine of estoppel, the mortgagor may sue for all outstanding rent. If the mortgagor subsequently reacquires the ownership of the property the tenancy by estoppel becomes an entirely legal tenancy.

Bruton v London & Quadrant Housing Trust [2000] 1 AC 406 - London and Quadrant had a license to use some property as temporary accommodation for homeless people. It offered a license of one of the units to Mr Bruton who later claimed he had a lease since it had the essential elements of a lease identified by Lord Templeman in ***Street v Mountford***. The House of Lords agreed that there was a tenancy created, although inadvertently and although the Housing Trust only had a license, they were prevented from relying on their inadvertence.

LANDLORD AND TENANT - RIGHTS AND PROTECTION

Implied and expressed covenants tend to guide the relationship between landlord and tenant. Common law and statutory provisions helps to protect and also to guide the behaviours of both parties.

Common law, given its harsh nature, will be inclined to skew the relationship of landlord and tenant in favour of the landlord. Where the landlord honours his covenants he is entitled to enforce his rights against the tenant for any breach of the tenant's covenants. However, statutory provisions have provided some relief for tenants. In Jamaica, the common law right of distress against a tenant's property has been removed by statute. And in Trinidad and Tobago the Courts have held that there can be no distress against chattel house.

TERMINATION OF A LEASE

A lease or tenancy may be terminated in any of the following ways depending on the type of lease:

a. Forfeiture
b. Surrender
c. Merger
d. Effluxion of time
e. Notice to quit
f. Frustration

Forfeiture

By virtue of provisions within the lease, the landlord may re-enter the demised premises in the event there are any breaches of covenant by the tenant under the lease. Where there is a breach, the lease would then be forfeited. A lease becomes voidable at the instance of a breach by the lessee. This means the landlord has the option to terminate or not. The landlord must of necessity exercise the right to re-enter by a clear, unambiguous act that leaves the lessee being absolutely clear of the landlord's intention. Three modes of doing so are:

1. Landlord's actual re-entry
2. Granting of a new lease of the premises to a third party
3. Court proceedings for ejectment for recovery of possession.

The right to forfeiture or actual re-entry may be waive by the landlord

1. if there is evidence that he is aware of the breach; and
2. does nothing about it

An acceptance of rent does not constitute a waiver where there is a continuing breach. An example of a continuing breach is a breach of a repairing covenant. So that, if the landlord collects rent and then the breach continues, there may be no waiver. However, if rent is collected after the breach continues then there may be a waiver of forfeiture.

Where the tenant has not paid rent, the landlord must ensure that he makes formal demand before re-entry. To avoid this formal demand before re-entry, the landlord should include a term in the lease agreement to the effect that non-payment of rent will result in forfeiture.

The court has discretion in equity, on the application of the tenant, to grant relief from forfeiture. The tenant has to satisfy the court that there has been an absence of inordinate behaviours on the tenant's part or that there are mitigating circumstances.

In the case of covenants other than the nonpayment of rent, as long as the landlord has served the required statutory notice and subsequently re-enters the premises, the tenant loses the right to relief against forfeiture. A statutory notice must be served on the tenant by the landlord for breaches of covenants other than to pay rent, setting out:

1. the particulars of the breach,
2. requiring a remedy to the breach, where possible; and
3. requiring compensation for the breach.

Colonial Minerals Ltd v Joseph Dew and Son Ltd (no.1) [1959] 20ECSLR 243, a decision from Antigua where Manning J said that the requirement for the statutory notice was "clearly to curb landlords in insisting on their rights of re-entry and forfeiture accruing from breaches of the covenants by tenants…"

A sublease will be destroyed where the main lease is forfeited.

Surrender

For a surrender to take effect, both parties must act in a way which indicates their intention to surrender the lease. The tenant should vacate the premises and handover the keys to the landlord or an agent as a clear indication that they are surrendering the lease. Thus if the landlord grants the tenant a right to occupy the premises as a licensee, the terms of the occupancy have changed, the lease having been surrendered.

If there were existing subleases granted by the tenant, the land lord will be bound by those. Where there is surrender, the landlord and tenant are released from any future obligations but are bound by obligations already incurred.

Merger

Where the interest by way of a lease is joined with the interest in fee simple in the same person, there is a merger. As a result of this coming together of both interests, the lease dies since both interest cannot be held by the same person.

Effluxion of time

This is the expiration of a lease and is particularly relevant to long leases. There is usually no problem with both parties knowing when a lease expires. The problem usually arises where the tenant holds over and the landlord needs possession. In **Scott v Lerner Shop Ltd [1988] 25 JLR 219** The Jamaican Court of Appeal was of the view that the tenant should be afforded reasonable time to find a suitable alternative accommodation.

Notice to quit

A periodic tenancy can be determined by the service of a notice to quit. A notice to quit may be served by either the landlord or the tenant. In the absence of an express term in the lease, or statutory provisions, the period of notice required is determined by the rules at common law. A person may limit his right to serve a notice to quit but may not deprive himself of that same right.

Where the parties have not made an express agreement, the period of notice required to determine a periodic tenancy are as follows: -

1. A yearly tenancy - 6 month's notice
2. A quarterly tenancy - one quarters notice
3. A monthly tenancy - one month's notice
4. Weekly one week's notice

Where the period of the tenancy is of unusual duration such as 7 months, it is wise to set the notice period. Where there is a fixed tenancy this may also be determined by notice this should usually be included in the lease agreement.

The Rent Restriction Act and The Conveyancing Act provide guidance on dealing with notices.

Expiration of Notice to Quit

At common law, the notice to quit must not only satisfy the requirements relating to the period of the notice, but it must also expire at the end of a period of the tenancy. If this requirement is not satisfied, the notice will be invalid. The courts have construed the end of the period of the tenancy to include the anniversary of the commencement of the tenancy. So that if a yearly tenancy began on January 1, a notice to quit would be effective if it took effect either on January 1, or December 31.

Form of Notice

A notice must show a clear intention to terminate. The notice must be clear and unambiguous, though it need not be in any specific form unless required by the terms of the tenancy or statutory provisions. It may be given orally although this is unadvisable because of the evidential difficulties that this causes. It must not be conditional and it must relate to the whole of the premises.

Service of Notice

The notice to quit must be given by the landlord to his immediate tenant, or by the tenant to his immediate landlord, or the authorised agent of either. In the case of joint tenants, notice to, or by any one of them binds all of them. It may be given by ordinary post, by registered post or as prescribed by the lease, or by personal service. It may be served on a spouse or employee provided it is made clear to the recipient that the notice is to be delivered. If it is left on the premises, it must be shown that it came to the attention of the tenant in time.

Frustration

The Courts have not been willing to hold that a lease can be frustrated. However, in **National Carriers Ltd v Panalpina Northern Ltd [1981] 1 ALL ER 161,** the House of Lords posited that on very rare occasions, the doctrine could apply to a lease on the arguments as frustration of a contract. Their Lordships took the view that a lease might be frustrated

> "*not only by physical catastrophe, such as where some vast convulsion of nature swallowed up the property altogether, or buried it in the depths of the sea, but also by a supervening event so far beyond the contemplation of the parties that it would be unjust to enforce the lease*".

The facts of **Panalpina** are that the local authority closed the only road that led to the warehouse for a period of 20 months which interrupted a lease that was entered into between the parties for a term of 10 years. It was held that the lease was not frustrated and rent remained payable by the tenant.

In **Cricklewood Property and Investment Trust Ltd v Leighton's Investment Trust Ltd [1945] AC 221**, it was held that wartime legislations did not frustrate a building lease that was agreed for 99 years from May 1936 and rent remained also remained payable.

Distress

Distress is an ancient common law remedy which can be used to coerce a tenant into payment of outstanding rent. It is not a remedy that is available to enforce any covenants other than covenants for payment of rent. It is a self-help remedy that allows the landlord to get his money and not an empty property. This remedy has been abolished in Jamaica.

A warrant of Levy may be obtained by the landlord which empowers a bailiff to seize the tenant's goods in Jamaica, where the Court has made an order for payment of rental and the tenant defies that order.

A landlord may not distrain on the tenant's goods on Sunday or between sunset and sunrise. In addition, the landlord can only distrain on another premises where it is known that the tenant has illegally and clandestinely taken the goods. **Thompson v Facey [1976] 14 JLR 158**

As to what goods are distrainable, the Jamaican case of **White v Brown [1969] 13 WIR 523** demonstrated that only goods which have been fraudulently and clandestinely removed from the premises may be destrained upon by the landlord. This case may be decided differently in the Bahamas as landlords may distrain against goods within six months of the termination of the lease. Generally speaking and Jamaica in particular as at the time of the decision, could only destrain during the currency of the lease. Jamaica has since abolished that area of law.

There are some items which at common law cannot be distrained for. These include: -

1. Animals ferae naturae
2. Fixtures
3. Items being used
4. Loose money (although money in a bag or chest could be distrained)
5. Property delivered to persons carrying on a public trade to be used in the exercise of this trade
6. Property in the custody of the law, belonging to the government or belonging to persons with diplomatic privilege

These provisions apply in all jurisdictions where distress is available and in some jurisdictions, perishable goods cannot be distrained upon.

A chattel house may not be distrained against.
This can be seen in **Doolan v. Ramlakan and Abdool [1967] 12 W1R 146** where it was held that only goods and chattels may be distrained for arrears of rent and that fixtures could not be held.

Baptiste v. Supersad [1967] 12 W1R 140 - It was made clear that Trinidad and Tobago like England all had the remedy available to a landlord given by s. 8 of the Landlord and Tenant Ordinance to distrain for the recovery of rent in arrears.
At common law any goods on the premises belonging to a lodger are also distrainable. This provision has been restricted by:

a. The concept of privileged goods; and
b. Statutory provisions, designed to protect third parties from seizure of their chattels

Privileged goods include goods actually in use by the tenant, also goods used in trade, and his ordinary clothing.

The third party must show for example, in Belize, Guyana and Trinidad and Tobago, where there are statutory provisions which protect the third party from having his good seized, that the tenant has no interest in the goods and may enter into an agreement to pay rent directly to the landlord. This is a frequent occurrence where there is a cohabiting relationship.

Once the goods have been distrained upon, the landlord is under duty to ensure that they are kept securely and are not damaged. They must not be used by the landlord who holds (or impounds) them as security until payment. There is also a requirement for the bailiff in Trinidad and Tobago to provide the tenant with a notice of distress, along with "an inventory and a statement of authorised changes".

By a procedure called *replevin*, sometimes known as "claim and delivery," a tenant is able to recover goods unlawfully withheld from his or her possession, by means of a special form of legal process in which a court may require a defendant to return specific goods to the plaintiff at the outset of the action (i.e. before judgment).

Note also that, in the jurisdictions where this is allowed, the landlord must not distrain in a manner which is illegal, excessive or irregular.

OBLIGATION OF LANDLORD'S AND TENANT'S COVENANTS

A landlord and or a tenant's obligation, implied or expressed may be guided by statute or common law.

Landlord's Implied Covenant Quiet Enjoyment

This covenant is not speaking of "silence" per se. It speaks of disturbances to include blocking the tenant's access to outdoor facilities. In addition, the landlord cannot enter upon the land in a manner which is repugnant to the tenant's interest, such as using a bulldozer to demolish structures on the property or to put loads of marl in the driveway as a means of harassing the tenant to vacate the premises. These actions will be seen as breach of the covenant of quiet enjoyment.

Once the tenant has been put in possession, the covenant implied in law is that a landlord will not engage in any activity which will disturb the tenant who has right to enjoy the premises quietly, that is, without disturbance or hindrance.

In **Douglas v. Bowen [1974] 22WIR 333,** a Jamaican Court of Appeal precedent that awarded compensatory damages to the respondent who operated a saloon which was destroyed along with the premises by the appellant landlord.

All the cases indicate that the breach complained of by the tenant must be a physical interference with the demised property.

Non derogation from grant

This covenant looks a lot like that for quiet enjoyment. It is an obligation implied on the part of a landlord to not give with one hand and take with another. The purpose for which the property was leased by the tenant is generally known by the landlord and so he is not allowed to offend this covenant by frustrating the tenant from enjoying the property for the purpose for which he leased it.

The act complained of must be such as to make the property less suitable for the purpose for which it was required. Where the tenant is particularly sensitive, he may not succeed in a claim.

Fitness for Human habitation

Although the common law does not impose any such obligation on the landlord, as a general rule, the demand and practices of modern dwelling have created some obligations. These are in respect of:

(a) Furniture in a furnished apartment must be capable of being used as such..

(b) Common areas in apartments must be available and habitable. The place must be well lit, there must be garbage disposal.

(c) Statutory provisions. **Hamblin v. Samuel [1966] 11W1R 48** provides for a good reading on what is meant by premises being fit for "human habitation". The appellant erected a one-storey building on her lot of land which sloped downwards at the back, so that the supporting pillars were about 3 ft. high in the front and about 7 ft. high in the rear. Later, in or about the year 1962, she did more excavation under the house, so as to get a uniform level of land about 10 ft. under the building and replacing the pillars as well. She concreted the floor and built two self contained apartments. The height from floor to ceiling was no more than 7 ft. 8 ins when concluded. This was evidence that the apartment was not fit for human habitation.

The Board also found that a plan for the proposed new construction may not have been submitted to the local health authority for approval and that was a breach of the statute. It was for this reason that they held, on their interpretation of certain dicta of the former full court in **Gibson v Martin ((1961), 3 WIR 335),** that she had failed to prove that the converted basement structure was not originally constructed for human habitation. There was evidence also that the ventilation of the two new basement apartments was inadequate, that the one bedroom window in each of them could not be opened at all and that the one sitting room window in each had to be generally kept closed because of the prevailing dust. The Board concluded that the conditions to which the apartments were subject was almost, if not wholly, sub-human and that the structure was not fit for human habitation.

Covenant to repair

The landlord's covenant where express refers to keeping the premises in "tenantable repair with normal wear and tears excepted". Common law does not impose the same obligation on a landlord to do more repairs than would a reasonable man; it has developed into an implied covenant through practice. In some leases one might see an obligation placed on the tenant to do small repairs of a stated small sum.

Milo Butler and Sons Investment Co. Ltd v. Monarch Investments Ltd. shows the situation where the tenant notifies the landlord of the need for repairs and the landlord fails to effect them, the tenant after notifying the landlord of his intention to conduct those repairs, may do so, deducing the cost from rent due to be paid. Because this is an area that is very contentious, it is to be exercised as a last resort.

Tenant's Implied Covenants not to commit waste

We have already looked at types of waste earlier in our reading. By way of reminder therefore, a tenant must avoid committing acts of waste on the demised premises. Acts of waste generally reduces the value of the property.

Express Covenants

The covenants to which they have bound themselves are often found in writing or by deed. The covenant in each lease will vary depending on who the parties are, their varying needs and the user of the property. Some express covenants follow:

(a) Covenant to pay rent
(b) Covenant of repair
(c) Not to sub-let or assign without landlord's permissions.

Covenant to pay rent

Payment is done in arrear at common law, however common practice has seen rent being paid in advance. The rent is often an agreed amount and paid at a particular/specific time. If the property is destroyed, what about the tenant's liability to pay rent? In one case, **Cricklewood Property and Investment Trust Ltd. v. Leighton's Investment Trust Ltd. [1945] A.C.** the House of Lords held that war-time building restrictions did not frustrate a 99 year lease agreement. Payment of rental would still be required from the lessee. One of their Lordships opining that frustration might occur in some instances. In **Denman v Brise [1949] 1KB 22** it was said that a lease can be frustrated.

Covenant of repair

Common law places the standard of repairs in which tenanted premises are to be on "the locality, character and age of the premises at the date of the lease" and in such condition as "a reasonably minded owner would keep them". The standard of repair may be seen from the dictum of Lord Esher MR in **Proudfoot v. Hart [1890] 25Q.B.D.42** where he defined good tenantable repair as:

> *"...such repairs as, having regard to the age, character and locality of the house, would make it reasonably fit for the occupation of a reasonably-minded tenant of the class who would be likely to take it. The age of this the house must be taken into account, because nobody could reasonably expect that a house 200 years should be in the same condition of repair as a house lately built; the character of the house must be taken into account, because the same class of repair as would be necessary to a palace would be wholly unnecessary to a cottage; and the locality of the house must be taken*

> *into account, because the state of repair necessary for Grosvenor Square would be wholly different from the state of repair necessary for a house in Spitafields…" (At pages 52-53)*

Lord Esher's dictum must be looked at in light of: the length of the lease, changes in the character of the neighborhood and the introduction of modern facilities in order to determine what is reasonable.

CONSEQUENCES OF BREACH OF COVENANTS

The consequence of a breach may lie on a landlord or a tenant whether or not such covenant be expressed or implied. If a third party is affected, they may be liable together or individually to that party as well. The liability has to be shown to be one that touches and concerns the land.

Liability of the landlord for breach to the tenant and third parties

As you would already know, the landlord's covenants cover a covenant for quiet enjoyment or covenants to keep in reasonable repair. For breach of these covenants the landlord, the tenant may be entitled to compensating by way of damages. Because of privity of estate, like the tenant, the landlord's successors are bound by covenants which "run with the land". They are not enforceable against a successor where the landlord's covenants do not run with the land but are personal between him and the tenant as tenant.

In **Thomas v Hayward [1869]** the tenant's successor to a tavern failed to enforce a restraint of trade covenant that the landlord would not build a tavern within half mile radius of the leased property as the nature of the agreement was not one that touched and concerned land. The situation is even more complicated in the case of a sub-lease. It is therefore significant that the sub-lessee to insist on a covenant with the sublessor that the covenants under the head lease will apply. In **Dewar v Goodman [1909]**, a lessee disregarded a covenant to repair. A subtenant was evicted following forfeiture proceedings and failed to recover damages from the sublessor's successor for the breach.

Liability of the tenant for breach to the landlord and third parties
Where the tenant has a personal agreement with the sub lessee which does not touch and concern the land, this arrangement is not enforceable against the tenant's successor. This is illustrated in **Hand v Blow [1901]**, where a tenant covenanted with his landlord to replace chattels and machinery which were not fixtures and it was held that the covenant could not be enforced against the tenant's assignee as it did not run with the land. The landlord may seek to terminate a lease or enforce its covenant where the tenant is in breach of the covenant.

LICENSES

Thomas v Sorrell (1673) the statement was made that "a dispensation or license properly passeth no interest, nor alters or transfers property in anything, but only makes an action lawful, which without it had been unlawful". This was translated to mean that a licensee does not have an estate in land but is authorized to be on the land so that he is not trespassing.

According to Denning LJ in **Facchini v Bryson [1952]** "…there has been something in the circumstances, such as a family arrangement, an act of friendship or generosity, or such like to negative any intention to create a tenancy". A license often arises from informal arrangements, particularly when relationships are going well. The question of legal and equitable rights comes in issue when the relationship is not so harmonious. There are different types of license:

Types of licenses

There are four (4) types of licenses:

i. Bare license
ii. License coupled with an interest
iii. Contractual license
iv. License by estoppel, or "the license coupled with an equity"

Bare license

This license is very fickle. It can be revoked at any time. It is usually permission given to do something without consideration being exchanged. Once this license is revoked, the former licensee must be given a reasonable period in which to leave the property and when that period is exhausted he will become a trespasser if he remains on the property. In **Robson v Hallett [1967]**

2 QB 939 some police officers were licensees and were within their rights when they approached a citizen's door and knocked. Without a search warrant or other authority permitting the officers to insist on remaining, their license could be revoked by the householder who should be given reasonable time to exit the property.

License coupled with an interest

This occurs where the licensor grants the licensee permission to enter upon his land and to take something from it e.g. marl from the pit or a crop of mangoes. There is also the situation where the proprietor sells lumber to a purchaser. He cannot then prevent the purchaser from collecting the items. It is not revocable as long as the proprietary interest continues.

Contractual license

This is a license that is conferred by way of a contract. In this regard consideration moves from the licensee to obtain a benefit upon the licensor's property. An all-inclusive vacation is an example. Also, the purchase of tickets to attend and watch cricket at Bourda, Arnos Vale, or Sabina Park in Jamaica. A contract can be implied or imposed based on the intention of the parties.

License by estoppel

This is also referred to as "proprietary estoppel" on the part of equity. It prevents the licensor from insisting on his legal rights in circumstances where it would be unjust for him to do so. Equity looks for evidence of unconscionable behaviours and frowns upon it. In addition to the behavior of the licensor, equity will look at the extent to which there is unjust enrichment to the detriment of the licensee.

The leading case on this point is **Central London Property Trust Ltd v High Trees House Ltd [1947]** where Lord Denning made the point:

> *"...the first principle upon which all courts of equity proceed, that is, prevent a person from insisting on his strict legal rights - whether arising under a contract or on his title deeds or by statute - when it would be inequitable for him to do so having regard to the dealings which have taken place between the parties".*

In **Inwards v Baker** a father permitted his son to build a bungalow on his land. The son occupied the bungalow in reliance on his father's permission and the expectation that he would live there all his life. The father died and did not leave the property to his son. The Court of Appeal held that the trustees could not dispossess the son after he acquired an interest in the property purely from his father's encouragement and at the son's expense.

ACTIVITY SHEET – LEASES

1. Have a look at least three cases that were decided before **Street v Mountford**. How do you think they would have been decided today?

2. **(a)** Define the term license.
   (b) Aunt Norma allows her niece, Karen, to stay in an apartment downstairs in her house until Karen can find an apartment to rent. Karen and her husband moves in and have been living at the apartment for the past 15 years. Aunt Norma dies and her daughter, Jamelia, informs Karen that she needs the apartment. However, Karen refuses to move out, saying that her aunt had given her the apartment. Jamelia wants to sue Karen to get back the apartment from her.

   Advise Jamelia as to what recourse she has against Karen and her likelihood of success, referring to at least one decided case.

3. **(a)** Explain each of the following phrases. Give one example of each
   i. A contractual license
   ii. A license by estoppel
   (b) Aiken allows his friend, Berty, to occupy his beach cottage in the last two weeks of August every year. That is the time when Aiken and his family usually go overseas for their holidays. He does not charge Berty. Aiken returns from his holiday early and passes by the cottage to say hello to Berty. To Aitken's surprise, he sees Morty and his family there and learns that for the past few years Berty has been renting the cottage to Morty for a week.
   i. Identify and discuss the license given by Aiken to Berty
   ii. If Aiken asks Morty and his family to leave the cottage, does Morty have any legal right to remain? Give reasons to support your answer.
4. Discuss the conditions under which one of the following remedies may be exercised:
   i. Forfeiture
   ii. Distress
   iii. Notice to Quit

5. Mr Morris has bought a bigger house in Jack's Hill and has decided to move into it. He has agreed to lease his house in Barbican where he now lives to Ms. Laura for one year at a monthly rent of $15000. The lease contains a clause giving Mr Morris a right of re-entry

   i. Explain to Mr Morris three of his implied covenants under the lease

   ii. Advise Ms Laura on one of her implied obligations under the lease.

6. Mr Mensie is operating his restaurant in a building which belongs to Mrs Cole. Mr
   Mensie has been paying his rent faithfully. In August there are severe floods in the area and Mr Mensie's restaurant is flooded. He loses all of his stocks and supplies. It takes him six months to get his restaurant functioning again and he has not been able to pay his rent for these six months, Mrs. Cole is very upset about this and wants to terminate the lease. There is no forfeiture clause in the lease agreement.

   i. Advise Mrs Cole on the legal remedies available to her
   ii. What relief, if any, is Mr Mensie likely to obtain?

7. Phinias lived in the Caribbean. He had one son, Pherb, who emigrated to America, and two nieces, Sade and Mary. In 2001, Sade told him about her plans to do agriculture and Phinias offered her the use of an unoccupied cottage he owned in the countryside. "you are welcome to use it" he said. "It needs quite a lot of work to make it habitable, but you don't need to pay me any rent."

Sade moved into the cottage, made it habitable and started her poultry business.

Mary was unemployed, and in 2007, when Phinia's housekeeper died, he suggested to Mary that she should come and live with him in his house in the city and assist him as unpaid housekeeper and secretary. In 2009, when Phinias was ill, he told Mary not to worry about the future as he was leaving her the city house in his will. In 2010, Phinias retired and sold the city house and bought a bungalow by the sea. He and Mary lived in the bungalow for a short time until his death later that year. In his will Phinias left his whole estate to his son, Pherb, who now seeks possession of both the cottage in the country and the bungalow.

(i) Sade has brought action against Pherb claiming a right to the countryside cottage.
(ii) Advise Pherb whether there is any likelihood of Sade succeeding in her claim.
(iii) Advise Mary on whether she has any legal interest in her uncle's property.

8. Explain any two of the following types of leasehold interests:

   a. Periodic tenancy
   b. Tenancy at will
   c. Tenancy at sufferance

Chapter 16

EASEMENT

An Easement is a legal or equitable interest that one land owner has over the land of another. When the various examples of an easement are explored, the common strand to all these arrangements is that they are all rights exercised by one person over land which belongs to another person. Danckwerts J in **Re Ellenborough Park [1956]** describes an easement as having four elements:

(i) There must be a dominant and a servient tenement
(ii) The easement must accommodate the dominant tenement, that is, it must be connected with its enjoyment and be for its benefit
(iii) The dominant and servient owners must be different persons
(iv) The right claimed must be capable of forming the subject matter of a grant

There must be a dominant and a servient tenement

There must be a servient tenement over which the right is exercised. Where one has to use the property belonging to another (servient tenement) to access his land (dominant tenement) this is an easement. So that, if there is no dominant tenement, there is only the servient tenement. If one is simply using the servient tenement then that is a license and not an easement. There cannot be an easement in gross, that is, an easement cannot exist where the claimant has no interest in a dominant tenement, the enjoyment of which is dependent on an easement over a servient tenement.

The easement must accommodate the dominant tenement

This rule requires that the right must confer an advantage on the dominant land. It is not sufficient that only a mere personal advantage is being enjoyed but must be a right for the better enjoyment of the dominant tenement.

The dominant and servient tenements need not be adjacent to each other, though this is usually the case. An example of this is where a utility company is granted an easement to place its pole and wires over X's land, even though the utility company's land, the dominant tenement, may be far away from X's land, the servient tenement.

On, personal advantages, the leading case of **Hill v Tupper [1861-1873] All ER Rep 696** is instructive. The facts are that a canal company leased Tupper land adjacent to the canal and exclusive rights to put pleasure boats on the said canal. Tupper claimed a right by way of an easement enforceable against Hill, the landlord of the nearby inn whom he claimed had interfered with his trade when the defendant Hill, placed rival boats on the canal. Tupper's claim was dismissed by the court of appeal. With Pollock CB stating that "*a new species of incorporeal hereditament cannot be created at the will and pleasure of the owner of the property*" and Martin B positing that such a right as claimed by Tupper "*would lead to the creation of an infinite variety of interests in land, and an indefinite increase of possible estates*". Their Lordships were loath to grant rights which seemed to them too broad and without definite borders.

The dominant and servient owners must be different

This is how the rule is stated in **Re Ellenborough Park**, but is perhaps easier to understand if one says that the two tenements must not be both owned and occupied by the same person. An easement is essentially a right over another's land for the benefit of one's own, and one cannot exercise a right against oneself. Thus, if a person owns two pieces of land and has to walk across one to reach the other, he is not exercising an easement. However, this same situation can give rise to a "quasi-easement" as seen in **Wheeldon v Burrows,** a potential easement which could develop into an easement if the plots came into separate hands.

The right claimed must be capable of forming the subject matter of a grant

The easement must be precise enough to be identifiable so that the grantee is able to assign it as he can with other real property. Rights to privacy or to view or for branches of a tree to overhang another's land are not easements because they are not identifiable enough. However, rights to fix a sign board on a neighbouring house, to have a building supported by the wall of another building and to hang clothes on a line which passes over another's land are examples of identifiable easements.

No expenditure of money by the servient owner

The servient owner must not be required to expend money for the maintenance of the easement. An easement of fencing is an exception. An easement of support may also be an exception, although such an easement does not impose on the servient owner any obligation to maintain a supporting building in repair

Rights against land

The right must be against the other land. It is not a right of possession of land. In **Copeland v Greenhalf [1951] Ch 488**, it was held that a claim to park an unlimited number of vehicles on a plot of land did not constitute an easement, but rather that it tended towards a joint possession of the land.

ACQUISTION OF AN EASEMENT

An easement may be acquired by (i) statute or by (ii) a grant or reservation

By Statute

Easements may be granted by way of legislation. Some examples could be the laying of mains and pipes by utility companies.

By Grant or Reservation

Acquisition by grant

The Grant or reservation of an easement may be expressed or implied, or be by prescription. An Express Grant arises by means of express words of grant and by means of statute. An Implied Grant arises where, in the circumstances of the grantee's enjoyment and use of his land, an easement is implied. Some circumstances are identifiable:

- Necessity
- Intended easement
- Easement under the Rule in **Wheeldon v Burrows**

Necessity
An easement of necessity is an easement which is so essential to the enjoyment of the land that the land cannot be used without the easement. It can be said that such easements would be implied into a transaction because to do otherwise would be to allow the grantor to derogate from his grant. A good example of such an easement is the situation where the land is totally inaccessible, unless an easement be permitted to access. Megarry V-C made the point that:

> *"there is a rule of public policy that no transaction should, without good reason be treated as being effectual to deprive any land of a suitable means of access. Alternatively, the point might be put as a matter of construction: any transaction which, without good reason, appears to deprive land of any suitable means of access should, if at all possible, be construed as not producing this result"*
> **Nickerson v Barraclough [1980] Ch 325.**

Intended Easement
For the express reservation to apply it must be specifically stated in the instrument of transfer or deed of conveyance. In other words, a claim for an intended easement will fail as it cannot be implied.

In **Wheeldon v Burrowes** the claim was for an implied reservation of the right of access to light. Such right was claimed as being impliedly reserved in the conveyance. The Court of Appeal held that a reservation can only arise where it is expressly stated in the conveyance.

Situations where there will be implied reservations are:

(a) necessity; and
(b) common intention.

EXTINGUISHING EASEMENTS

(1) One party being the dominant and servient tenement simultaneously
(2) Express or implied release- legal easements can be extinguished by way of a deed within which it was previously documented. Equity will recognize an informal release if it would be inequitable to allow the releasing owner to go back on his word. In general, as it relates to implied release, the mere lack of use of an easement once it has been acquired will not lead to extinguishment of the right because one is never obliged to exercise the rights which one may have. However, a prolonged non-use may be used as evidence that the dominant owner has impliedly abandoned his right. It should however be noted that if the dominant owner explains the non-use he or she may still be regarded as not having abandoned the right. Thus in **James v Stevenson [1893] AC 162** a right was not lost due to a long period of non- use because the dominant owner explained that he had simply no occasion to exercise the right but presumably may wish to do so in the future.

In **Benn v Hardinge [1992]** the Court of Appeal said that non- use even for 175 years was not enough on its own to indicate an intention to abandon. The Court also commented that the abandonment of such a right would not be lightly inferred

ACTIVITY SHEET – EASEMENT

(1) Describe the ways by which an easement may be acquired. Support your answer with reference to legal authorities.

(2) Edeno and Danny own adjoining properties and for over twenty years Edeno used a narrow, unpaved private road that has been formed overtime by the constant use, from his property over Danny's land to the main road. Whenever it rains heavily, this road becomes slippery and almost unusable. Edeno and Danny have been friends and Danny has never objected to Edeno's use of the road. Edeno and Danny quarrel and when Edeno starts to pave the road to make it passable to vehicles, Danny writes him "withdrawing the permission I gave you to use the road." Danny then erects a fence across the road, barring access to Edeno's farm. Advise Edeno on:

i. Whether he has acquired an easement over Danny's land
ii. The remedies that would be available to him to protect his legal interest

(3) **(a)** With the use of illustrations, explain the requirements for an easement.
(b) Outline any two methods of acquiring an easement.

(4) Explain how an easement may be
i. acquired
ii. extinguished

Chapter 17
RESTRICTIVE COVENANTS

Restrictive covenants are generally placed on titles to ensure the preservation of the character of a particular community. This could be a farming, residential or commercial community. Character of a community could refer to value of property, user of land. They are usually negative by nature, for example, a covenant may be to the effect that no building in that community is used to be used as a shop, church or school. Covenant may also be positive, for example, the covenantee will maintain a fence in good repair. Gray and Symes defines a covenant as follows:

> *"In the context of real property, a "covenant" is an arrangement under seal in which one party ("the covenantor") promises another party ("the covenantee") that he will or will not engage in some specified activity in relation to a defined area of land. A covenant is therefore an agreement which creates an obligation and which is contained in a deed. Such an agreement has legal efficacy because the seal imports consideration and averts the strict question of whether consideration has been provided for the promise given by the covenantor. The covenant is therefore clearly enforceable between covenantor and covenantee as a form of contract."*

According to Gray and Symes, the essential elements of a covenant are:

1) Mutual benefit and benefit and burden
2) Mutual obligations

3) Presence of consideration
4) Enforceability as contract

"The test of a restrictive covenant is always a test of substance". This is according to Gray and Symes who stated that:

> *"A rule of thumb commonly used to test the nature of a covenant of dubious status is the question whether the covenant requires the expenditure of money for its performance. If the covenantor is required to "put his hand into his pocket", the covenant cannot be negative in nature."* (p.617)

Transmission of Benefit and Burden
Benefit at Common law

It is very important that the covenant "touches and concerns" the land. In order to benefit from the covenant, the covenantee must have a legal, not an equitable interest in the land affected by the covenant, but the covenantor need not have any land to be burdened, that is, there is no requirement for a servient tenement. Also, an assignee of land must have a legal, not an equitable interest in the land which benefits from the covenant.
The Prior's Case illustrates the point that there need not be a servient tenement. There, where a Prior had covenanted with the Lord of the manor to sing divine service in the manor chapel, the lord's successor in title was held to be able to sue the prior for breach of the covenant to perform.

The well-known case of **Smith and Snipes Hall Farm Ltd. v. River Douglas Catchment Area [1949] 2K.B. 500** is helpful. In that case, the facts were as follows:
In 1938, the defendants entered into a covenant with eleven landowners who owned land along a certain stream. On a landowner's payment of a part of the cost, the defendants then undertake to improve the banks on the stream and maintain the banks in the future. Two years later, in 1940, one landowner sold her land to Smith who, in 1944, leased the land to Snipes Hall Farm Ltd.

In 1946, a flood burst the banks of the river and flooded the adjoining land, because of the defendant's negligence in maintaining the banks, in breach of the 1938 covenant in not maintaining the banks of the river. It was held that the plaintiffs could enforce the covenant as it touched and concerned the land. The covenant was for the benefit of the land and was therefore transferred with it. Accordingly, the contractual principle of privity of contract was not applicable in this instance and the defendants could not rely upon it in a case where there was a mutual benefit and burden, based upon the 1938 covenant. A third party who took an interest in the land benefited and was therefore bound by it and could therefore enforce the covenant.

The Benefit in Equity

Where common law poses the usual hardship, equity brings relief in maintaining that there is a benefit which runs with the land. Kodilinye very neatly highlights these circumstances, as follows:

a. Where the covenantee or the assignee are merely equitable owners of the land benefitted
b. Where the covenantor is no longer the owner of the servient tenement but has assigned it, so that the enforcement against the assignee of the servient tenement depends upon the rule in **Tulk v Moxhay**
c. Where only part of the benefitted land is assigned to the plaintiff, since at common law the benefit cannot be assigned in pieces
d. Where the plaintiff relies upon his land being part of a scheme of development (Kodilinye, 2000 p.150)

Burdens at common law

The basic rule is that the burden of the covenants does not run at common law. Common law dislikes restraints being placed on your use of your own estate, and accordingly applies the strict rules of privity of contract in such cases. The leading decision on this issue is **Austerberry v Oldham Corporation [1885] 29 Ch D 750**, in which it was held that, at common law, the obligation to make up a road and keep it in good repair could not pass to the successor in title of the original covenantor. Lindley LJ puts the position succinctly, as follows:

> *"[I am] not prepared to say that any covenant which imposes a burden upon land does run with the land, unless the covenant does, upon the time of construction of the deed containing the covenant, amount to either a grant of an easement, or a rent charge, or some estate or interest in land. A mere covenant to repair, or to do something of that kind, does not seem to me, I confess, to run with the land in such a way as to bind those who may acquire it"* p.781

This position was reaffirmed in **Rhone v Stephens [1994] 2 AC 310**, in the case of a covenant to maintain a roof.

Professor HWR Wade believes the common law position is too strict and that "the law has failed to provide any mechanism by which the necessary obligations can be made to run satisfactorily with freehold land" in an era where shared facilities are common place.

Mechanisms have been introduced to circumvent the rigidity of the common law. One of these is:

1. The "chain of covenants" by which the successors in title of the covenantee, contract to indemnify his predecessor in title for any future breaches. In essence, each purchaser of the burdened lands covenants separately with their immediate predecessor to carry out the positive covenant. Thus, if the original covenantor is sued on the covenant, he will be able to recover any damages paid from the person he sold the land.
2. The "doctrine of mutual benefits and burdens" which posits that one does not take an interest in land without taking the benefits and burdens and passing them equally to successors in title.

The burden in equity

The foundation of the law in this area is the leading case, **Tulk v Moxhay [1848]**. The criteria which must be satisfied for the burden of a covenant to be enforceable are as follows: The burden must have intended to run with the land and the covenant must be negative by nature

The benefit must have been made to benefit land which the covenantee held at the time he made the covenant.

Covenants in equity

The mid - nineteenth century saw a balancing act between the desires for industrial development and the preservation of residential amenities for the private householder.

The courts found it necessary to protect land usage from the "fancy and caprice of owners" and in **Keppell v Bailey [1834]**, Lord Brougham declined to enforce the burden of a covenant, against a successor in title holding the view that to do so would "fetter the use and development of the land in perpetuity".

Equity reared its head and began to intervene, bringing relief where previously the common law restrictions caused hardship. The leading case of **Tulk v Moxhay** advanced the position further. In that case, the plaintiff was the owner of several plots in Leicester Square. In 1808 he sold one plot to Elms who covenanted for himself, his heirs and assigns to keep and maintain the land "in an open state, uncovered with any building, in neat and ornamental order". The land was subsequently sold to the defendant who claimed a right to construct building upon it. He admitted that he had notice of the covenant, but claimed that he was not bound by it. It was held that an injunction would be granted to restrain the defendant from the building on the land, because there was a jurisdiction in Equity to prevent the defendant from acting contrary to the provisions of the covenant, as he had notice of it.

The decision in **Tulk v Moxhay** was applied with great enthusiasm in ensuing years. Overtime, the Courts began to limit its application, seeing the need to prevent a contractual right from being enlarged into proprietary right. Limitations took the form of something akin to the enforcement of easements. Equity therefore imposed a number of requirements, for example, that there should be a dominant and a servient tenement.

Among the requirements of equity are the following as set out in (Gray and Symes pp. 616 - 619):

1. The covenant must be restrictive or negative. Thus in **Heywood v Brunswick Permanent Benefit Building Society [1881]**, it was held that equity had no jurisdiction to enforce a positive covenant to build and repair.
2. The covenant must accommodate the dominant tenement. Thus in **London County Council v Allen [1914]**, it was held that a plaintiff could not enforce a restrictive covenant against the covenantor's successors where the plaintiff was not in possession of, or having an interest in land benefitting from the covenant. Statute reversed this decision, to enable such bodies as local authorities and the National Trust to be able to enforce covenants even where they do not possess a dominant tenement to benefit from the covenant. Also instructive is **Re Ballards Conveyance [1937],** where approximately 1,700 acres of land were retained by the covenantee, it was held that his successor in title could not benefit from the covenant, as it could not practicably be conceived that the covenant's benefits were intended for such an extensive holding.
3. The covenant must have been intended to run with the covenantor's land.

Annexation

By annexation, the benefit of the restrictive covenant is nailed to a specific plot of the covenantee's land. It allows the purchaser of the benefited land to acquire rights to enforce covenants. It is done in such a way that the benefit passes with every subsequent transfer of the land. It may be express, implied, or statutory.

Express annexation

Where "words of annexation" are used, the benefit of the covenant is annexed or attached to the land, so that for ever after it passes automatically with the land to the new owner. In order to achieve express annexation, it is necessary that the words of the covenant should show that the original parties intended the benefit to run, and one way of doing this is to state expressly that the covenant is made expressly "for the benefit of" named land. This is illustrated in the case of **Rogers v Hosegood [1900] 2Ch 388.** Another method which will have the same effect is for the covenant to be made with the covenantee as estate owner, that is, describing him as the owner of the land to be benefitted.

Implied annexation

This form of annexation is somewhat controversial, as may be perceived from its very nature. The Courts, already making rules to make express annexation specific, have greater difficulty with this type of annexation. See **Jamaica Mutual Life Assurance Society v Hillsborough Ltd [1989] 1 WLR 1101.** Where words of express annexation are lacking, some cases suggest that it may still be possible for the court to identify the benefited land by looking at the circumstances. Where the facts are held to indicate with reasonable certainty the land which is to be benefited, the benefit will thereafter run with the land. This way of proceeding has been called implied annexation.

Statutory annexation

Federated Homes Ltd v Mill Lodge Properties Ltd [1980] 1 All ER 371 has shown by way of statute that any covenant that is 'related to any land' of the covenantee is 'annexed' to that land. The facts are set out below.

In 1970 M Ltd, the owner of a site which included three areas of land, the red, green and blue land, obtained outline planning permission to develop the site by erecting a certain number of dwellings. The permission was valid for three years.

In February 1971 M Ltd as vendor conveyed the blue land to the defendants. By a restrictive covenant contained in cl 5(iv) of the conveyance the defendants covenanted with the vendor that in carrying out the development of the blue land they would not build "at a greater density than a total of 300 dwellings so as not to reduce the number of units which the vendor might eventually erect on the retained land under the existing planning consent".

The retained land "was described as "any adjoining or adjacent property" retained by M Ltd and therefore meant the red and green land, together with some additional land. By a series of transfers the plaintiffs became the owners of the red and the green land. In the case of the green land the transfers contained an unbroken chain of express assignments of the benefit of the restrictive covenant. However, in the case of the red land, the transfer to the plaintiffs did not contain any express assignment of the benefit of the covenant and the chain of assignments of the benefit of the covenant was broken.

In 1977 the plaintiffs obtained planning permission to develop the red and green land. They then discovered that the defendants had obtained permission to develop the blue land at a higher density than permitted by the restrictive covenant, and that that density was likely to prejudice development of the red and green land. The plaintiffs accordingly brought an action to restrain the defendants from building on the blue land at a density which would be in breach of the restrictive covenant. By their defence the defendants contended, inter alia, that, if the restrictive covenant was capable of assignment and was not spent on the lapse of the 1970 planning permission, the benefit of the covenant had not been transmitted to the plaintiffs.

The judge held that the covenant was capable of assignment and was not spent, but that the benefit of it had not been annexed to the retained land because the conveyance to the defendants had not expressly or impliedly annexed it and because s 78 of the Law of Property Act 1925 did not have the effect of annexing the benefit of the covenant to the retained land. However, he held that in the case of the green land, the unbroken chain of assignments of the benefit of the covenant vested the benefit of it in the plaintiffs as the owner of the green land, and that under s 62 of the 1925 Act, which implies general words into a conveyance of land, the benefit of the covenant was carried to the plaintiffs as the owners of the red land. The judge granted the plaintiffs an injunction restraining breach of the covenant by the defendants.

The defendants appealed. On the appeal, the court having concluded that the restrictive covenant was capable of assignment and was not spent, the question arose whether the benefit of it had been transmitted to the plaintiffs as the owner of the red land.

Held: Where there was a restrictive covenant which related to or touched and concerned the covenantee's land, s 78(1) of the 1925 Act had the effect of annexing the benefit of the covenant to the covenantee's land, and did not merely provide a statutory shorthand for shortening a conveyance. The language of s 78(1) implied that such a restrictive covenant was enforceable at the suit of

(i) the covenantee and his successors in title,
(ii) A person deriving title under him or them and
(iii) The owner or occupier of the benefited land, and, therefore, under s 78(1) such a covenant ran with the covenanter's land and was annexed to it.
(iv) Since cl 5 of the conveyance to the defendants showed that the restrictive covenant was for the benefit of the retained land and that land was sufficiently described in the conveyance for the purposes of annexation, the covenant related to, or touched and concerned, the land of the covenantee (M Ltd) and s 78(1) had the effect of annexing the benefit of the covenant to the retained land for the benefit of M Ltd, its successors in title and the persons deriving title under it or them including the owners for the time being of the retained land.

Furthermore, if on the proper construction of a document a restrictive covenant was annexed to land, prima facie it was annexed to every part of the land. It followed that s 78(1) had caused the benefit of the restrictive covenant to run with the red land and be annexed to it, and that the plaintiffs, both as the owners of the red land and as the owners of the green land, were entitled to enforce the covenant against the defendants. The appeal would therefore be dismissed.

Restrictive Covenants and scheme of development

Schemes of development will generally have restrictive covenants noted on their certificate of title. This is done in order to maintain the desirable character of the development. These covenants are used as guidelines on how the owners should or should not operate. Upon receipt of planning permission for a building scheme or housing scheme the local authority will grant approval subject to a number of restrictive covenants which, when accepted by the developer, are endorsed on the certificate of title.

The conditions which must be satisfied to secure restrictive covenants were laid down in **Elliston v Reacher [1908] 2 Ch 374**

(1) The area of the scheme must be clearly defined
(2) The vendor must have laid out the estate in plots, or sold plots of a size which the purchasers required
(3) The vendor must have extracted restrictive covenants from the purchasers
(4) Each purchaser must have covenanted that covenants are enforceable against each other
(5) The vendor must have intended the restrictive covenants to be for the benefit of all the plots sold in the scheme

Extinguishing the Restrictive Covenants

Where both the dominant and the servient tenements become owned by the same person, the restrictive covenant is extinguished, except in a scheme development.

Discharge and Modification of Restrictive Covenants

A restrictive covenant can be discharged or modified where the character of a neighbourhood has changed to the extent that the restrictive covenants no longer apply. A residential community may have slowly adopted commercial status or a residential community may find that it is now located so close to an area that has become commercial that it makes good sense to discharge or modify the restriction. Where the covenantees have acquiesced to the breaches of covenants in their neighbourhood, the Court will exercise its inherent jurisdiction to modify or discharge a restrictive covenant, as the circumstances require on an application from another covenantee.

A covenantee may want to modify the restrictions in order to build a more financially viable structure on the property. It may be the case that he may want to construct an apartment complex that will house more persons and thus earning more income from his property.

The applicant has to assist the court in justifying the need for discharge or modification of restrictive covenants. He has to show that:

(1) **The covenant has become obsolete**

Stephenson v Liverant [1972] 18 WIR 323 - In this case, the applicants owned two lots which formed part of a subdivision containing some twenty lots. This subdivision was laid out in 1950 as a private residential area, and formed an enclave or peninsula with areas of industrial and commercial activity surrounding it where it was not open to the sea. In close proximity thereto are lands accommodating an industrial complex. Covenants endorsed on the titles to the several lots were directed to preserving the subdivisions as a private residential area. The relevant covenants prohibited, inter alia, (i) the erection on any lot of any building other than a private dwelling house with appropriate out-buildings, and (ii) the use of any building erected as a shop, etc., and the carrying on of any business. The applicants sought the modification of these covenants to enable them to erect certain apartment blocks for the purpose of letting to tourists. They relied on two grounds in support of their application, namely:

(a) that by reason of changes in the character of the neighbourhood and breaches of the relevant covenants, the restrictions imposed by those covenants had become obsolete; and

(b) that the proposed modification would not injure persons entitled to the benefit of these covenants. All, save one, of the owners of the other lots in the subdivision indicated that they had no objection to the grant of the application.

With regard to ground (a), evidence on affidavit disclosed a breach by all lot owners who had erected dwelling houses of one covenant designed to govern the geographical arrangements of the buildings on a lot, and the breach by the owners of two lots of another covenant prohibiting the erection of more than one dwelling house. There was also evidence in affidavits filed by the applicants that there had been considerable growth and expansion of commercial activity (including the erection of a block of apartments) on lands adjoining the subdivision since its creation, and that in respect of some ten lots their owners rented the buildings thereon, or some of them, to tourists. At the hearing of the application it was argued that in the result the character of the neighbourhood of the subdivision had changed, and that the original object of the relevant covenants had disappeared since in the majority of cases the houses erected were not being used as in a purely private residential area.

With regard to ground (b) the applicants endeavoured to show that the extended user of their lots would improve the quality of the neighbourhood and that there would be no aesthetic, financial or other injury to anyone entitled to the benefit of the covenants. The opposers, on the other hand, claimed that the privacy they enjoyed would be adversely affected by the project itself and that the modification proposed would amount to an expropriation of a viable extant right and render the covenants vulnerable to the action of the court. The trial judge held that the applicants had failed to satisfy him that there was any material on which he could exercise his discretion in their favour by allowing the modification sought.

On appeal it was held that:

(i) Viewing the subdivision as a neighbourhood of its own, no change in its character had been shown since, inter alia, a dwelling house may be used as such even when the person residing therein is a tenant of the owner and it did not cease to be used as a private dwelling house because the tenant happened to be a tourist who occupied the house as his dwelling house. The restrictions imposed by the relevant covenants remained substantially intact and this notwithstanding the proved or admitted breaches thereof;

(ii) that the modification proposed would interfere with the privacy enjoyed by the objectors thereby adversely affecting one of the original purposes of the subdivision sought to be ensured by the covenants;

(iii) that those dwelling houses which were being rented solely to tourists were being used as holiday resort houses and not as private dwelling houses, and this involved carrying on a business, albeit in limited form. The proved or admitted breaches of the restrictions imposed did not alter the character of the subdivision since neither the presence of additional buildings, nor the fact that all buildings were erected in contravention of the covenants, nor the limited form of business done in respect of some of the lots, resulted in any change in its private residential nature;

(iv) that the benefit of the restrictions was a proprietary right vested in the owner of each lot which could be enforced in order to preserve the private residential character of the subdivision. Any project which, if implemented, was capable of destroying or causing a change in this character was therefore bound to cause injury to an owner who objected to the change. The appeal was dismissed.

2. Neighbours have acquiesced to the change in user, not having objected to the applicant's or other occupant's use of their property contrary to the provisions of the covenants.

Re Federal Motors Ltd [1969] 9 WIR 375, the applicants FM Ltd were the registered proprietors in fee simple of land known as 8 Marescaux Road in St Andrew, Jamaica registered at Volume 89, Folio 40, subject to the following restrictive covenants: "(1) That no building other than showrooms and offices of a value of not less than £25,000 in connection with the business of dealers in motor vehicles and buildings for business or professional offices shall be erected on the said land or any part thereof. (2)

That no trade or business other than the sale of motor vehicles which shall be displayed in a showroom and that of business and professional offices shall be carried on upon any part of the said land."
The applicants sought the discharge of these restrictions in order to enable them to do heavy servicing of motor vehicles on the land and to enable them more readily to get a loan on the business. A number of objections to the application were filed by persons entitled to the benefit of the restrictions.

It was held that the restriction could not be modified because on none of the grounds on which they relied was the court satisfied that the restrictions ought to be either wholly or partially discharged or modified.

3. The discharge or modification would not injure or affect negatively the objectors.
Re Bay Distributors an application under this ground failed since the applicant was unable to produce sufficient evidence to show that the practical benefits of peace, privacy and seclusion, enjoyed by the objectors, would not be adversely affected by the proposed modification.

4. The continued existence of the covenant would impede the reasonable user of the land.
Stannard v Issa [1987] AC 175, was an appeal from an order of the Court of Appeal of Jamaica made on 12th April 1984 allowing the respondent's appeal from the Supreme Court of Jamaica dated 22nd June 1983 and ordering that certain restrictive covenants affecting the respondent's land at Harmony Hall in the parish of St. Mary be modified.

The judge asked the following questions: "what was the original intention of the restriction and is it still being achieved?" and "does the restriction achieve some practical benefit and if so, is it a benefit of sufficient weight to justify the continuance of the restrictions without modification?" If the evidence indicates that the purpose of the covenants is still capable of fulfillment, then in my judgment the onus on the [respondent] would not have been discharged."

ACTIVITY SHEET - RESTRICTIVE COVENANTS

Victor owns two lots of land that are adjacent to each other, Montclair and Chantel House. He sells Montclair to Sasha who covenants that she will keep the fence between the two properties in good repair and that she will not carry on any business on the Monclair premises. Sasha then sells the property to Margaret who refuses to maintain the fence, which has fallen into disrepair, and also wants to build a roti business on the premises.

(a) (a) Using the information given above, answer the following questions:

i. Identify the positive and the negative covenant or covenants, if any
ii. Who has the benefit of the covenant and who has the burden?
iii. Who is the covenantor and who is the covenantee?

(b) What is the common law concerning the running of the benefits of a covenant with respect to a successor in title to the covenantee

Chapter 18

MORTGAGES

A mortgage is a loan in which your house functions as the collateral. The homeowner (Mortgagor) is able to access financing from financial institutions (Mortgagee) that hold the property as security for the money while the legal interest remains with the landowner. Building Societies play a very key role in this regard. However, there is the National Housing Trust (NHT), in Jamaica that also does financing at a very low or competitive interest rates. In Jamaica, employers and employees pay a small percentage of wages and salaries into a fund operated by the latter institution from which persons can benefit. It is important to note that self-employed persons can also place money in this fund with the NHT and thereafter derive housing benefits.

Lindley MR in **Santley v Wilde [1899] 2 Ch 474**, defined a mortgage as a disposition of an interest in land or other property as a security for the payment of a debt or the discharge of some other obligation for which it is given. It has also been defined as "as a conveyance or other disposition of an interest in property designed to secure the payment of money or the discharge of some other obligation".

As is the case with many interests in land, mortgages can be either legal or equitable.

A legal mortgage arises where all legal formalities in terms of the registration of a mortgage in favour of a mortgagee has been observed. The title in this instance will also reflect the fact of registration.

An equitable mortgage is one in which the lender is secured by taking the deposit of title deeds given by the owner of an estate, for money borrowed with an accompanying agreement to execute a regular mortgage, or by the mere deposit of the title without any further arrangements. In other words, an equitable mortgage may arise in any of the following ways:

(a) The owner of an equitable interest in land assigning his interest to a mortgagee
(b) The owner of a legal interest effecting an informal mortgage
(c) The deposition of title deeds by owner with the intention that the mortgagee should hold them as security for the loan.

PROTECTION OF THE MORTGAGOR

There are circumstances in which it would be unfair for the mortgagor to be allowed to sell the property. Equity has always insisted that there should be no unfair advantage taken of the mortgagor. Schemes devised to deprive the mortgagor of the "equity of redemption", were often struck down, unless bargaining was done at arm's length. Thus, if the mortgage interest is only a few months in arrears and the mortgagor can show that he will be in a position to pay his debts very shortly it would be undesirable to allow the mortgagee to insist on sale. Equity's rules are deeply embedded in a philosophy expressed by Lord Eldon LC in 1802, "once a mortgage, always a mortgage".

What is the Equity of Redemption?

Lord Hardwicke LC in an old case, **Casborne v Scarfe [1738]** gave a definition which is still applicable today. His Lordship said:

> *"an equity of redemption has always been considered as an estate in the land, for it may be devised, granted, or entailed with remainders…the person therefore entitled to the equity of redemption, is considered as the owner of the land….The interest of the land must be somewhere, and cannot be in abeyance, but it is not in the mortgagee, and therefore must remain in the mortgagor".*

Based on his lordship's classic definition, equity devised the rules which are designed to protect the mortgagor scrutinizing each transaction to protect the mortgagor from harsh or unconscionable terms imposed by the mortgagee.

"Once a mortgage always a mortgage"

The equity of redemption belongs to the mortgagor. As such, commercial transactions must adhere to the requirements of equity and the terms of the contract must not deprive or appear to deprive the mortgagor of the equity of redemption. Terms that are at odds with a mortgage and are favourable to the mortgagee are generally void. The following case illustrates the point.

Samuel v Jarrah Timber and Wood Paving Corporation Ltd [1904] AC 323

A first mortgage was given to Samuel for 30000 pounds to secure an advance of 5000 pounds at 6%. The mortgagee, Samuel had an "option to purchase the whole or part of such stock at 40% at any time within twelve months". The principal was payable with interest upon 30 days notice on either side. The mortgagee sought to exercise the option to purchase, over the whole stock, within the twelve month period. The mortgagor brought an action to redeem the equity and for a declaration that the option was illegal and void.

The House of Lords held that the option was void and that the mortgagor could redeem. Per Lord MacNaghten: "this court, as a court of conscience, is very jealous of persons taking securities for a loan and converting such securities into purchases".

The judges commented that they dislike meddling into contracts entered into freely by business men. However, equity abhors mortgages that are clothed as a purchase. Where an arrangement is attached to a mortgage and can be construed to the disadvantage of the mortgagor, the courts may be willing to separate the transactions in order to facilitate good business practices. This point is illustrated in the case of **Reeve v Lisle [1902] AC 461** where property was mortgaged to secure a loan of money. The parties to the mortgage agreed that if the loan was not repaid within five years, the mortgagees should elect to enter into a partnership with the mortgagors. A term of the agreement was that if the partnership was entered into, the mortgagors' liability for the mortgage would cease and a ship, which was not part of the security, would be transferred from the mortgagors to the partnership.

The House of Lords held that the two transactions were separate and independent. The mortgagor was bound by the agreement.

There should be no clogs on the equity of redemption
This equitable principle talks about the fact that nothing should prevent the equity of redemption from returning to the mortgagor. The principle affords protection to the mortgagor to the effect that any attempt by the mortgagee to prevent the mortgagor from exercising the right to reduce is void.

Collateral advantages after redemption

(1) Restricting redemption
Sometimes in commercial transactions the parties agree that the mortgagee will continue to have some advantages, in respect of the mortgagor's business, after the equity of redemption has been exercised by the mortgagor. This usually arises in "tied" arrangements. **Kreglinger v New Patagonia Meat and Cold Storage Co. Ltd [1914]** offers some instructions on this point.

In Kreglinger, Viscount Haldane enumerated the three cardinal tenets upon which equity relies:

(i) "the most general of these was that if the transaction was once found to be a mortgage, it must be treated as always a mortgage and nothing but a mortgage"

(ii) "......the second rule that a mortgagee should not stipulate for a collateral advantage which would make his remuneration for a loan exceed a proper rate of interest".

(iii) "The result is that a collateral advantage may now be stipulated for by the mortgagee provided that he has not acted unfairly or oppressively, and provided that the bargain does not conflict with the third principle. This is that a mortgage…cannot be made irredeemable, and that any stipulation which restricts or clogs the equity of redemption is void".

Bradley v Carritt - Bradley owned a number of shares in a tea company. He mortgaged them to Carritt, a tea broker, who wished to become sole broker for Bradley's teas. Bradley undertook to grant Carritt sole brokerage and, if teas from his company were sold to any other broker, to pay Carritt the commission he would have earned, had he sold the teas. The shares were later mortgaged to a different mortgagee, after the debt to Carritt was repaid. The new mortgagee ousted Carritt from the position he previously occupied as sole broker. Carritt sued to recover damages for breach of contract and for recovery of lost commission.

It was held that the covenant was void as a clog on the equity of redemption. Carritt's action failed.

(2) Unfairness and unconscionability

Questions of unfairness and unconscionability are important in determining what conduct the Court will uphold or condemn. One case which illustrates the point very well is **Multiservice Bookbinding Ltd v Marden** where, in 1966 the plaintiffs, a small but prosperous company, needed cash to enable them to buy larger premises, costing £36,000, so that they could expand their business.

They approached the defendant, who had £36,000 available, with a view to obtaining a loan. The defendant told them that he wanted to use the money in a way which would preserve its real purchasing power and would provide security for his retirement. He said that he would be willing to lend them the £36,000 provided that their liability to repay the capital and interest was linked to the value of the Swiss franc. Each side instructed separate solicitors who agreed a form of mortgage which was executed on 7 September 1966. The mortgage deed provided, inter alia:

(i) that the plaintiffs would pay interest, at two per cent above bank rate, quarterly in advance on the whole of the £36,000 throughout the period of the loan notwithstanding the capital repayments;
(ii) that arrears of interest would be capitalised after 21 days;
(iii) that the loan could not be called in nor the mortgage redeemed during the first ten years of its life; and
(iv) in cl 6 ("the Swiss franc uplift" provision) that any sum paid on account of interest or in repayment of the capital sum should be increased proportionately or decreased proportionately if at the close of business on the day preceding the day on which payment was to be made the rate of exchange between the Swiss franc and the pound sterling should vary by more than three per cent from the rate of 12.07 5/8 francs to the pound sterling prevailing on 7 September 1966.

In the decade which followed, the pound greatly depreciated in value against the Swiss franc. In February 1976 the plaintiffs gave the defendant notice of their intention to redeem on 7 September 1976. They then brought a redemption action claiming the usual accounts which were duly ordered. When the redemption statement was prepared the rate of exchange was just over 4 Swiss francs to the pound.

Although £24,355·57 had by then been repaid on capital account, the repayments had operated to reduce the nominal amount of the debt by only £15,000 leaving £21,000 nominal still to be discharged, which, after adding the Swiss franc uplift, meant that a further actual payment of £63,202·65 would be required, with the result that the defendant, who had advanced £36,000 in 1966, would receive £87,588·22 in repayment of capital.

The combined effect of a high minimum lending rate and cl 6 of the mortgage deed had had a similar effect on the interest payable. The interest due totaled £45,380 (i.e. £31,051 basic interest + £14,329 Swiss franc uplift) which meant that the average rate of interest over the ten year period was 16·01 per cent.

The plaintiffs applied to the court for the determination of the following questions which arose in taking the accounts:

(i) whether cl 6 was void or unenforceable as being contrary to public policy;
(ii) whether cl 6 or the terms of the mortgage, taken together, were unreasonable and as such unenforceable.

It was held that:

(i) An index-linked money obligation in a contract made between two parties within the United Kingdom was not contrary to public policy; cl 6 was not therefore void or unenforceable as being contrary to public policy (see p 496 g, p 497 e and p 504 c, post); dictum of Denning LJ in **Treseder-Griffin v Co-operative Insurance Society Ltd [1956] 2 All ER** at 36 not followed.
(ii) The test of the enforceability of the terms of the mortgage was not whether they were reasonable but whether they were unfair and unconscionable. The court would hold that a bargain was unfair and unconscionable only where it was shown that one of the parties to it had imposed objectionable terms in a morally reprehensible manner. On the evidence there was nothing unfair, oppressive or morally reprehensible in the terms of the mortgage. The defendant had struck a hard bargain but had done nothing that he was not entitled to do by stipulating that he should be repaid the real value of the loan and had not been guilty of any sharp practice. The plaintiffs had entered into the bargain with their eyes open, with the benefit of independent advice and without any compelling necessity to accept the £36,000 on the terms offered. They were accordingly bound to comply with all the terms of the mortgage.

In **Re Petrol Filling Station, Vauxhall Bridge Road, London [1968]**, the plaintiffs owned a petrol station. They entered into an agreement with the defendants, agreeing to sell only the defendant's products. Sometime after entering into this agreement, the plaintiff mortgaged their property to the defendants, for the purpose of modernization. They entered into a number of covenants including giving the defendants a right of pre-emption and keeping the "tied" arrangements in force during the continuance of the mortgage.

The plaintiffs sought to redeem the mortgage. It was held that they were bound by the terms of the mortgage.

Restraint of Trade

Collateral agreements are prima facie void and will be struck down where they are perceived to be in restraint of trade. A court of equity will be interested in whether the mortgagee can show that the arrangement was reasonable as between parties and the public interest.

Rights of the Mortgagor in Possession

The mortgagor, though obligated to pay the monthly installments to the mortgagee, retains rights over the property without having to account to the mortgagee. Some of these retained rights are:

(a) A right to rents and profits obtained from the property
(b) A right to sue for trespass against a trespasser
(c) A right to grant valid leases.

PROTECTION OF THE MORTGAGEE

A number of devices have been utilized by financial institutions in order to protect their interest in the mortgaged property. The main device is the mortgagor can provide a free and unencumbered title on which will be noted, the fact of the mortgage. The following are other devices that a mortgagee may utilize to protect and or exercise his rights:

(a) Foreclosure
(b) Power of Sale
(c) Taking possession of the mortgaged property
(d) Appointing a Receiver
(e) Suit against the mortgagor on the covenant

Foreclosure

In Jamaica, s.109 of the Registration of Titles Act, states that the mortgagee or his transferee may also be entitled to foreclose the right of the mortgagor or his transferees to redeem the mortgaged land.

In order to balance the equitable right to redeem given to the mortgagor, equity gives the mortgagee a simultaneous right to foreclose the mortgage, that is, to bring an action in court in order to extinguish the equitable right to redeem and to acquire for himself the legal and equitable title to the property, freed from the equity of redemption.

Proceedings for foreclosure before the Registrar

Whenever a mortgagor is in default with his payments of the principal or interest money secured by a mortgage and such default continues for six months after the time for payment mentioned in the mortgage, the mortgagee or his transferee may make application in writing to the Registrar of Titles for an order for foreclosure.

Contents of application

(a) The application must state that such default has been made and has continued for the period of 6 months
(b) That the land mortgaged has been offered for sale at a public auction by a licensed auctioneer after notice of sale has been served
(c) That the amount of the highest bidding at such sale was not sufficient to satisfy the moneys secured by such mortgage, together with the expenses occasioned by such sale
(d) That notice in writing of the intention of the mortgagee or his transferee to make an application for foreclosure has been served on the mortgagor or his transferee by being given to him or them, or by being left on the mortgaged land, or by the same being sent through the post office by a registered letter directed to him or them at his or their address appearing in the Register Book
(e) and also that a like notice of such intention has been served on every person appearing by the Register Book to have any right, estate or interest, to or in the mortgaged land subsequently to such mortgage,

by being given to him or sent through the post office by a registered letter directed to him at his address appearing in the Register Book.

The application shall be accompanied by a certificate of the auctioneer by whom such land was put up for sale, and such other proof of the matters stated by the applicant as the Registrar may require, and the statements made in such application shall be verified by statutory declaration.

Effect of order for foreclosure

(a) The Registrar will publish a notice once in each of three successive weeks, in at least one published in the city of Kingston, offering such land for private sale, and
(b) The Registrar shall appoint a time (not less than one month from the date of the first of such advertisements) after which the Registrar shall issue to such applicant an order for foreclosure,
(c) every such order for foreclosure under the hand of the Registrar when entered in the Register book, shall have the effect of vesting in the mortgagee or his transferee the land mentioned in such order, free from all right and equity of redemption on the part of the mortgagor or of any person claiming through or under him subsequently to the mortgage; and
(d) such mortgagee or his transferee shall, upon such entry being made, be deemed a transferee of the mortgaged land, and become the proprietor thereof, and be entitled to receive a certificate of title to the same, in his own name, and
(e) shall cancel the previous certificate of title and duplicate thereof and register a new certificate.

Power of sale
Where there is default in payment of the mortgage sum due on a monthly basis, a notice must be sent to the mortgagor.

Default and notice
Section 105 of the Jamaican Registration of Titles Act, states that where there is default in the payment of the principal sum or the interest or in

the performance or observation of any covenant expressed or implied in the mortgage and such default continued for a month or such period that is expressly stated in the mortgage agreement, then the mortgagee or his transferees may give to the mortgagor or his grantor or transferees notice in writing to pay the money owing on such mortgage or to perform and observe the said covenants as the case may be.

Mode of giving notice

The notice must be:

(1) given to him or them; or
(2) left on some conspicuous place on the mortgaged land; or
(3) sent through the post by registered letter to the registered proprietor at his address appearing in the Register Book

Power of sale in cases of default

s.106 states that where the default in payment, or in performance or observance of the covenants continues for one month after the service of notice or for such other period that is fixed in the mortgage, then the mortgagee or his transferees may sell the land or any part of it either altogether or in lots.

How sale to be carried out

Sale may be effected by public auction or by private contract either at one or at several times and subject to such terms and conditions as may be deemed fit. The mortgagee or his transferee may buy in or vary or rescind any contract for sale and resell without being liable to the mortgagor or grantor for any loss occasioned. They have power to make and sign such transfers and do such acts and things as shall be necessary for effectuating any such sale.

Purchaser has no obligation to enquire into default

It is not the purview of a purchaser to inquire whether there was default on the part of the mortgagor, whether it continued or whether a notice indicating default was served on the mortgagor or to enquire into the propriety or regularity of a sale.

Therefore the Registration of Titles Act (RTA) confers a statutory power of sale on the Mortgagee. But it does not define or indicate the obligations of the mortgagee when exercising his power of sale. However, the following ought to be examined when a power of sale is being exercised:

1. both on principle and authority a mortgagee in exercising his power of sale owes a duty to take reasonable precaution to obtain the true market value of the mortgaged property at the date on which he decided to sell;
2. Where a mortgagee sells by virtue of a power of sale, the sale must be closely examined and a heavy onus lies on the mortgagee to show that in all respects he acted fairly to the borrower and used his best endeavours to obtain the best price reasonably obtainable for the mortgagor's property. Sale by auction does not necessarily prove the validity of the transaction. Have a look at **Diane Jobson v Capital & Credit Merchant Bank Limited -PC Appeal # 52/2006** where In 1980 the appellant Diane Jobson, who was then an attorney at law, bought a small fruit farm at Above Rocks, St Catherine. In 1989 she borrowed $50,000 from the respondent, Capital & Credit Merchant Bank Ltd ("the bank", then known as Tower Merchant Bank and Trust Company) to repair hurricane damage. As security she executed on 8 September 1989 an Instrument of Mortgage of the property. The mortgage recited that it was made under the Registration of Titles Act and contained covenants to pay monthly sums by way of interest and in reduction of the outstanding capital. Clause 10 provided:

"*That the Powers of Sale and of distress and of appointing a Receiver and all ancillary powers conferred on Mortgagees by the Registration of Titles Act shall be conferred upon and be exercisable by the Mortgagee under this instrument without any Notice or demand to or consent by the Mortgagor NOT ONLY on the happening of the events mentioned in the said Laws BUT ALSO whenever the whole or any part of the Principal Sum or the whole or any part of any monthly installment of interest shall remain unpaid for THIRTY DAYS after the dates hereinbefore covenanted*

> *for payment thereof respectively or whenever there shall be any breach or non-observance or non-performance of any covenant or condition herein contained or implied..."*
>
> *In October 1989 Ms Jobson paid the first monthly instalment. But she paid nothing more. On 14 February 1990 the bank sent a standard form letter to Ms Jobson, notifying her that she was in arrears with her payments and saying that unless she paid within 10 days, the bank would exercise the power of sale. The letter was sent by hand but the trial judge found that Ms Jobson never received it. On 26 April 1990 the bank sold the property by auction to a Mr and Mrs Taylor for $260,000. This compares with the $350,000 valuation which the bank obtained for the purposes of the mortgage the previous September.*
>
> *On 5 June 1990, pursuant to the contract made at the auction, the bank executed a transfer to the Taylors and their title was registered on 23 August 1990. But Ms Jobson refused to yield up possession. The Taylors commenced proceedings against her and she issued a third party notice against the bank, claiming that it had not been entitled to exercise the power of sale.*
>
> ***Findings***
>
> *The trial judge (Harrison J) found that the Taylors had acted in good faith and that, whatever might be said about the bank's right to sell, their title was unassailable. A challenge to this finding was unsuccessful in the Court of Appeal and has been abandoned before the Board. In the CA the proceedings concerned solely with the validity of the exercise of the power of sale. The judge rejected submissions that the bank's exercise of the power of sale had been negligent or otherwise than in good faith.*

Application of purchase money

s.107 of the RTA states how the purchase money from the sale of the mortgaged property should be applied. Firstly, the mortgagee or transferee must pay the expenses of and incidental to the sale and consequent to the default. Secondly, he must pay the moneys which may be due or owing on the mortgage. Thirdly, any subsequent mortgages must be paid. If there is any surplus it must be paid to the mortgagor.

But if there is any subsequent charge on the property the remaining purchase moneys shall be deposited in names of the chargees.

Effect of registration of a transfer by mortgagee

s.108 of the RTA states that where the mortgagee registers a transfer signed by him or his transferees for the purpose of effecting a sale, the estate and interest of the mortgagor or grantor in the land, at the time of the registration of the mortgage or which he was then entitled or able to transfer or dispose of under any power of appointment or disposition, or under any power under the Act, shall pass to and vest in the purchaser.

The purchaser will get an estate or interest freed and discharged from all liability on account of such mortgage and of any mortgage or encumbrance subsequently registered on that title except a lease to which the mortgagee or his transferees have consented to in writing. And when the purchaser is registered as the proprietor he shall be deemed a transferee of such land, and shall be entitled to receive a certificate of title to the same.

Taking Possession

In some jurisdictions a mortgagee may enter mortgaged premises and take possession, unless otherwise agreed. In Barbados, the common law right has been abolished and the mortgagee is required by statute to seek a Court order for such entry. Equity stipulates strict rules in the case of property occupied by the mortgagor as his home. The mortgagee must bring an action for recovery of possession. The right is usually exercised as pre-requisite to the exercise of a power of sale so that the mortgagee may sell with possession.

Four Maids Ltd. v. Dudley Marshall (Properties) Ltd. [1957] Ch 317

The legal charge provided that the principal would not be called in for some 2 years 10 months if the interest was paid punctually. Interest was late 6 months after the loan was made. The lender called in the principal.

The arrears were then paid. The lender claimed the whole sum and brought an action for recovery of possession. It was held that the mortgagee was entitled to possession. Parliament has since sought to grant some relief in the case of dwelling houses

Appointment of a receiver

s.125 of the RTA gives the mortgagee power to appoint a receiver:

(1) A mortgagee of any land under this Act shall have power, whenever he shall be entitled to sell the mortgaged property, or any part thereof, by writing under his hand, to appoint a receiver of the income of the mortgaged property, or any part thereof.

(2) The appointment shall be registered in manner hereinbefore provided, before or within thirty days of it being acted upon.

(3) The receiver shall be deemed to be the agent of the mortgagor; and the mortgagor shall be solely responsible for the receiver's acts or defaults, unless the mortgage deed otherwise provides.

(4) The receiver shall have power to demand and recover all the income of the property of which he is appointed receiver, by action, distress, or otherwise in the name either of the mortgagor, or of the mortgagee, to the full extent of the estate or interest which the mortgagor could dispose of, and to give effectual receipts accordingly for the same.

(5) A person paying money to the receiver shall not be concerned to enquire whether any case has happened to authorize the receiver to act.

(6) The receiver may be removed, and a new receiver may be appointed from time to time by the mortgagee, by writing under his hand and registered as aforesaid.

(7) The receiver shall be entitled to retain, out of any money received by him, for his remuneration and in satisfaction of all costs, charges and expenses incurred by him as receiver, a commission at such rate, not exceeding five per centum on the gross amount of all money received, as is specified in his appointment, and if no rate is so specified, then at the rate of five per centum on that gross

amount, or at such higher rate as the court thinks fit to allow, on application made by him for that purpose.

(8) The receiver shall, if so directed in writing by the mortgagee, insure and keep insured against loss or damage by fire out of the money received by him, any building, effects or property comprised in the mortgage, whether affixed to the freehold or not, being of an insurable nature.

(9) The receiver shall apply all money received by him as follows, namely:

(a) in discharge of all rents, taxes, rates and outgoings whatever affecting the mortgaged property; and

(b) in keeping down all annual sums or other payments, and the interest on all principal sums having priority to the mortgage in right whereof he is receiver; and

(c) in payment of his commission and of the premiums on fire, life, or other insurances, if any, properly payable under the mortgage deed, or under this Act, and the cost of executing necessary or proper repairs directed in writing by the mortgagee; and

(d) in payment of the interest accruing due in respect of any principal money due under the mortgage, and shall pay the residue of the money received by him to the person who, but for the possession of the receiver, would have been entitled to receive the income of the mortgaged property, or who is otherwise entitled to that property.

Where a mortgage is made by deed, mortgagees have a statutory right to appoint a Receiver. The receiver is regarded as the agent of the mortgagor and manages the property, obtaining all monies earned therefrom and using them to discharge obligations on the property, including the mortgage arrears. His duty ceases when the affairs of the property are regularized.

Suing the mortgagor on personal covenant

The mortgagee may sue the mortgagor for failing, neglecting or refusing to make a payment when it becomes due. This is not a much practiced remedy as it is time consuming and costly and less effective than other remedies.

Rights of Equitable Mortgagee

Like the legal mortgagee, the equitable mortgagee has the right to sue the mortgagor and to foreclose, exercise a power of sale, or appoint a receiver. The Court may also make an order of possession in his favour.

Equitable interests are very fickle and as such the holder of this interest needs to be very alert in order to ensure protection. A Power of Attorney is just one means of such protection. This instrument will enable him to convey the legal interest to himself where a mortgagor does not honour his obligation. The equitable mortgagor may also be requested to ratify a term in a mortgage contract that allows him to hold the legal interest in the property on trust for the mortgagee.

Priority of Mortgages

An equitable mortgage can sometimes take priority over a legal mortgage. This will be the case where there are vitiating factors that contribute to the acquisition of a mortgage. In **Oliver v. Hilton [1899] 2 Ch 264**, the plaintiff, O, brought an action that she was entitled as an equitable mortgagee to certain premises, against the defendant H, who had purchased them. A solicitor had conveyed the property to O who was represented by an agent, who was not a solicitor. The agent had asked to see the deed but the solicitor declined to show him, on the basis that other property was involved. It was held that O was entitled to priority over H who had purchased the legal estate.

Tacking

This is the right to add a further loan to an earlier one secured by a mortgage so that the additional loan shares the priority of the earlier debt and thus takes priority over intervening mortgages. The following illustration makes the point:

> *National Mortgage Bank approved a loan to Felisha Holt on January 05th, 2010. This ranks first in order of priority. Felisha secured a second mortgage on the said land from First Region Mortgage Bank on March 20th 2011. She then took another loan from National Mortgage Bank on the 06th of June 2012.*

The loan received by Felisha in June 2012 can be "tacked" onto the loan dated January 05th 2010 and would share first priority over the March 2011 loan.

Consolidation

The right of the mortgagee to refuse to allow the mortgagor to redeem one mortgage unless some other mortgage is redeemed at the same time.

ACTIVITY SHEET – MORTGAGES

1. "Once a mortgage always a mortgage". With reference to at least three decided cases, explain how the courts protect the interest of the mortgagor.

2. In July, 2005 Mrs Harold takes a loan of $1,500,000 at 10% interest from Jamdung Bank Ltd to build her house in Paddington. She agrees to pay the bank monthly installments of $48,500. One year later, in July 2006, Mrs Harold falls seriously ill and is unable to continue working. She is now 12 months in arrears on her loan. The bank writes to Mrs Harold giving her an extension of time to pay the outstanding money but to date she has been able to do so.

Advise the bank on the remedies they have against Mrs Harold. Use relevant statutory provisions or decided cases to support your answer.

3. (a) Explain three remedies available to a mortgagee to enforce his security.
   (b) Describe the circumstances which may influence the mortgagee to choose among the available remedies.

4. (a) Explain what is meant by the "equity of redemption".
   (b) List four ways in which the equity of redemption can be destroyed

5. "Now there is a principle which I will accept without qualification… that on a mortgage you cannot by contract between the mortgagor and mortgagee, clog, as it is termed, the equity of redemption so as to prevent the mortgagor from redeeming on payment of principal, interest and costs." Discuss

6. (a) List four rights which protect the mortgagee in enforcing the payments of what is due under a mortgage.
   (b) of the rights named in (a), which two are considered the most important to the mortgagee? Give reasons for your answer.

TORT LAW

Chapter 19

INTRODUCTION TO THE LAW OF TORT

A tort is a wrongful act or a civil wrong which may have been caused intentionally or accidentally and which results in injury to someone. Some examples or torts include all negligence and intentional wrongs such as assault, battery, wrongful death, fraud, and conversion trespass on property, and defamation.

OBJECTIVES

The main objectives of tort law are outlined below:

Compensation
The main focus of tort law is to compensate victims for injuries and losses that they suffer. Tort law allows liability to be attributed to an offender and requisite compensation assessed and awarded.

Protection of interests
Various torts have been developed to protect a person's interest in for example, land and reputation. The tort of nuisance seeks to protect a person's use or enjoyment of land, the tort of defamation protects reputation, and the tort of negligence seeks to protect the breaches of more general duties owed to a person.

Deterrence
Tort law also seeks to encourage persons to be aware of their actions and effect on other persons and property. This type of law serves to restrain

behaviours and so persons may behave in a more reasonable manner, taking fewer risks that are likely to harm other people.

Retribution

"We want justice!" is an exclamation that we hear in the different media almost daily. People are often anxious to litigate a matter in court because of the "principle of the thing". However, civil matters unlike criminal matters are rarely heard by a jury and several matters are settled outside the court and sometimes by insurance companies. The claimant it is submitted is often very satisfied that the defendant is spared no expense regarding the settling of the matter - out of court or by way of a trial.

Vindication

A matter is often brought before the court because conflicting parties cannot agree on an issue of dispute and so, in addition to retribution, a claimant is frequently very happy to be declared innocent or right as it relates to the matter brought to the court.

Loss distribution

The cost of compensation for harm suffered is generally shifted from the claimant to the defendant or the defendant's insurance company. Tort law is the medium that is used to attribute liability to the defendant and thus taking the burden of the loss away from the claimant who has been injured.

Punishment of wrongful conduct

In addition, to compensation, vindication and retribution, tort law allows a civil wrong to be appropriately punished. While the punishment is not custodial in nature, the objective of the remedy often seeks to punish the actual wrongful act of the defendant.

DIFFERENCES BETWEEN TORT LAW, CRIMINAL LAW AND CONTRACT LAW

Tort is a civil wrong, that is, a wrong between private individuals and must be distinguished from a crime which is an offence against the State.

Crime versus tort - criminal proceedings are proceedings between the state and the wrongdoer and the person injured serves as a witness for the state. He or she is not compensated financially. On the other hand, in tort proceedings, the injured party sues the wrongdoer for compensation.

Criminal law is concerned primarily with punishing a wrongdoer for wrongful acts while the law of torts is predominantly about compensation of the injured party for wrongful act or omission and to a lesser extent, punishment. It is possible for a particular breach to be both a tort and a crime, for example, public nuisance. A claim in tort can also be derived from a criminal matter such as an accident on the road that severely injures an employee and causes him to lose income over an extended period of time.

Contract versus tort - both contract and law of torts are concerned with civil obligations. However, the law of contract is about the enforcement of obligations established between the parties. In the law of tort, these duties are not established by any agreement between persons but rather by the law itself.

ACTIVITY – INTRODUCTION

1. Using illustrations, distinguish between a breach of contract and
   a. A tort
   b. A crime

2. 2. In groups of four explain at least four objectives of Tort law. Be as creative as possible in showing how these objectives ensures a win-win situation for both Defendant and Claimant.

Chapter 20

TORT OF NEGLIGENCE

DUTY OF CARE

The paragraph below represents Lord Atkins mantra in ***Donoghue v Stevenson*** where he attempted to lay down a general principle of liability for negligence.

> *"The rule that you are to love your neighbour becomes in law, you must not injure your neighbour; and the lawyer's question, Who is my neighbour? receives a restricted reply. You must take reasonable care to avoid acts or omissions which you can reasonably foresee would be likely to injure your neighbour. Who, then, in law is my neighbour? The answer seems to be persons who are so closely and directly affected by my act that I ought reasonably to have them in contemplation as being so affected when I am directing my mind to the acts or omissions which are called in question."*

Prior to this statement, there was no general principle outside of the obvious duty situations. A duty before 1932 was only owed in obvious cases where, for example, there is a road accident or dangerous goods.

This test has made it easier for lawyers to argue that there is liability in previously unknown situations but it has been criticized in many cases as being too wide. However, even in the 1970's it remained almost entrenched with Lord Reid affirming in **Home Office v Dorset Yacht Co** that the "neighbour principle" was to be applied unless there was some "justification or valid explanation for its exclusion".

Public policy considerations

The test of reasonable foreseeability which was dubbed to be too wide by virtue of **Donoghue v Stevenson** was narrowed by policy considerations by Lord Wilberforce in **Caparo v Dickman. Caparo**, in addition to foreseeability and proximity added the element of whether it would be, fair, just and reasonable to hold someone liable". As such, a duty of care may be denied in the following instances:

(a) The claimant is the author of his own misfortune (**Philcox v Civil Aviation Authority, The Times, 8 June 1995).**
(b) A duty of care would lead to unduly defensive practices by defendants seeking to avoid claims for negligence with detrimental effects on their performance of some public duty.
(c) Awards of damages against a public authority exercising a public function would have an impact upon the resources available to the authority to perform its duties, both in terms of the damages and costs, and in terms of the resources required to investigate and defend spurious claims.
(d) A duty of care would cut across a complex statutory framework established by Parliament for regulating particular circumstances, such as the regulation of financial markets.
(e) There is an alternative remedy available to an aggrieved claimant, such as a statutory right of appeal from the decision of a government officer or department, or judicial review, or another cause of action, such as a claim for breach of contract, even where the action would be against a different defendant.
(f) Where a duty of care would tend to undermine the requirements of other causes of action, particularly in the case of complex commercial contracts where the parties have had the opportunity to negotiate a detailed structure of contractual negotiations.

ACTS AND OMISSIONS

A duty of care may be made out for acts as well as omissions. Unlike acts, the general rule is that there is no duty on a person to take action in order to prevent harm being sustained by others.
Omission falls into two categories:

(1) A person may fail to take appropriate precautions, which would be regarded as a negligent act.
(2) It may refer to passive inaction where a person does not take any action.

Lord Goff looked at this latter rule and came up with the following exceptions:

(a) there is an undertaking by the defendant;
(b) there is a special relationship between claimant and defendant;
(c) the defendant has control over a third party who causes damage to the claimant; or
(d) the defendant has control over land or something likely to be dangerous if interfered with.

Undertaking

It is an agreement to be responsible for something or someone. It is a situation where a person undertakes to perform a task and thus by doing so, assumes a duty to act carefully in carrying it out.

Relationship between claimant and defendant

The relationship between employer and employee, parent and child, captain and passenger, referee and player, hotelier and patron, the organiser of a dangerous competition and a visibly drunken participant, and occupier and visitor are all examples of relationships that give rise to a duty to prevent harm. In other words, a duty of care is inherent in these relationships.

Control over third parties
Employer and employee, parent and child, gaoler and prisoner, mental hospital and patient and even car owner and an incompetent or drunken driver are examples of relationships that involves a third party and hence a duty exist to control the third party's behavior so as to prevent harm to another. This duty to control the third party's behavior exists within the context of a special relationship.

In **P Perl (Exporters) Ltd v Camden LBC (1984)**, Thieves used the defendant's flat to gain access to the plaintiff's flat. There was no compulsion vested on the defendants to prevent such a break-in although such instances were foreseeable. Perl was followed in the case of **King v Liverpool City Council**.

In **King v Liverpool**, Vandals accessed and damaged the plaintiff's flat through the defendant's vacant and unprotected property. The court held that all that is required is reasonable effort on the part of the defendant to protect the property which could not include 24 monitoring daily.

In **Smith v Littlewoods Organization Ltd**, it was held that the defendant could be responsible for the acts of third parties if, special circumstances existed as follows:

1. Special relationship between plaintiff and defendant
2. Source of danger negligently created by the defendant and reasonably foreseeable that third parties would interfere
3. The defendant had knowledge or means of knowledge that a third party had created or was creating a risk of danger on his property and failed to take reasonable steps to abate it

Foreseeability of damage was not a factor in Littlewoods and as such the defendants could not be liable.

Control of land or dangerous substances or objects
Where a defendant brings substance or objects of a dangerous nature on his land, the occupier is consequently clothe with an obligation and a duty

of care breach of which results in strict liability because of the extent of harm which may occur. **Rylands v. Fletcher**

TYPES OF CLAIMANT

Trespassers are owed a common duty of care by the occupiers of premises. This is by virtue of the Jamaican Occupiers' Liability Act, 1969. Section 3 of the Act is outlined below:

> *An occupier of premises owes the same duty (in this Act referred to as the "common duty of care") to all his visitors, except in so far as he is free to and does extend, restrict, modify or exclude his duty to any visitor by agreement or otherwise.*
>
> *The common duty of care is the duty to take such care as in all the circumstances of the case is reasonable to see that the visitor will be reasonably safe in using the premises for the purposes for which he is invited or permitted by the occupier to be there.*
>
> *The circumstances relevant for the present purpose include the degree of care and of want of care, which would ordinarily be looked for in such a visitor and so, in proper cases, and without prejudice to the generality of the foregoing-*
>
> *(a) an occupier must be prepared for children to be less careful than adults;*
>
> *(b) an occupier may expect that a person, in the exercise of his calling, will appreciate and guard against any special risks ordinarily incident to it, so far as the occupier leaves him free to do so.*
>
> *determining whether the occupier of premises has discharged the common duty of care to a visitor, regard is to be had to all the circumstances.*
>
> *Where damage is caused to a visitor by a danger of which he had been warned by the occupier, the warning is not to be treated without more as absolving the occupier from liability, unless in*

> *all the circumstances it was enough to enable the visitor to be reasonably safe.*
>
> *Where damage is caused to a visitor by a danger due to the faulty execution of any work of construction, maintenance or repair by an independent contractor, the occupier is not to be treated without more as answerable for the danger if in all the circumstances he had acted reasonably in entrusting the work to an independent contractor and had taken such steps, if any, as he reasonably ought in order to satisfy himself that the contractor was competent and that the work had been properly done.*
>
> *The common duty of care does not impose on an occupier any obligation to a visitor in respect of risks willingly accepted as his by the visitor (the question whether a risk was so accepted to be decided on the same principles as in other cases in which one person owes a duty of care to another).*
>
> *For the purposes of this section, persons who enter premises for any purpose in the exercise of a right conferred by law are to be treated as permitted by the occupier to be there for that purpose, whether they in fact have his permission or not.*

Generally a participant in a crime may not be owed a duty of care by another party in the same crime.

A duty of care is also owed to a rescuer. Cardoza J in **Wagner v International Railway**
The had this to say, "Danger invites rescue. The cry of distress is the summons to relief. The wrong that imperils life is a wrong to the imperiled victim; it is a wrong also to his rescuer"

In **Haynes v Harwood [1935] 1 KB 146** the plaintiff, a police constable, was on duty inside a police station in a street in which, at the material time, were a large number of people, including children. Seeing the defendants' runaway horses with a van attached coming down the street he rushed out and eventually stopped them, sustaining injuries in consequence, in respect of which he claimed damages:-

It was held that:

(1) On the evidence the defendants' servant was guilty of negligence in leaving the horses unattended in a busy street;
(2) as the defendants must or ought to have contemplated that someone might attempt to stop the horses in an endeavour to prevent injury to life and limb, and as the police were under a general duty to intervene to protect life and property, the act of, and injuries to, the plaintiff were the natural and probable consequences of the defendants' negligence; and
(3) the maxim 'volenti non fit injuria' did not apply to prevent the plaintiff recovering.

ECONOMIC LOSS

General position

No compensation for pure economic loss can be claimed in the law of torts. Pure economic loss is financial loss which is not as a result of physical damage to the property or person of the plaintiff. However, economic loss which is consequent upon physical damage to the plaintiff or his property is recoverable.

A simple example as taken from Kodilinye, (2000) may clarify the distinction: if D negligently runs down P, a fashion model, with his car, P can recover damages for loss of earnings, including such items as a lucrative modeling contract which P is prevented, by her injuries, from obtaining. But P's agent, Q, who expected to earn a large commission from the modeling contract, cannot recover damages for his loss of earnings caused by the injuries to P, because his loss is not consequent upon any physical damage to him; it is consequent only upon damage to P.

The leading case on this point is **Spartan Steel and Alloys Ltd v Martin and Co Ltd** where it was held that a person who negligently damaged a cable belonging to the power authority, thereby cutting off electricity supply to the plaintiff's nearby factory, was not liable to the plaintiffs for loss of profits arising from the stoppage of steel production during the power cut, because there was no duty to avoid causing purely economic loss. It is significant, however, that in this case the plaintiff did recover for financial loss for loss arising from damage to molten metal which was in their furnace at the time of the power cut, because this loss was consequent upon physical damage to the metal.

Exceptions:

One exception to the rule that damages for pure economic loss are not recoverable in the law of torts is the principle that damages can be recovered for negligent misstatement. This principle can be found in the case of **Hedley Byrne and Co v Heller and Partners** which established that damages can be recovered in tort for economic loss caused by careless misstatements. A negligent misstatement may result in a person sustaining physical damage by relying on this careless statement or a purely financial loss to such a person. To secure damages under this heading, it has to be shown that a special relationship existed at the time of making the statement and that loss was suffered as a result of relying on this same statement.

Another important exception to the rule that compensation for pure economic loss is not recoverable in tort arose in **Ross v Caunters.** The spouse of a beneficiary witnessed a Will which invalidated the gift to the beneficiary. The solicitor had negligently failed to communicate this information to the testator and the beneficiary brought an action in negligence against the solicitor. The defendant's negligence caused a loss to a third party, the plaintiff under the **Donoghue v Stevenson** principle.

The decision made the point that economic loss was recoverable as the solicitor had a proximate relationship with his specific client and should have reasonably foreseen that his negligence would cause a loss. It was determined that in such a case, it is easier for the court to find the existence of a duty of care because there is no danger of liability in an "indeterminate amount…to an indeterminate class of persons".

WHAT IS NEGLIGENT MISTATEMENT?

Negligent misstatement, simply stated, refers to situations where statements are carelessly made, written or oral and is relied on by another party to their disadvantage. Statements may have been made by a professional on social occasion and may have even been passed on without the consent of the speaker.

There is no requirement of contractual relation for a claim to succeed for negligent misstatement but there needs to be a special relationship and proximity existing between the parties.

A special relationship will arise where there is experience or special knowledge on the part of the advisor who knows or ought to have known that the other party is relying on his expertise. The facts of **Hedley Byrne v Heller**, which is the leading case on this point, are instructive.

The appellants, becoming doubtful about the financial position of Easipower Ltd, asked their bank to communicate with Easipower's bankers, the Respondents. This they did by telephone asking the Respondent's, in confidence, and without liability on the Respondent's part, whether Easipower would be good for a contract of 8000 to 9000 pounds. The Respondents replied that they believed Easipower "to be respectably constituted and considered good for normal business engagements". Six months later the appellant's bank wrote to the respondents to ask whether they considered Easipower trustworthy, in the way of business, to the extent of 100,000 pounds per annum contract and the respondents replied: "Respectably constituted company, considered good for its ordinary business engagements". The appellants relied upon the respondent's statements and as a result lost over 17000 pounds when Easipower Ltd went into liquidation. The appellants sought to recover this loss from the respondents as damages on the ground that the respondent's replies were given negligently and in breach of the respondent's duty to exercise care in giving them.

It was held that assuming that negligence could be established, persons in the respondent's position might have been liable but the disclaimer here was adequate to exclude their assumption of a legal duty of care.

Where a person assumes the responsibility of advising another in a professional capacity, he assumes a duty to that other person to act or advise with care. A court will not, generally, attribute a duty of care where there is an exchange in a social or domestic context.

However, see **Chaudhry v Prabhaker [1988] 3 ALL ER 718** where the Court of Appeal held that the standard of care owed by an unpaid agent to his principal was an objective one, such as to be expected of him in all the circumstances…as such a friend was found liable for loss suffered when, in breach of his duty, he recommended to the claimant the purchase of a second hand car which turned out to be both unroadworthy and valueless…

In order to establish the existence of a "special relationship", the court will need to consider whether or not:-

(i) there was reliance on the defendant's skill or knowledge,
(ii) the person giving the advice knew or ought to have known that the injured party was relying on the advice; and
(iii) the plaintiff was reasonable in relying on this advice.

NERVOUS SHOCK AND DUTY OF CARE

Emotional distress which may be suffered by normal individuals where someone is injured or killed must be distinguished from nervous shock which is a medically recognized illness or disorder that includes mental illness, neurosis and personality change. Unlike nervous shock, compensation is not available for emotional distress, anguish or grief unless these defects lead to some psychiatric illness such as heart attack, nervous breakdown or even depression, among others.

(a) Primary victims

A person who was physically injured or could foreseeably have been physically injured as a result of another person's negligence is a "primary victim". Such a claimant can recover damages for his vehicle, his injuries, if any, and the nervous shock he had suffered. "Primary victims" also include rescuers such as firemen, policemen or volunteers who put themselves in the way of danger and suffer psychiatric shock as a result.

Liability was originally limited to, shock suffered as a result of the claimant fearing for their own physical safety as a result of the defendant's negligence. The courts were traditionally cautious about admitting claims for psychiatric harm which were not the result of physical injury to the claimant. This was the result in the following early decision:

Dulieu v White [1901] 2 KB 669 where A, being pregnant, alleged that while she was sitting behind the bar of her husband's public-house B.'s servant negligently drove a pair-horse van belonging to B. into the public-house. A. suffered a severe shock which led to her suffering a miscarriage. The baby survived but suffered from mental illness.

It was held that her statement of claim disclosed a good cause of action against B and that mere fright not followed by consequent physical damage will not support an action, but if it is followed by consequent physical damage, then, if the fright was the natural result of the defendants' negligence, an action lies, and the physical damage is not too remote to support it. It was also said that where there is a legal duty on the defendant not to frighten the plaintiff by his negligence, then fright with consequent physical damage will support an action.

However, damages were awarded by the House of Lords in **Page v Smith** for psychiatric injury although only physical injury was sustained and foreseeable. It was decided in this case involving primary victims that, there should be no distinction between physical and psychiatric injury.

Dulieu was later overruled and it was held that a claimant could recover on the basis of fear of injury to self and even to relatives. This was aptly illustrated in the following case:

Hambrook v Stokes Bros [1925] 1 KB 141 - The defendants' servant left a motor lorry at the top of a steep and narrow street unattended, with the engine running, and without having taken proper precautions to secure it. The lorry started off by itself and ran violently down the incline. The plaintiff's wife, who had been walking up the street with her children, had just parted with them a little while before at a point where the street makes a bend, when she saw the lorry rushing round the bend towards her.

She became very frightened for the safety of her children, who by that time were out of sight round the bend, and who she knew must have met the lorry in its course. She was almost immediately afterwards informed by bystanders that a child the description of one of hers had been injured. In consequence of her fright and anxiety she suffered a nervous shock which eventually caused her death, whereby her husband lost the benefit of her services.

In an action by the husband under the Fatal Accidents Act it was held that, on the assumption that the shock was caused by what the woman saw with her own eyes as distinguished from what she was told by bystanders, the plaintiff was entitled to recover, notwithstanding that the shock was brought about by fear for her children's safety and not by fear for her own.

There are factors that will limit the extent to which a claimant will be able to recover. These include:

(a) The psychiatric injury must have been the product of what the claimant perceived with his or her own unaided senses.
(b) The nature of the relationship between the accident victim and the person who suffered the psychiatric injury is important.
(c) The test of liability for shock is foreseeability of injury by shock, thus separating psychiatric damage from other forms of personal injury.
(d) When applying the test of foreseeability of injury by shock it has to be demonstrated that the claimant is a person of reasonable fortitude and is not unduly susceptible to some form of psychiatric reaction.

(b) Secondary victims

A "secondary victim" is a person who suffers nervous shock without himself being exposed to danger.

To establish liability, the secondary victim has to establish the following elements:

(a) reasonable foreseeability of psychiatric illness arising from the close relationship of love and affection between the claimant and the primary victim of the defendant's negligence;
(b) proximity in terms of physical and temporal connection between the claimant and the accident caused by the defendant;
(c) the psychiatric harm must come through the claimant's own sight or hearing of the event or its immediate aftermath.

Greatorex v Greatorex and Others [2000] Times Law Report May 5 - There was no duty of care owed by a victim of self-inflicted injuries towards a secondary party who suffered only psychiatric illness as a result of having witnessed the event causing the injuries or its aftermath. The policy considerations against there being such a duty owed clearly outweighed the arguments in favour, since to impose liability for causing psychiatric harm in such circumstances, particularly where the parties were members of the same family, would be potentially productive of acute family strife.

The facts of the case are that the defendant carelessly injured himself in a road accident and the claimant, who was a fire officer and the claimant's father, was called to the scene. As a result of what he saw the claimant suffered post-traumatic stress disorder. It was held by Cazalet J that even as a direct witness of the defendant's injuries, the claimant who had a recognized relationship of love and affection with the defendant, was not owed a duty of care…it was also held that the defendant did not owe the claimant a duty of care even as a rescuer because the a had not been exposed to danger, nor had he reasonably believed himself to be so exposed…

Employees

Employers may be responsible for psychiatric injury caused to employees. In other words, they owe a duty of care to employees for psychiatric injury suffered as the following cases will illustrate:

Dooley v Cammell Laird [1951] 1 Lloyd's Rep 271 - The claimant, an employee of the defendant was operating a sling on a crane when the sling broke and the cargo it was moving fell on the ship. The claimant suffered psychiatric shock as he felt fear for his colleagues' safety who were somewhere on the now damaged ship. Judgment was granted in his favour and against his employers for breach of their statutory duty and against the owner of the crane in negligence.

Young v Charles Church Ltd (1997) 39 BMLR 146 - was a case arising out of the fatal electrocution of the plaintiff's workmate with whom he was erecting scaffolding in the course of employment. While the plaintiff's back was turned, the deceased touched an overhead electric cable with a scaffolding pole and was electrocuted, dying instantly. On hearing a loud bang and hissing sound, the plaintiff immediately looked behind and saw that the workmate had been killed and that the surrounding ground had burst into flames. He ran 600 yards to the security office to summon help and returned to the scene of the accident to wait for the arrival of the ambulance. As a result of what he saw and heard he suffered psychiatric injury and claimed damages for nervous shock as a primary victim of the defendant's negligence and breach of statutory duty.

NEGLIGENCE: BREACH OF DUTY

If it is found that the defendant owes the claimant a duty of care, the next step is to establish whether the duty has been breached. To establish or find that there is a breach, the defendant will be judged on the standard established by a reasonable person. This is an objective standard and disregards the individual peculiarities of the defendant. Everyone is judged by the same standard with the exception of: skilled professionals, children, the insane and physically ill.

UNFORESEEABLE HARM

If the standard of a reasonable man is the basis upon which breach has to be established, then the fact that harm was not foreseen by a reasonable objective man, a defendant will not be found to be in breach where he fails to take safety measures against a named hazard.

The greater the likelihood that the defendant's conduct will cause harm, the greater the amount of caution required of him. According to Lord Wright in **Northern Utilities Ltd v London Guarantee and Accident Co Ltd [1936] AC 108**, the degree of care which the duty involves must be proportioned to the degree of risk involved if the duty should not be fulfilled".

FACTORS TO BE WEIGHED IN ESTABLISHING BREACH

1. MAGNITUDE OF HARM

Where there is a small risk but the potential harm that may occur is great then a reasonable man would be expected to take precautions.

Paris v Stepney BC (1951) - The plaintiff was blind in one eye. While he was working for the defendants, a metal chip entered his good eye and rendered him totally blind. The defendants were found to be negligent in failing to supply him with goggles as, even though there had only been a small risk, the consequences were serious.

2. DEFENDANT'S PURPOSE

If the defendant is doing something that is deemed to be a valuable act, then he may have been justified in taking greater risks. The greater the social utility, the greater the likelihood of the defendant's behavior being assessed as reasonable. This was seen in the case of **Watt v Hertfordshire CC[1954]** 1, in which firemen, in a hurry to rescue a woman trapped under a vehicle, failed properly to secure a heavy jack on the back of their lorry (the vehicle properly equipped for such a task being unavailable). The jack slipped and injured the plaintiff, one of the firemen. In the circumstances it was found that the authorities had not been negligent. Lord Denning indicated that the decision might have gone the other way had the defendants been engaged in ordinary commercial pursuits.

3. PRACTICABILITY OF PRECAUTIONS

The courts expect people to take only reasonable precautions in guarding against harm to others. This argument corroborates our earlier argument on foreseeability. That is to say, "the greater the likelihood that the defendant's conduct will cause harm, the greater the amount of caution required of him". The cost of avoiding a risk is a material factor in the standard of care. The defendant will not be expected to spend vast sums of money on avoiding a risk which is very small. In **Latimer v AEC Ltd (1953)**, the defendant's factory was flooded; the water mixed with factory oil and made the floor slippery. Sawdust was spread on the surface, but not enough to cover the whole affected area. The employers were held not to be negligent.

4. GENERAL PRACTICE

If the defendant acted in accordance with the common practice of others this will be strong evidence that he has not been negligent. For example, see:

Gray v Stead [1999] 2 Lloyd's Rep 559 - Mr. Alan Gray was employed as a fisherman on board the motor fishing vessel, Progress which was owned by the defendant, Mr. Keith Stead. At all material times progress was manned solely by Mr. Stead and Mr. Gray. On July 26, 1994 at about 2215 Progress sailed from Hartlepool on a fishing trip of a routine nature.

The fishing grounds were about 18 miles to the north of Hartlepool and about eight miles east of South Shields. The vessel shot her gear at about 0345 to 0350. It was then just breaking daylight and in accordance with normal practice it was agreed that Mr. Gray should be on watch first. This involved him being in the wheelhouse. At all material times visibility, wind and sea conditions were good.

The system of fishing involved Progress proceeding on automatic pilot at about three knots over the ground, turning to starboard gently in manual steering and then on reaching the return leg and settling on the new course, proceeding again on automatic pilot. After shooting the gear Mr. Gray stood the first watch. At about 0415 Mr. Stead turned in. At about 0635 he felt the boat jolt slightly indicating that she had come fast on her gear. He went into the wheelhouse and discovered that Mr. Gray was not there. He looked at the Decca navigator and could see immediately that Progress was approximately three to four miles south of where she should have been and on a south easterly rather than west south westerly heading.

The steering was in manual. At about 0830 the body of Mr. Gray was found floating face down. A postmortem examination and inquest held on Oct. 11, 1994 found that the cause of death was accidental drowning.

It was common ground that how and why and where on "Progress" Mr. Gray fell into the sea would forever remain a mystery and it also became clear that had Mr. Gray been wearing a single chamber inflatable lifejacket he probably would have survived. It was common ground that it was not in 1994 nor nowadays the practice for single chamber inflatable lifejackets to be kept on small fishing vessels such as Progress. The defendant asserted in evidence that no fisherman in practice ever wore such lifejackets and there was no evidence to contradict him.

The plaintiff, as the widow of and administratrix of the estate of Mr. Alan Gray brought an action for damages the principal issue being whether Progress should have been furnished with a single chamber inflatable lifejacket by Mr. Stead and whether Mr. Stead should have instructed Mr. Gray on the importance of wearing it whenever he went on deck alone. The plaintiff contended that the risk of a seaman such as Mr. Gray falling overboard unobserved (with a virtual certainty of drowning) when alone on deck was such that Mr. Stead ought to have applied his mind to it and concluded that the single chamber inflatable lifejacket was the solution and so instructed Mr. Gray. Quantum was agreed at £61,000 subject to liability.

Held, by Q.B. (Mr. Geoffrey Brice, Q.C.), that:

(1) in determining whether the employer had acted reasonably one was entitled to consider the ambit of published guidance and regulations available to him prior to the accident and the practices within the industry;

(2) at the date of the accident the legislation relating to the carriage of lifejackets on fishing vessels was contained in s. 3 of the Safety at Sea Act, 1986 and on the regulations made thereunder namely the Fishing Vessels (Life-Saving Appliances) Regulations, 1988 (S.I. 1988 No. 38); there was no dispute that Progress carried the lifejackets which complied with these regulations but these

lifejackets were bulky and it was not suggested that Mr. Gray should have been instructed to wear one of these lifejackets as opposed to the single chamber inflatable lifejacket;

(3) it was accepted that Mr. Stead as the employer of Mr. Gray owed him a general duty to exercise reasonable care as regards his safety and that a fisherman going out on deck alone was vulnerable;

(4) there was a duty on each employer of a fisherman on an inshore trawler to apply his mind to the safety of such a fisherman and not simply to follow convention and practice without further thought; so far as the use of the single chamber inflatable lifejacket was concerned, this the defendant did not do; the danger of falling overboard and drowning in the case of a fisherman such as Mr. Gray on watch alone (but who was expected at times to go on deck), was small but sufficient for a prudent employer to conclude that notwithstanding existing practice on other trawlers an instruction to wear a lifejacket such as a single chamber inflatable lifejacket would minimize if not wholly eliminate the risk of such an accident;

(5) if, as appeared to be the case, there was a general practice of not having and wearing lifejackets of any type on small trawlers when on deck such practice was unsafe; the defendant failed to exercise the duty of reasonable care in respect of the safety of Mr. Gray; that failure caused his death by drowning and the plaintiff was entitled to judgment in the sum of £61,000 (including interest).

The defendant appealed, the principal issue being whether in 1994 the standard of care required of an employer to his employee fishermen extended to a duty to provide him with a single chamber inflatable lifejacket and a duty to instruct him to wear it whenever alone on deck.

It was held, by C.A. (Lord Bingham of Cornhill, C.J., Otton and Robert Walker, L.JJ.), that

(1) there was no statute or statutory regulation requiring employers to provide buoyancy aids on trawlers; it was clear that fishermen in practice never wore buoyancy aids at the time of the accident; and the evidence

confirmed that this was a general and recognized practice among fishermen even when working on deck; in 1994 there was nothing to indicate that the practice was "clearly bad" or "folly" in the sense of creating a potential liability in negligence at any time before 1994 and the reasonable and prudent employer, weighing up the risks and potential consequences was entitled to follow or permit the practice; there was evidence that the defendant did take positive thought for the safety of his workers (see p. 564, col. 2; p. 565, col. 1);

(2) applying the correct standard of care the proper conclusion was that the duty of care of the reasonable and prudent employer in 1994 did not require the provision of single chamber lifejackets and a system of work such that they were worn at all times when on deck; there was no justification for imposing on Mr. Stead a more stringent duty than the responsible authorities, after research and testing, were prepared to recommend; Mr. Stead had no reason to expect Mr. Gray to be working on deck nor was there any evidence that he was doing so at the time he went overboard; the appeal would be allowed on this ground alone (see p. 565, col. 2);

(3) the learned Judge correctly found that if Mr. Gray had been wearing a buoyancy aid when he fell overboard he probably would have survived; but the learned Judge could not reasonably have found that if a lifejacket had been provided and if the instructions to wear it at all times when on deck were given Mr. Gray would have departed from the practice of all fishermen and put on a lifejacket for such a short period of time; it was inherently unlikely that in the circumstances Mr. Gray would have worn a lifejacket; the vessel was found to be in manual steering suggesting that he was anticipating being away for a short period only and returning before it was time to put the steering back into automatic at the completion of the turn; the appeal would be allowed on this ground also and the judgment in favour of the plaintiff set aside.

The abovementioned case illustrates that if the defendant acted in accordance with general and approved practice then this may be strong evidence that he has not been negligent. However, this is not an absolute position and a defendant may still be negligent even though he acted in accordance with a common practice. There is an obligation on the defendant to keep up to date with developments and to change practices in light of new knowledge.

It will not be a defence to say that the general and approved practice has been followed if it is an "obvious folly" to do so. "Neglect of duty does not by repetition cease to be neglect of duty". The doctrine of "obvious folly" was articulated in the Zeebrugge ferry disaster where the master of the ship claimed that it was general and approved practice for him not to check that the bow doors were closed prior to setting out to sea. It was held that the general and approved practice constituted an "obvious folly" and should not have been followed.

SPECIAL STANDARDS APPROPRIATE TO PROFESSIONALS

A professional will be judged by the standard of the ordinary professional that has the same skill. This is the basis of the 'Bolam test'. McNair J in **Bolam v Friern Hospital Management Committee (1957)** made the point that:

> *"The test is the standard of the ordinary skilled man exercising and professing to have that particular skill. A man need not possess the highest expert skill at the risk of being found negligent. It is well established law that it is sufficient if he exercises the ordinary skill of an ordinary competent man exercising that particular art".*

In the realm of tort law, the general rule is that everyone is judged by the same standard. However, skilled persons are held to a higher standard than the ordinary man. Often there are conflicting views within a particular profession as to which practice is approved and so skilled professionals often have a difficulty when trying to utilize the defence of "generally approved practice". Bolam dealt with this dilemma when it made the statement that a doctor acting in accordance with a respectable body of opinion was not negligent merely because another body of opinion took a contrary view.

Slight modifications were made to the Bolam test in **Bolitho v City and Hackney Health Authority (1997)**. The plaintiff's son was admitted into hospital for respiratory problems. He was not attended to in a timely manner by the doctors and suffered further complications. The defendants' argument was that their decision not to have intubated the boy earlier could be confirmed by a reasonable body of medical opinion. There was evidence from one expert witness that he would not have intubated, whereas five other experts said that they would have done so.

The House of Lords held that there would have to be a logical basis for the opinion not to intubate. This would involve a weighing of risks against benefit in order to achieve a defensible conclusion. In effect, this means that a judge will be entitled to choose between two bodies of expert opinion and to reject an opinion which is, logically indefensible.

A young, inexperienced doctor is judged by the standards of a competent experienced doctor. This is illustrated by the case of **Wilsher v Essex Area Health Authority.**

Persons outside the medical arena who exercise special skills are generally judged by the standard of a reasonably competent man professing that skill. This was seen in **Wells v Cooper** where the Court of Appeal held that a householder performing a DIY task was judged by the standard of a reasonably competent carpenter.

See also the case of **Phillips v William Whiteley**, where the court rejected the idea that a jeweler who pierced ears should be judged by the standard of surgeon but instead the court said that she should be judged by the standard of a reasonably competent jeweler that pierces ears.

In **Nettleship v Weston,** a learner driver was judged by the standard of a "competent and experienced driver" as she held herself out as possessing a certain standard of skill and experience.

STANDARD APPLIED IN SPORTING SITUATIONS

Wooldridge v Sumner confirms that spectators at a sporting event take the risk of any injury from competitors acting in the course of play, unless the competitor's actions show a reckless disregard for the spectator's safety. In Wooldridge a snow jumper was not found to be negligent when there was a momentary lapse on the part of the snow jumper. The competitor was guilty of an "error or errors of judgment or lapse of skill…but this was not enough to constitute a breach of the duty of reasonable care which a participant owes to a spectator…".

On the facts of the case in **Smoldon v Whitworth [1997] PIQR P133** the referee was liable for spinal injuries caused by a collapsed scrum. The decision confirms that a referee who oversees a match may also owe a duty of care to see that players are not injured.

STANDARD APPLIED TO CHILDREN

Unlike criminal law, children cannot plead infancy as a defence to a tort. However, where a tort is committed and the defence is raised, children and young people will usually be judged by the objective standard of the ordinarily prudent and reasonable child of the same age.

If a young person deliberately commits an action with an obvious risk of harm, they may be judged by the standards of an adult. This was the situation in **Williams v Humphrey, The Times, February 20 1975** where it was decided that school authorities or parents, may be liable in negligence for failing to adequately supervise a child who causes harm to another. In this case, the defendant pushed the plaintiff into a swimming pool with the result that the latter was injured when his foot struck the side of the pool. The defendant did not intend to cause harm, Talbot J found that the reasonable man would have foreseen the likelihood of harm to the plaintiff and as such, the plaintiff succeeded in negligence.

PROOF OF NEGLIGENCE

IMPORTANCE OF EVIDENCE IN ESTABLISHING PROOF OF BREACH

The claimant has to prove on the civil standard (balance of probabilities) that the defendant was negligent. However, in some situations a claimant may be able to rely on the maxim res ipsa loquitur, i.e. the thing speaks for itself and in this instance the burden shifts and it is the defendant who will be required to disprove negligence. By this rule of evidence, the mere fact of an accident occurring raises the inference of the defendant's negligence, so that a prima facie case exists. "You may presume negligence from the mere fact that it happens" (**Ballard v North British Railway (1923) SC 43**).

WHEN THE MAXIM 'RES IPSA LOQUITUR' APPLIES

There are three conditions that must be fulfilled before res ipsa loquitur applies.

(a) The damage must have been caused by something that the defendant has control of.
(b) Carelessness generally, must be blamed for the occurrence of such accidents. **Scott v London and St Katherine Docks (1865) 3 H & C 596**…the servants of the defendants were lowering bags of sugar by means of a crane or hoist, and that by the negligence of the defendant's servants a bag of sugar fell upon the plaintiff and injured him…
(c) The cause of the accident must be unknown.

ITS EFFECT

There are two opinions as to the effect of res ipsa loquitur.

(a) The burden of proof remains with the claimant. The defendant has evidential burden and if this is believed, then the ball is back in the court of the claimant to prove negligence.
(b) whether the burden of proof shifts to the defendant.

The opinion of the Privy Council in **Ng Chun Pui v Lee Chuen Tat [1988] RTR 298**, is that burden of proof does not shift to the defendant but remains with the claimant throughout the case.

NEGLIGENCE - CAUSATION AND REMOTENESS

The claimant having established that the defendant owes him a duty of care and that the duty has been breached, also has to proof that the plaintiff suffered damage that has been caused by the defendant. There are two aspects to this element:

1. Causation in fact or law
2. Remoteness of damage

CAUSATION IN FACT

THE "BUT FOR" TEST

The claimant must prove that harm would not have occurred 'but for' the negligence of the defendant. In other words, would the claimant not have suffered the damage "but for" the event brought about by the defendant? A negative response to this question means that it is likely that the defendant's wrong factually caused the claimant's damage. If the damage would have been sustained irrespective of the defendant's wrong, there will be no liability. This was highlighted in the case of **Barnett v Chelsea and Kensington Hospital** where Mr. Barnett went to the hospital complaining of severe stomach pains and vomiting. He was seen by the nurse who telephoned the doctor on duty. The doctor told the nurse to send home Mr. Barnett and contact his GP in the morning. Mr. Barnett died five hours later from arsenic poisoning.

The doctor owed the plaintiff's husband a duty of care. The doctor had breached his duty of care in failing to examine the plaintiff's husband, but the hospital was held not to be liable as the breach had not caused the death. The plaintiff's husband would have died even if the doctor had examined him.

MULTIPLE CAUSES

The but for test is relevant for cases in which there is one breach of duty by one defendant. It is not adequate, however, to deal with cases where there are two or more breaches of duty, that is, where there are multiple causes of damages and two or more tortfeasors. Kodilinye, 2000 aptly illustrates the point thus:

D1 and D2 both negligently start fires, and the two independent fires converge simultaneously on P's house and destroy it. Assuming that either fire alone would have been sufficient to destroy the house, the result of applying the "but for test" would be that neither D1 nor D2 would be liable for the damage, since it could not be said that the damage would not have occurred "but for" D1's fire or, equally, 'but for' D2's fire. The courts, therefore, do not apply the test to such cases, but simply hold both tortfeasors fully liable for the whole loss, subject to the right of each to obtain a contribution from the other.

Have a look at **Fairchild v Glenhaven Funeral Services (2002)**

SEVERAL SUCCESSIVE CAUSES

The "but for test", again will not assist where there are concurrent events that cause injury. In this type of situation, there is usually a sequence of events and every act in the sequence is a relevant cause as far as the claimant's damage is concerned and so the court will always have to look at the operative cause of the claimant's damage.

The courts have not always been consistent in their approach. One method is to establish whether the later even has added to the claimant's damage; if not then the person who caused the original injury will be liable.

In **Performance Cars Ltd v Abraham (1962),** the plaintiff's Rolls Royce had been involved in an accident and the damage involved the cost of respraying the car. Two weeks later, before the respray had been carried out, the defendant was involved in an accident with the plaintiff for which the defendant accepted responsibility. This time, there was damage to the wing and bumper which necessitated a respray of the lower part of the car.

The defendant was not liable as he had not contributed any more damage than had occurred after the first accident.

A similar sequence of events took place in **Baker v Willoughby (1970)**. As a result of the defendant's negligence, the plaintiff suffered an injury to his left leg. Before the trial and while working at a new job, the plaintiff was the victim of an armed robbery and suffered gunshot wounds to his left leg, which then had to be amputated. The defendants argued that their liability was extinguished by the second incident. In other words, they were liable only from the date of the accident to the date of the bank robbery. The House of Lords rejected this. They held that the plaintiff was being compensated for his loss of amenity, that is, the loss of a good left leg, the difference between a damaged leg and a sound leg. The fact that the leg was further damaged at some later date did not alter the fact that he had already been deprived of a perfectly good left leg.

In both of these cases there have been two successive incidents and the second incident has not added to the plaintiff's loss, so the perpetrator of the first incident has remained liable. This can be contrasted with **Jobling v Associated Dairies Ltd**. The facts were that the defendants negligently caused an injury to the plaintiff's back. Three years later and before the trial, the plaintiff was diagnosed as suffering from a condition called mylopathy, which was unrelated to the accident. This time it was accepted, in contrast to other cases, that the second incident extinguished liability. The main differences between these cases have been identified as follows:

1. In **Jobling**, the second incident occurred as a result of a natural condition, whereas in **Baker v Willoughby** there was an intervention by a third party
2. Policy decisions on the part of the court. If the court had accepted that the second incident extinguished liability in **Baker**, this would have left the defendant without compensation after the second incident.

PROOF OF CAUSATION

The claimant must prove, on the civil standard of proof that the defendant's breach of duty caused the harm.

LOSS OF CHANCE

A claimant may lose because of a solicitor's negligence an opportunity to bring legal proceedings, or because of a doctor's negligence a good chance of recovery. Loss of chance is actionable in contract (**Chaplin v Hicks [1911] 2 KB 786**) but its extent in tort is unclear. The House of Lords has held that questions of loss of chance do not arise where there are positive findings of fact on the issue of causation. Such a case may be an 'all or nothing' case. This was the argument in **Hotson v East Berkshire Health Authority [1987] 2 All ER 909** where the claimant had an injured leg (an injury sustained in a non-tortious context) from which there was a chance (assessed by the trial judge as approximately 25%) of a full recovery. However, after negligent medical treatment for the injury the leg was permanently damaged. His claim against the Health Authority for loss of the chance of a full recovery was allowed by the trial judge and the Court of Appeal. The House of Lords held, however, reversing the decision of the Court of Appeal, that there is no principle in tort which would allow a percentage of a full financial recovery based on probabilities. A claimant's claim could only be worked out on an all or nothing basis. It was necessary to establish the claimant's status at the time of the negligence; in this case was he on the balance of probabilities a person already irretrievably damaged, or a person destined to recover? In view of the finding of fact on the likelihood of recovery, he clearly fell into the former category and therefore the negligence of the doctor was deemed not to be causally relevant.

INTERVENING ACTS THAT BREAK THE CHAIN OF CAUSATION

"Where subsequently to the defendant's breach of duty, an independent event occurs which cause damage to the plaintiff, the question arises as to whether the defendant is to be liable for the damage, or whether the intervening event is to be treated as a *novus actus interveniens* which snaps the chain of causation and thus relieves the defendant from liability". (*Kodilinye*, 2000)

This event was described by Lord Wright in the **Oropesa (1943)** as "a new cause which disturbs the sequence of events, something which can be described as either unreasonable or extraneous or extrinsic".

The facts of **The Oropesa** were that two ships collided. The captain of one ship put out to sea in heavy weather in a lifeboat to discuss the situation with the captain of the other ship and was drowned. It was argued that this constituted a *novus actus*, but this was rejected as it was held that the decision to put out to sea was reasonable in the circumstances.

As long as the peril is active, a rescuer's intervention that turns out to be fatal or adverse will not break the chain of causation. This was illustrated in **Haynes v Harwood** where a horse and cart took off along a busy street because the horse had been frightened as a result of a young boy throwing a stone; all this was put down to the defendant's negligence. The claimant, a policeman, in trying to prevent injury to the public, was injured when he stopped the horse. He was awarded damages, as a rescuer, against the defendant.

Haynes was followed in **Baker v Hopkins and Sons Ltd [1958] 3 All ER 147**, in which a doctor went to the rescue of workmen endangered by their employer's negligence. The men were working at the bottom of an open shaft, and had been overcome by carbon monoxide fumes leading from a faulty compressor unit. Unknown to anyone at the time, the men were dead, but the doctor insisted on being lowered down the fume filled shaft, secured only by a rope tied round his waist. No breathing apparatus was available, in fact firemen were waiting for it to arrive. The doctor, like the men, succumbed to the fumes and his widow was awarded damages against the men's employer, the defendant, for breach of its duty to the doctor as a rescuer.

Note: A person who places himself in danger owes a duty of care to a rescuer using the principles in **Baker.**

In **Rouse v Squires (1973)** the court decided that not every illegal act constitutes a *novus actus interveniens.* They required reckless, negligent act. The facts of the case are that a lorry driver caused an accident which blocked two lanes of motorway. The plaintiff was killed when a second driver negligently drove into the obstruction caused by the first accident. The chain of causation was not broken as the intervening conduct had not been so reckless as to constitute a *novus actus.*

In **Wright v Lodge**, the first defendant negligently left her car on the carriageway in the thick fog. The second defendant was deemed to be driving recklessly when he collided with the first defendant's car while driving at 60 mph before swerving across the carriageway and crashing into several other cars. It was held that the second driver's recklessness broke the chain of causation and the first defendant could not be held liable for the damage suffered by the other drivers.

In **Knightley v Johns**, Stephenson LJ stated that the court looks at the "common sense rather than logic on the facts and circumstances of each case" to make a determination as to whether the chain of causation has been broken. In this case, the first defendant, Johns, had caused an accident in a road tunnel within which operated a one-way traffic system. A police inspector, who was in charge of the situation, realized that he had failed to close the tunnel to oncoming traffic and ordered two constables (one of whom was the claimant) to go back against the oncoming traffic in the tunnel to remedy his mistake. The claimant was injured when he collided with a car; the motorist was not negligent. In acting as they did both the inspector and the claimant had broken police standing orders. The claimant claimed damages from Johns, the police inspector and the chief constable (vicarious liability).

The Court of Appeal found that though the claimant had added to the danger by his behavior, not having acted in a wantonly or foolhardy way, he was not guilty of negligence and was not responsible for his own injuries. The appeal was heard on the issue of whether the inspector had been negligent, and whether that negligence was a *novus actus interveniens* breaking the chain of causation between John's negligence and the claimant's injuries.

The court held that:

a. the inspector had been negligent
b. in considering whether a *novus actus interveniens* had occurred it was necessary to ask the question "was the damage the natural and probable, ie, reasonably foreseeable, result of the defendant's negligence? put another way, was something similar likely to happen? if the answer was yes, no event in the sequence of events was a *novus actus interveniens*. Common sense, rather than logic would show what was and what was not reasonably foreseeable;
c. the inspector's negligence in the present case was the real cause of the claimant's injuries; it was a new cause and not a concurrent cause with the negligence of Johns. It broke the chain of causation between the latter's negligent act and the claimant's injuries.

The Inspector and the chief constable were liable to the claimant.

ACTS OF THIRD PARTIES

Liability to the defendant may derive from the actions of third parties that are foreseeable. This can be seen in **Stansbie v Troman [1948] 2All ER 48** where the claimant, a householder, enlisted the services of the defendant, a painter. The claimant had to be absent from his house for a while and he left the defendant there working alone. Later, the defendant went out for two hours leaving the front door unlocked. He had been warned by the claimant to lock the door whenever he left the house. While both defendant and claimant were gone, someone entered it by way of the unlocked front door and stole some of the claimant's possessions. The defendant was held liable for the claimant's loss for, although the criminal action of a third party was involved, the possibility of theft from the unlocked house was one which should have occurred to the defendant.

ACTS OF THE CLAIMANT

Acts of the claimant can amount to a *novus actus*, as in **McKew v Holland and Hannen and Cubitts (1969)**, where the plaintiff suffered injury at work which caused stiffening and weakening of his leg. Shortly afterwards he went to inspect a flat, access to which was provided by a steep staircase with no handrail. As he was about to descend the stairs, his leg gave way, and to avoid going down head first, he threw himself and landed on his right leg, breaking his ankle. The House of Lords rejected the argument that the defender should be liable for this damage. Lord Reid held that, although it was quite foreseeable that the plaintiff would attempt to do what he did, the attempt to descend the stairs was an unreasonable act for which the defendant was not responsible.

However, the chain of causation was not broken in **Wieland v Cyril Lord Carpets (1969)** when the defendant's negligence caused injury to the claimant's neck that forced her to wear a surgical collar. The claimant wore bifocals which were inhibited by the surgical collar. She fell, as she had been unable to use her bifocal spectacles with her usual skill, and suffered further injuries. It was held that all the injuries combined were attributable to the defendant's original negligence.

A defendant may be responsible where the claimant commits suicide following the defendants' negligence. In **Kirkham v Chief Constable of Greater Manchester (1990).** The plaintiff's husband was taken into custody by the police. The police were told that the husband was a suicide risk. When the husband was remanded into custody to the prison authorities, that information was not passed on to the authority. The husband committed suicide and it was held that the suicide of a prisoner in police custody was not a *novus actus interveniens* as the police were under a duty to guard the prisoner to prevent that type of incident and thus the police were liable to the plaintiff.

REMOTENESS OF DAMAGE

Remoteness is designed as a limit or control on the extent of the defendant's liability and also to ensure that the amount he pays in terms of damages will be a fair amount. The defendant cannot be liable indeterminately and so the remoteness of damage principle is used to scrutinize how much, if anything, the defendant will be responsible for financially.

"Direct consequences" and "foreseeable consequences" are the tests that are popularly used to determine remoteness.

In the former test, direct consequences, "the defendant could find himself liable for all the direct consequences of his act suffered by the claimant and it would not matter that a reasonable man would have foreseen them or not, no matter how unusual or unexpected". This was the decision in **Re Polemis and Furness, Withy & Co Ltd (1921)** which is no longer considered good law and which gave way to the forseeability test.

The new test was laid down in **Overseas Tankship (UK) v Morts Dock & Engineering** where a large amount of bunkering oil was spilt into the bay through the carelessness of the appellant's servant while a vessel was dispensing gasoline products and taking in oil. Evidence was brought to prove that the appellants did not know, and could not reasonably have foreseen, that the oil was capable of being set alight when spread on water. Melted hot metal from the respondent's wharf set fire to some cotton fibres floating in the oil, this ignited the oil and the fire ensued resulting in damage to the respondent's wharf and equipment. It was held that the appellants were not liable for the damage since they could not reasonably have foreseen it.

If the type of injury is foreseeable then the manner in which it occurs need not be foreseeable. In **Hughes v Lord Advocate (1963)** the facts were that on 8 November 1958, the appellant, who was then aged eight, was in company with another boy aged ten in Russell Road, Edinburgh. There, near the edge of the roadway, was a manhole, some nine feet deep, over which a shelter tent had been erected, and four paraffin warning lamps were placed at its corners. Post office employees opened the manhole for the purpose of getting access to a telephone cable. The time was about 5 pm, and the site was unattended, the employees having left for a tea-break. They had removed the ladder from the manhole, leaving the ladder beside the shelter; and they had pulled a tarpaulin cover over the entrance to the shelter, leaving a space of about two feet between the lower edge of the tarpaulin and the ground. The lamps were left burning. The boys took one of the paraffin lamps and the ladder into the tent to explore. Shortly thereafter the appellant tripped over the lamp, which fell into the manhole. An explosion followed. The appellant was thrown into the manhole and suffered severe burns. On the evidence the cause of the explosion was found to be that paraffin from the lamp escaped, formed vapour and was ignited by the flame; this particular development of events was not reasonably foreseeable, according to the expert evidence, but there was no other feasible explanation and this explanation was accepted as established.

It was held that although in the law of negligence the duty to take reasonable care was confined to reasonably foreseeable dangers, the fact that the danger actually materialising was not identical with the danger reasonably foreseeable did not necessarily result in liability not arising; in the present case the happening of an accident of the type that did occur, an accident to a child through burns, was reasonably foreseeable, and the further fact that the development of the accident as it actually happened (the occurrence of the explosion) could not reasonably have been foreseen did not absolve the defendants from liability, and accordingly the plaintiff was entitled to recover damages for negligence.

In **Tremain v Pike (1969)**, the farm assistant contracted leptospirosis, a rare disease, transmitted by way of the handling of rat's urine. It was held that the defendant was not liable as it was not known at the time that leptospirosis could be contracted by handling materials contaminated with rat's urine. The decision may have been different had the farm assistant been bitten by rats.

The 'thin-skull rule' and extent of damages

Where the type of damage sustained is reasonably foreseeable, it does not matter that it is in fact more serious than could reasonably have been foreseen. The defendant will be liable for its full extent. This is so even if the damage is greater than could have been foreseen due to some peculiar susceptibility of the claimant, for example, a "thin skull". The thin skull concept mirrors the liability for direct loss concept that we already discussed in **Polemis.**

In **Smith v Leech Brain & Co (1962)**, the claimant was burnt on the lip as a result of the defendant's negligence. He had a precancerous condition, which became cancerous as a result of the burn, and the defendant was held liable for the full result of the negligence.

Also in **Bradford v Robinson Rentals (1967)**, the defendants were liable for the frost bite suffered by the plaintiff when he was subjected to extreme cold. This was so even though this was greater than could have been foreseen. Remember to contrast this case with **Tremain** above, where the type of injury was not foreseeable.

The Claimant's impecuniosity

The claimant generally has a duty to mitigate his loss. He is to do what he can, so that his loss is not increased unduly. There are instances where a claimant cannot mitigate his loss because his resources are simply too limited. The court's approach has not always been predictable:

In **Liesbosch Dredger v SS Edison (1933)**, the plaintiffs incurred exorbitant expenses in order to fulfill a contract because they were too poor to buy a substitute dredger for the one which had been damaged by the defendants. It was held that the plaintiff's impecuniosity had to be disregarded and they were unable to recover the additional expenses.

A contrasting decision was made in the cases of **Dodd Properties Ltd v Canterbury City Council (1980)** and **Martindale v Duncan (1973)**, when the cost of substitute hire vehicles were allowed where delays in repair caused by the impecuniosity of the claimants.

This trend continued in **Alcoa Minerals v Broderick (2001)** where the Privy Council confirmed that Liesbosch Dredger did not solidify any rule that damages attributable to impecuniosity were barred from recovery. The facts are that there was damage to Mr Broderick's roof caused by emissions from Alcoa's aluminum plant…it was held that where a plaintiff was unable to pay immediately for repair caused to his property by the defendant's nuisance and, owing to rampant inflation, the cost of repairs had quadrupled between the date on which the damage occurred and the date of judgment, the plaintiff was entitled to recover as damages the cost of repairs at the date of judgment.

ACTIVITY - NEGLIGENCE

1. With reference to decided cases, explain how the elements of duty, breach and damage are dealt with by the courts in determining tortuous liability for negligence.
2. Zara visits Dr. Scale, a dermatologist, as she wants to remove warts from her face and neck. She has just completed a series of treatment for chicken pox that was given to her by Dr Scale. Dr Scale gives Zara a prescription which she fills and uses to assist in the removal of the warts. She suffers severe burns to her neck and face after using the medication and upon consulting another dermatologist, it turns out that the medication is too strong for her sensitive skin, about which she had told Dr Scale. Advise Zara on the likelihood of her success in a claim against Dr Scale. Support your answer with reference to decided cases.
3. (a) List three elements of the tort of negligence

   (b) Briefly explain the "neighbor principle" laid down in the well known case of Donoghue v Stevenson

   (c) List three situations in which it is established that a duty of care exists
4. Explain two of the following phrases with respect to the tort of negligence:

   a. The "but for" test

   b. Pre-existing conditions

   c. Successive caused

   d. Novus actus interviniens
5. Merrick has been unemployed for a while and so he is low on cash. He then decides to write a book entitled "how to win at the Races Everytime". Merrick makes a large amount of money from the sale of the book through its wide circulation to the public. Ian Jones, a popular newscaster interviewed Merrick while promoting the book on his show. Ian Jones promotes the book in his book club and kept recommending the formula in the book as one that cannot fail.

Courts Furniture Store is threatening to repossess Christena's furniture and she watches the promotion on Ian's show and was persuaded to purchase the book. After reading it she uses money her friend lent her to stop the repossession proceedings and places a bet at the races following with precision the formula in Merrick's book. Christena loses all her money and her furniture. In fact, Merrick knows very little about horse racing and the book is erroneous in many respects.

a. Explain the elements of the tort of negligent misstatement

b. Does either Merrick or Ian Jones owe a duty of care to Christena? Give reasons for your answer.

Chapter 21

DEFAMATION

DEFINITION

A defamatory statement is one which is communicated to a person other than the claimant and puts the claimant in a negative light. It is a statement that tends to expose the claimant, according to ***Sim v Stretch [1936] 2All ER 1237***, to "hatred, contempt, or ridicule, or which tends to lower him in the esteem of right-thinking members of society".

OBJECTIVES OF THE TORT AND WHAT HAS TO BE PROVED

The principal objectives of the law relating to defamation are to:

(a) provide effective and fair remedies for persons whose reputations are harmed by the publication of defamatory matter.
(b) Promote speedy and non- litigious methods of resolving disputes concerning the publication of defamatory matter; and
(c) Ensure that the law relating to the tort of defamation does not place unreasonable limits on freedom of expression and, in particular, on the publication and discussion of topics of public interest and importance.

Consequently, Tort of Defamation can only be proved when the claimant can show:

(1) that the statement in issue was defamatory,
(2) that the statement referred to him, and
(3) that the statement was communicated to a third party (published).

The defendant can chose among the following defences which will be discussed later in this chapter:

(1) truth
(2) fair comment
(3) Innocent Dissemination
(4) Privilege

DISTINCTION BETWEEN LIBEL AND SLANDER

Section 6 of The Jamaican Defamation Act, 2013 has effectively abolished the distinction between libel and slander. It is instructive nonetheless to examine the three distinctions between the two arms of defamation:

(1) Libel is a defamatory statement that is in permanent, written or printed form. Some examples of what may be construed as libel are dramatizations or plays, radio and television presentations, movie films and wax images. The following are cases that illustrate the nature of libelous situations.

Monson v Tussaud's Ltd [1894] 1 QB 671 - Lopes LJ stated that "libels are generally in writing or printing, but this is not necessary; the defamatory matter may be conveyed in some other permanent form. For instance, a statute, a caricature, an effigy, chalk marks on a wall, signs or pictures may constitute libel".

Youssoupoff v MGM Pictures Ltd (1934) 50 TLR 581 - The plaintiff sued for libel in relation to suggestions in the film, Rasputin, the Mad Monk, that she (called Princess Natasha in the film) had been seduced and raped by the eponymous figure of Rasputin. She was awarded 25000 by the jury for damages. The defendants appealed and it was dismissed on the argument of:

> Slesser LJ who commented that "*this action is one of libel and raises at the outset an interesting and difficult problem which, I believe, to be a novel problem, whether the product of the combined photographic and talking instrument which produces these modern films does, if it throws upon the screen and impresses upon the ear defamatory matter, produce that which can be complained of as libel or slander.*
>
> *In my view, this action…was properly framed in libel. There can be no doubt that, so far as the photographic part of the exhibition is concerned, that is a permanent matter to be seen by the eye, and is the proper subject of an action for libel, if defamatory. I regard the speech which is synchronized with the photographic reproduction and forms part of the complex, common exhibition as an ancillary circumstance, part of the surroundings explaining that which is to be seen…*"

The ratio decidendi of the abovementioned case is that cinematographic images, that can be viewed, and being permanent in the sense that the film stock (similar to a video tape) is retained, will be libel and not slander. This case provides good guidance on the point that defamation in the form of an anecdote (story) in the sound track (recorded music), unaccompanied by any image, will be libel…

Slander is a defamatory statement in a transitory or fleeting form. The statement made is not permanent.

(2) Libel is actionable without proof of special damage while damage must be proved for slander, except in four instances:

i. Where there is an allegation that the claimant has committed an imprisonable offence;

ii. Where there is an imputation that the claimant is suffering from a contagious disease, such as venereal disease, leprosy, plague and, arguably, HIV/AIDS;
iii. Where there is an imputation that a woman has committed adultery or otherwise behaved in an 'unchaste' fashion; or
iv. Where there is an imputation that the claimant is unfit to carry on his trade, profession or calling.

(3) Historically libel was a crime as well as a tort while slander was a tort. Criminal libel has now been abolished and consequently we are left with the Tort of Defamation.

THE JUDGE AND JURY: THEIR ROLES

All actions for the Tort of defamation must be commenced in our Supreme Court and unless the court orders otherwise, a claimant or defendant in defamation proceedings may elect for the proceedings to be tried by jury.

> *s.17(1)…*
>
> *s.17(2) Where there is an election for a jury trial, the jury is to determine whether the defendant has published defamatory matter about the claimant and, if so, whether any defence raised by the defendant has been established.*
>
> *If the jury finds that the defendant has published defamatory matter about the claimant and that no defence has been established, the judge and not the jury is to determine the amount of damages (if any) that should be awarded to the claimant and all unresolved issues of fact and law relating to the determination of that amount.*
> Defamation Act, 2013

We await precedents in this area of law to determine whether this reform to the law has helped or hindered awards to deserving Claimants who are determined by the court to have had their reputation tarnished.

INGREDIENTS OF DEFAMATION

(1) WORDS MUST BE DEFAMATORY

The statement in issue must be one that causes right-thinking people of society to think less of the claimant and may also cause them to avoid him or her. The words must be of such that they cause the claimant to be "estranged". Lord Atkin puts it thus, "the statement made must tend to lower the claimant in the estimation of right-thinking members of society generally, and in particular cause him to be regarded with feelings of hatred, contempt, ridicule, fear and disesteem". The statement must be false and thus the defendant has the burden of proving that the statement made is true.

Mere abuse is not defamatory

Speaking in a loud or offensive manner is not defamation. Mansfield CJ made the point in that for a mere general abuse spoken no action lies". Further, abusive or venomous words spoken are not actionable if they were understood to be so by those who heard them. The same is true for words spoken or uttered as a joke.

Innuendo can be defamatory

Statements are not always openly defamatory. They may have innuendo (hidden meaning, implied criticism or suggestion) that make them defamatory. Such statements or innuendos may be actionable. To be successful using this argument, persons who knew the claimant could understand that the hidden meaning referred to him or her. In **Lewis v Daily Telegraph (1963) 2 ALL ER 151**, the defendant published articles headlined, Fraud Squad Probe Firm" and "Inquiry on firm by City Police". It was evident that the articles were about the claimant and the company he operates. The judges disagreed with the claimant who alleged that the words meant not only that there was an investigation, but by implication or inference, that there was ground for suspicion, or even a presumption of guilt.

In **Cassidy v Daily Mirror [1929] 2 KB 331**, the defendant published a picture of Mr. Cassidy and Miss X, "celebrating their engagement". The claimant, Mrs. Cassidy, legally married to Mr. Cassidy. Although they were separated, Mr. Cassidy did visit with her occasionally. Mrs.Cassidy alleges that the effect of the picture was to lead her friends and neighbours to the conclusion that she was not married to Mr. Cassidy but was his kept mistress. She succeeded in her claim.

(2) STATEMENT IDENTIFIED THE CLAIMANT

The claimant must have been identified, directly or indirectly, in the statement made by the defendant. So that, in addition to proving that the statement in issue is defamatory, the claimant has to show that an ordinary, reasonable reader or listener, including persons of the claimant's social circle would take the statement as referring to him. It does not matter that the public at large might not make the same assumption.

In **J'Anson v Stuart (1787)** a newspaper referred to "a swindler", describing the person meant in the words "his diabolic character, has but one eye, and is well known to all persons acquainted with the name of a certain noble circumnavigator". The claimant had only one eye, and his name was very similar to the name of a famous admiral; he was able to prove that the statement referred to him, even though he was never mentioned.

There is also the situation where the statement in issue was intended to refer to a invented or fictitious character, or to someone other than the claimant. The defendant will still be liable for defamation if a reasonable person would think the statement referred to the claimant. **Hulton v Jones (1910)** is a good case in point. The facts are that the defendants published a humorous newspaper story of the discreditable behavior in Dieppe of a fictitious character called Artemus Jones. He was said to be a churchwarden in Peckham. Unknown to the author or the editor, the claimant was also known as Artemus Jones, although he had actually been baptized Thomas Jones. He was a barrister not a churchwarden, did not live in Peckham and had never visited Dieppe. But he had contributed articles to the newspaper in the past and some of his friends thought that the article referred to him. He sued the owner of the newspaper for libel and was awarded 1750 pounds, and the House of Lords agreed. It did not matter that the defendants did not intend to defame him; all that mattered was what a reasonable person would understand the words to mean.

Defamation of a class

Where a defamatory statement refers to a class or group of people such as all nurses are cruel or all politicians are corrupt, it is not usually possible for that group of people to sue for defamation. No one member of that named group will be able to sue on the grounds that the remark libels them personally.

In **Knupffer v London Express Newspapers Ltd (1944)**, the defendants published an article describing the Young Russia party, a group of Russian émigrés, as a Fascist organization. The group had approximately 2,000 members, 24 of whom were based in the UK. The claimant, a Russian emigrant living in London, sued on the basis that, as a member of the group, the statement defamed him personally. The House of Lords refused his claim, on the grounds that the statement was aimed at a large class of people, and nothing in it singled him out.

However, where the group is small and the statement could be construed as referring to all of them, one or all of them may be able to successfully sue. In **Riches v News Group (1986)**, the News of the World published a letter from a man who held his children hostage, which made serious allegations against the, Banbury CID, although without naming any of the officers. Ten members of the Banbury CID successfully sued the paper for damages.

(3) STATEMENT MUST BE PUBLISHED

Communication of the statement must be made to someone other than the claimant.

Communication to a defendant's husband or wife is generally not publication. Publication can take place by way of newspapers, magazines or books, or sometimes radio and television.

Where publication was not foreseeable, the defendant may not be liability. In **Huth v Huth (1915)**, a letter was sent in an unsealed envelope by the defendant to the claimant. The letter was taken out of the envelope and secretly read by the butler who was a servant at the house and had no authority to read mails. It was held that there was no evidence of publication and as such libel was not made out.

However, in **Theaker v Richardson**, communication amounted to publication because it was foreseeable that a third party would access the information. A letter was written by the defendant stating that the claimant was "a lying, low down brothel keeping whore and thief". The letter was placed after being sealed, through the claimant's door. The letter was subsequently opened and read by the claimant's husband and thus the defendant was held liable for defamation as it was foreseeable that the letter might be opened by a person other than the claimant.

Distributors

A person is not generally considered to be the author, editor or publisher of a statement if he is only the printer, producer, distributor, or seller of printed material containing the statement, or the broadcaster of a live programme. Book sellers and distributors are generally able to use the defence of 'innocent dissemination' where they are accused of distributing materials that are libelous.

A person has a defence if he shows that:

i. he was not the editor, author, or publisher of the statement;
ii. he took reasonable precautions in publishing the statement;
iii. he had no idea that the statement was defamatory; and
iv. he had no reason to believe that what he did, caused or contributed to the publication of defamatory statement.

In **Godfrey v Demon Internet (1999)**, it was stated that an internet service provider could be said to have published messages posted on its server by users. However, this will only apply in situations where an internet service provider's part in publishing the words is broadly speaking, comparable to the role of a book or newspaper publisher.

Bunt v Tilley (2006) a number of Internet service providers were sued over defamatory remarks published online. However, unlike Demon, they did not host the websites complained of, but merely provided the system by which the messages were conveyed from the writer to the websites. This made them more like a telephone or postal service than a publisher, and so it was held that they could not be liable.

Consent

Where the claimant himself publishes to other persons a defamatory statement which the defendant wanted only the claimant to see, a situation is created where there is technically, no publication and therefore no defamation can be made out. Publication therefore cannot be made by the claimant.

DEFENCES

A defendant will generally feel he has a right to make a particular statement. It is not a defence to a claim in defamation that the circumstances of the publication of the matter complained of were such that the person defamed was not likely to suffer harm. It is generally the claimant's prerogative to make the assertion that he or she has been defamed and thus bring a claim.

Where a defendant exercises his right to utter a particular statement and the statement is said to be defamatory, he may have the following defences available to him:

(1) TRUTH

The defence of justification has been abolished and is now known primarily as truth. The defence of truth shall succeed:

(a) if the defendant proves that the imputations contained in the matter that is the subject of a proceeding were true or not materially different from the truth; or

(b) Where the proceedings are based on all or any of the matter contained in a publication, the defendant proves that the publication taken as a whole was in substance true, or was in substance not materially different from the truth, if the words not proven to be true do not materially injure the claimant's reputation having regard to the truth of the remaining imputations.

(2) FAIR COMMENT

This is a defence to an action for the tort of defamation. It gives protection to a defendant who seeks to criticize claimants. These statements or criticisms must be made fairly, honestly and must be based on facts that are true and relates to matters of public interest. The defence is very useful to publishers of newspapers but can be used by one who wants to exercise their right to freedom of expression on matters of public concern.

In an action for defamation in respect of words, including or consisting of expressions of opinion, a defence of fair comment shall not fail only because the defendant has failed to prove the truth of every relevant assertion of fact relied on by him as a foundation for the opinion, provided that such of the assertions as are proved to be true are relevant and afford a foundation for the opinion.

Elements that must be proved for this defence include:

(a) The comment must be one of public interest where subject matter may include government issues, education, justice or the law, church matters and the conduct of politicians.
(b) Statement must be a comment or opinion. It is sometimes difficult to make a distinction between a comment or opinion and a fact. There are instances where it is evident that an opinion is being stated. These easy examples are identifiable by words such as 'I think she is a lousy housewife' or it appears that the minister knows not what he is doing'. However, where, for example, there is a controversy about whether a minister followed the proper procedure in issuing a warrant for someone's arrest, and a newspaper writes that the "DPP is stupid", the statement may sound like an opinion but it is not treated as such in law. It is stated as an expression of fact and on that basis, the defence of fair comment will not be available. The following recent cases are instructive.

In **Cornwell v Sunday People (1983),** the actress and singer Charlotte Cornwell sued the Sunday People over an article written by its television critic Nina Myskow. The article said of Ms. Cornwell that she couldn't sing or act, and had 'the kind of stage presence that jams lavatories'. The News of the World argued that this was comment on Ms Cornwell's performance, rather than assertions of fact, but the jury disagreed and found for Ms. Cornwell.

Burstein v Associated Newspapers (2007) concerned a review in London Evening Standard of an opera about suicide bombers. The reviewer described the opera as 'horribly leaden and unmusical' and concluded 'I found the tone depressingly anti-American, and the idea that there is anything heroic about suicide bombers is, frankly, a grievous insult.' The composer sued for defamation, claiming that the review implied that he sympathized with terrorist causes, and considered suicide bombers to be heroes. The Court of Appeal threw the case out, saying it was very clear that the review was a comment and not a statement of fact, and the fact that it might imply anything about Mr. Burnstein's motives did not mean it ceased to become a comment. The facts referred to in the review were accurate, and the opinions the reviewer formed on the basis of those facts were ones which could be honestly held.

In **Keays v Guardian Newspapers (2003),** The Guardian published a story about Sarah Keays, who was known as the former mistress of a cabinet minister and mother of his child. After long refusing to talk to the press, Ms Keays had recently decided to publish her story, and the Guardian article speculated about her motives. The judge held that the article could only be read as a comment, since the writer could not know as a fact what was in Keays' mind.

(c) The statement must be based on facts that are true – once it has been established that the words in question are comment, the court must ask whether that comment has a basis of truth. The facts need not be set out in full by the defendant. This was confirmed by the House of Lords in **Kemsley v Foot [1952] AC 345** in which Michael Foot, writing in Tribune, had described an article in the

Evening Standard as 'the foulest piece of journalism appearing in this country for many a year'. The piece appeared under the headline 'Lower than Kemsley'. Lord Kemsley, the proprietor of rival newspapers, sued for defamation. The House of Lords held that the reference to Kemsley sufficiently indicated the facts on which Foot had commented. It is known that the Kemsley Press had a bad reputation.

(d) The comment must not have been set in motion by malice. In other words, the defendant must not have acted with corrupt motive. The onus is on the plaintiff to prove that malice existed on the part of the defendant. If the statement is made and the writer does not honestly believe it to be true, this could be evidence of malice. In **Thomas v Bradbury, Agnew and Co Ltd (1906)**, the defendant had written a very unfavourable review of the claimant's book in the magazine, *Punch.* It became apparent that he had acted out of personal dislike for the writer and not genuine belief in what he said. He was liable for defamation.

(e) The comment must be honestly made

INNOCENT DISSEMINATION

It is a defence to the publication of defamatory matter if the defendant proves that

(a) he published the matter merely in the capacity of a distributor who is subordinate to the publisher of the matter alleged to be defamatory, or as an employee or agent of the distributor, or as an employee or agent of the distributor or in the capacity of a secondary publisher having received the matter from a reputable wire service;

(b) the defendant knew or ought reasonably to have known, that the matter was defamatory; and

(c) the defendant's lack of knowledge was not due to any negligence on the part of the defendant.

The defence is not available to a person who:

(a) knows, or ought reasonably to have known, that the matter was or could have been defamatory but proceeded to publish the matter anyway.
(b) fails to remove the defamatory matter from his publication or from circulation promptly after it has been brought to his attention

PRIVILEGE

(a) Absolute
Absolute privilege has the effect that a statement cannot be sued on as defamatory. This defence seeks to protect our fundamental right to freedom of speech and as such the defence is generally invincible. This is so even where there is a false or malicious statement. The following are incidents that attract the defence of 'absolute privilege':

i. Lawyer client communications
ii. Parliamentary statements
iii. Communication among officers of the state during the course of their official duty. An example of this is where issues of national security are being discussed.
iv. Statements made in judicial proceedings
v. Papers, reports, proceedings of parliament.

(b) Qualified
Qualified privilege, like absolute privilege seeks to protect freedom of speech in the form of statements made in certain forums. It is the judge that decides whether a particular statement is protected by qualified privilege. In addition reports must be fair and accurate and free from malice in order to qualify for this privilege and it is the jury that decided on the matters of good faith and malice.

Adam v Ward (1917) is the case in point that dictates where qualified privilege will be relevant. In this case, Lord Atkinson explained that "a privileged occasion is…an occasion where the person who makes a communication has an interest or duty, legal, social or moral, to make it to the person to whom it is made, and the person to whom it is so made has a corresponding interest or duty to receive it. This reciprocity is essential".

Reciprocity has been illustrated in many cases.

In **Bryanston Finance v De Vries (1975),** the defendant was found to be covered by qualified privilege when he made defamatory statements which were concerned with protecting his business interests in a memo to a secretary.

In **Adam v Ward**, the claimant had severely criticized an army general. These criticisms were protected by absolute privilege because they were made within Parliament, but after the army investigated his allegations and announced that they were totally unfounded, the claimant wrote to a newspaper defending his position, and again criticizing the general. The House of Lords held that the letter was covered by qualified privilege as the claimant was protecting his own reputation.

In **Watt v Longsdon (1930),** the claimant was working abroad for the company of which the defendant was director. While the claimant was away, the defendant received a letter saying that the claimant was, among other things, "a blackguard, a thief and a liar" who "lived exclusively to satisfy his own passions and lust". None of this was true. The defendant showed the letter to the chairman of the board of directors, and also to the claimant's wife, who decided to get a divorce as a result. When the claimant sued for defamation, it was held that showing the letter to the board was covered by qualified privilege because they had an interest in seeing it, and as a fellow officer of the company the defendant had a duty to show it to them. However, showing the letter to the claimant's wife was not covered by the privilege; although she had an interest in receiving the information, he had no duty to give it to her.

In **Croucher v Inglis (1889)**, it was stated that "when a person suspects that a crime has been committed, it is his right and his duty to inform the police".

"The Reynolds defence"

Traditionally, qualified privilege only protected a person who had a duty to make the statement and not someone who repeated it. As such, media reports were given little protection. So, by way of example, if a person reports a suspicion to the police, this person would be covered by the defence. This is so as the person has a duty, whether moral or legal to report what he saw and the police had a right to receive it. A newspaper carrying this report would not have been protected prior to Reynolds.

The defence would only cover the media where someone had a duty, social, moral or legal to make a report to the media and the media had the same duty to publish the statement received. This situation was adapted and morphed into the Reynolds defence. Media protection has been elevated where it acts responsibly in reporting matters of public interest.

Reynolds v Times Newspapers (1999) gave birth to the "Reynolds Defence". The case surrounds a story published by The Times about the curious resignation of the former Irish Prime Minister, Albert Reynolds. Mr. Reynolds' contention about the published article was that it gave the impression that he deceived the Irish Parliament. The Times claimed the defence of qualified privilege, and submitted that it should be applicable to discussions concerning matters of grave public interest. This they believe to be so because the media had a duty to report such matters and the public a duty to be knowledgeable about them.

The House of Lords agreed that it was of importance that matters of public interest should be available so that people can make decisions regarding their politician of choice. However, the Law Lords pointed out that it was also in the public interest for individuals such as politicians to be able to defend their reputations against false allegations because, to make an informed choice, voters needed to know who was good as well as who was bad.

In Reynolds, The House of Lords said that courts should look at the following ten factors in determining if the defence is available:

(1) The seriousness of the allegation. The more serious the allegation, the greater the care the press must show in handling it, but, on the other hand, if an allegation is not especially serious, it may be of insufficient public interest to be covered by the defence
(2) The nature of the information, and the extent to which it is the subject of public concern
(3) The source of the information. Important issues here will include whether the informants had direct knowledge of the events, whether they were being paid for their stories, and whether they had their own axes to grind
(4) The steps taken by the journalist to check the information.
(5) The status of the information. The allegation may have already been the subject of an investigation which commands respect.
(6) The urgency of the matter. News is often a perishable commodity
(7) Whether comment was sought from the plaintiff. He may have information others do not possess or have not disclosed. An approach to the plaintiff will not always be necessary.
(8) Whether the article contained the gist of the plaintiff's side of the story.
(9) The tone of the article. A newspaper can raise queries or call for an investigation. It need not adopt allegations as a statement of fact
(10) The circumstances of the publication, including the timing

Reynolds was applied successfully in **Loutchansky v Times Newspaper (2002)** where a defendant to a libel action who pleaded qualified privilege was not entitled to rely on matters of which he had no knowledge at the time of publication. Have a look also at **Jamell v Wall Street Journal (Europe) 2006**

RESOLUTION OF DEFAMATORY ISSUES WITHOUT COURT PROCEEDINGS

Where a person publishes any matter that is, or may be, or is alleged to be defamatory of another person, the publisher may make an offer to make amends to the aggrieved person. An offer to make amends maybe in relation to the matter in question generally or limited to any particular defamatory imputations that the publisher accepts that the matter in question carries.

An offer to make amends is to be taken to have been made without prejudice and shall be understood to mean an offer:

(i) to publish or join the publication of a suitable correction of the matter in question and a sufficient apology to the aggrieved person; or
(ii) where copies of the matter in question have been distributed by or with the knowledge of the person making the offer, to take steps as are reasonably practicable on his part for notifying persons to whom copies have been so distributed that the matter in question is alleged to be defamatory of the aggrieved person.

An offer to make amends may include payment of a specified sum or an offer of compensation and maybe accepted or rejected by or on behalf of the aggrieved person. This offer shall be in writing and shall be accompanied by a Voluntary Declaration. The effect of a claimant not accepting an offer to make amends, a defendant in proceedings for defamation may rely in mitigation of damages on this offer.

In any action for defamation, the defendant, in mitigation of damages, may make, or offer, an apology to the claimant for defamation before the commencement of the action in court. Where the action was commenced before there was an opportunity of making or offering the apology, as soon after the commencement of the action as he had an opportunity of doing so.

REMEDIES AVAILABLE TO A CLAIMANT

Damages

Where it is determined that a defamatory statement has placed someone's character in disrepute, damages may be awarded as compensation. In determining the amount of damages to be awarded in any defamation proceedings, the court shall ensure that there is an appropriate and rational relationship between the harm sustained by the claimant and the amount of damages awarded.

Further, evidence is also admissible on behalf of the defendant, in mitigation of damages for the publication of defamatory matter where the claimant has suffered no harm and is unlikely to suffer harm; the defendant has made an apology to the claimant; the defendant has published a correction of the defamatory matter; and the claimant has already recovered damages for defamation in relation to any other publication of matter having the same meaning or effect as the defamatory matter.

Declaration

A claimant may be entitled to declaration that the defendant is liable to the claimant in defamation. This remedy along with the award of cost for attorney-at-law and client fees, may be available.

Correction

In any proceedings for defamation, the claimant may seek an order from the court that the defendant publishes or cause to be published a correction of the matter that is the subject of the proceedings.

ACTIVITY - DEFAMATION

(1) **a.** What is a defamatory statement?
b. List the elements of a defamation
c. Explain at least two defences to a defamatory statement

(2) During the budget debate an opposition Member of Parliament in his speech said that it had been brought to his attention that Mr Gareth McKenzie, Minister of the Environment, had been paid millions of dollars by the Crudity Garbage Disposal Company for awarding them a million-dollar contract. The next day the headlines of the daily Horizon newspaper were: "Government Minster Entangled in Bribery".
Minister McKenzie wishes to sue the opposition Member of Parliament and the newspaper for defamation.

a. Explain the elements of the tort of defamation that Minister McKenzie must satisfy to succeed against the opposition Member of Parliament and the newspaper.
b. Outline two defences that could be raised by the newspaper and one defence that the opposition Member of Parliament might have.

Chapter 22

NUISANCE

DEFINITION

A person's behavior on their land may affect us on ours. The law relating to private nuisance is geared towards creating a balance in the use and enjoyment of land. It seeks to restrict an unreasonable interference with our use or enjoyment of land and in some instances, the interference with some right over the land.

ELEMENTS TO BE PROVED

1. continuous interference with enjoyment of the land
2. the interference was unreasonable
3. the claimant suffered damage

CONTINUOUS INTERFERENCE

The longer the interference with the claimant's use and enjoyment of land, the more likely the interference will be seen as a nuisance. In **De Keyser's Royal Hotel v Spicer Bros Ltd (1914)** 30 TLR 257, a noisy pile driving at night during temporary building works was held to be a private nuisance. One off incidents of interference with the use and enjoyment of land can amount to nuisance. This was seen in the case of **Crown River Cruises v Kimbolton Fireworks [1996] 2 Lloyd's Rep 533** where firework display for approximately 15-20 minutes had debris of a flammable nature falling upon nearby property and damaging the property when it caught fire.

UNLAWFUL INTERFERENCE/UNREASONABLENESS

The disposition of the court in dealing with issues of private nuisance is to perform a balancing act. The claimant must prove that the defendant's conduct was unreasonable, thereby making it unlawful. In the law of defamation, we are entitled to freedom of speech but we are not generally entitled to injure a person's reputation. It is the same concept that pervades the law of nuisance. We are entitled to use out property but we are not to injure our neighbor or prohibit their enjoyment of land.

The court uses several criteria to determine whether the defendant is being excessive or unreasonable in the use of his land:

The locality

It was stated in **Sturges v Bridgman (1879) 11 Ch D 852 t**hat: "What would be a nuisance in Belgravia Square would not necessarily be so in Bermondsey." This can be interpreted to mean that what is nuisance in an uptown community may not be a nuisance in a, downtown community

Sensitivity of the claimant

An individual who is abnormally sensitive is unlikely to succeed in a claim for private nuisance since the test is one of reasonable user. A reasonable user is not particularly sensitive. **Robinson v Kilvert (1889) 41 Ch D 88** made the point when the P's claim for damage to abnormally sensitive paper stored in a cellar which was affected by heat from adjoining premises failed because ordinary paper would not have been affected by the temperature. **McKinnon Industries v Walker [1951] 3 DLR 577** was also instructive. The facts are that fumes from the Defendant's factory damaged delicate orchids. Since the fumes would have damaged flowers of ordinary sensitivity there was a nuisance.

The utility of the defendant's conduct

Where an activity being carried out is for the benefit of the community, it is hardly likely that this activity will be seen as a nuisance. Have a look at the case of **Harrison v Southwark Water Co [1891] 2 Ch D 409** where building work carried out at reasonable times of the day did not amount to a nuisance. However, in **Adams v Ursell [1913] 1 Ch D 269** the activities of a business owner of a fried-fish shop was a nuisance in the residential part of a street because of the constant odour from the frying and an injunction was granted for him to stop the operation. The argument is that no hardship would have been caused to the Defendant and to the poor people who were his customers.

Malice

While it is not necessary to establish malicious behaviour on the part of the defendant, evidence of malice may refute reasonableness. In **Christie v Davey [1893] 1 Ch D 316**, the plaintiff had been giving music lessons in his semi-detached house for several years. The defendant, irritated by the noise, banged on the walls, shouted, blew whistles and beat tin trays with the malicious intention of annoying his neighbour and spoiling the music lessons. An injunction was granted to restrain the D's behaviour.

In **Bradford Corporation v Pickles [1895] AC 587**, the Plaintiff deliberately diverted water flowing through his land, away from his neighbour's property, rendering one of their dams useless. The Plaintiff intended to force them to buy his land at an inflated price. It was held that he was committing no legal wrong because no-one has a right to uninterrupted supplies of water which percolates through from adjoining property. Lord Halsbury LC held in that case that "if it was a lawful act, however ill the motive might be, he had a right to do it. If it was an unlawful act, however good his motive might be, he would have no right to do it."

Malice was also found in **Hollywood Silver Fox Farm v Emmett [1936] 2 KB 468** where as a result of a dispute between the plaintiff and the defendant, the defendant instructed his son to fire bird-scaring cartridges as near as possible to the breeding pens of the plaintiff silver foxes whilst remaining on the defendant's land. As a result, one vixen would not breed and another ate her cubs. The plaintiff was entitled to damages and an injunction for the loss as the malice rendered the discharge of the firearm an unreasonable user of land.

The state of the defendant's land

Where an occupier of land is aware of a naturally arising hazard but fails to take reasonable step to prevent injury, he may be liable for nuisance caused. This principle was seen in **Leakey v National Trust [1980] QB 485** where the defendants occupied land on which there was a large, naturally occurring mound known as Barrow Mump. After one very hot summer, they were aware that the area could be affected by landslides, because of the earth drying out, but they took no precautions against this. A landslide did occur, casting earth and trees onto neighboring land and the defendants refused to remove the debris.

The court held that they were liable for the nuisance, even though they had not actually done anything to cause it, but had merely failed to prevent it. It was made clear, however, that where the defendant had not actually caused the problem, only failed to do something about it, the law will take account of that fact in what it requires the defendant to do, and will take into account the defendant's resources. According to Lord Wilberforce, "the standard ought to be to require of the occupier what is reasonable to expect of him in his individual circumstances".

INTERFERENCE WITH THE USE OR ENJOYMENT OF LAND OR SOME RIGHT OVER OR IN CONNECTION WITH IT

The claimant must prove that there was interference of his use or enjoyment of land by a defendant. This interference must be indirect and are usually acts that are continuous rather than a one-off incident. Often, it is noise and or smells that constitute nuisance. However, in some instances there will be something that affects the claimant's land physically, such as overhanging tree branches from the defendant's property to the claimant's.

WHO MAY SUE

The owner or a person in occupation, such as a lessee can succeed in a claim for nuisance. In **Malone v Laskey [1907] 2 KB 141,** the plaintiff was using a toilet and the lavatory cistern fell on her head because of vibrations from machinery on adjoining property. Her claim failed as she was merely the wife of a licensee, and had no proprietary interest herself in the land. However, today she would be able to claim in negligence.

However, **Hunter v Canary Wharf** confirmed this principle and so only someone with a significant legal or beneficial interest can sue and succeed in nuisance.

WHO MAY BE SUED

Creator of the nuisance

Any person who creates the nuisance can be sued, regardless of whether that person owns or occupies the land from which the nuisance came. In **Thomas v National Union of Mineworkers (South Wales Area) (1985),** it was held that the striking miners participating in an industrial action outside of a factory could be liable for nuisance.

Occupiers

The owner of the land and the occupier, who can be a tenant, can be sued for nuisance. The occupier of land may be liable for nuisance caused by himself or his employees. In addition, as per **Matania v National Provincial Bank**, employers of independent contractors may be liable where the activities of the contractor involve a special danger of nuisance. Also, occupiers of land may be liable for acts of nuisance caused on that land by third parties such as trespassers, or previous occupiers, if the occupier is or ought to be aware of the potential for nuisance to be caused and fails to take steps to prevent it.

Landlord

A landlord may be liable for nuisances originating from his land. This may be so in any of the following three instances:

1. If nuisance was in existence as at the time of the lease and the owners knew or ought to have known about it.
2. Where the lease agreement makes a provision for repairs to be done by the landlord or there is a right reserved for him to deal with repairs. In **Wringe v Cohen (1940)** the defendant was responsible for keeping the premises repaired but failed to do so, and as a result, a wall collapsed and damaged the neighboring shop which belonged to the claimant. The defendant was held liable.

3. Where the landlord can be said to have authorized the nuisance. In **Tetley v Chitty (1986)**, the local council allowed a go-Kart club to use their land, and the noise from it disturbed local residents. The council claimed they were not liable because they had neither created the noise nor permitted it, but the court held that, as such noise was an inevitable result of the activities of a go-kart club, allowing the club to use the land amounted to permitting the nuisance, and thus the council were liable.

DEFENCES

Prescription

If the nuisance has been continued for 20 years without interruption and the claimant knew about it, the defendant will not be liable if he raises a defence of prescriptive right to the nuisance. In **Sturges v Bridgman (1879) 11 Ch D 852** a Doctor built a consulting room next to a confectioner's workshop which had been operating for over 20 years. The doctor successfully sued for nuisance created by way of the noise and the court held that the prescriptive right began when the doctor started using the property. This did not amount to 20 years.

Statutory authority

A statute may prescribe that some activity be done. Pursuing that activity may create a nuisance. There will be no liability because the statute is treated as having authorized the nuisance.

Allen Gulf Oil Refining Ltd (1981) is the leading case on this principle. In this case a statute authorized the defendants to carry out oil refinement works. The plaintiff complained of noise, smell and vibration. It was held that the defendants had a defence of statutory authority.

Coming to the nuisance no defence

It is no defence to prove that the claimant came to the nuisance. This was the situation in **Miller v Jackson (1977)** where cricket had been played on a village ground since 1905. In 1970, houses were built in such a place that cricket balls went into the garden. It was held that there was a nuisance. There was an interference with the reasonable enjoyment of land. It was no defence to say that the plaintiff had brought trouble onto his own head by moving there.

REMEDIES

Injunction
An injunction is an equitable remedy and is only granted at the discretion of the court. Where the tort of nuisance is established, the plaintiff can seek the court's assistance in getting an injunction against the defendant to cease the activity that has prevented him from using or enjoying land or rights to land.

Damages
Where a claimant is successful in a claim for nuisance, damages may be recovered for injury to the claimant's land, or the loss of enjoyment of it such as lack of sleep, or discomfort caused by noise or smells.

Abatement
This is a remedy that allows the claimant to take steps to end the nuisance. The claimant may enter the defendant's property with notice to build a drain or cut down a tree that has been hanging on the claimant's property. The claimant becomes a trespasser where he enters the defendant's property without notice or permission.

PUBLIC NUISANCE

Public nuisance is a crime as well as a tort and remedy for a public nuisance is a prosecution or relator action by the Attorney General on behalf of the public. A claimant who suffers particular damage, over and above the damage suffered by the rest of the public, may maintain an action in public nuisance.

A Public nuisance is committed where a person carries on some harmful activity which affects the public or a section of the public, for example, where the owners of a crop duster causes pesticides and other chemicals to pollute the atmosphere in the locality, or where there is an obstruction on the public highway. In addition, it is defined as, an act or omission which materially affects the reasonable comfort of a class of Her Majesty's subjects.

RYLANDS v FLETCHER

The Rule in Rylands deals with damage caused by isolated escapes from your neighbour's land. The best example is the case itself. The facts of **Rylands v Fletcher (1868) LR 3 HL 330**, are that the defendants employed independent contractors to construct a reservoir on their land. The contractors found disused mines when digging but failed to seal them properly. They filled the reservoir with water. As a result, water flooded through the mineshafts into the plaintiff's mines on the adjoining property. The plaintiff secured a verdict at Liverpool Assizes. The Court of Exchequer Chamber held the defendant liable and the House of Lords affirmed their decision.

The principle established in Rylands was stated by Blackburn J when he said "we think that the rule of law is that the person who for his own purposes brings on his lands and collects and keeps there anything likely to do mischief if it escapes, must keep it in at his peril, and, if he does not do so, is prima facie answerable for all the damage which is the natural consequence of its escape."

The Rule can be broken down as follows:

1. That the defendant brought something onto his land that is likely to do mischief;
2. The thing escapes
3. Escape caused by non natural use
4. Foreseeable damage caused

All four elements must be proved in order to establish liability

REQUIREMENTS

1. The defendant brought something onto his land

The dangerous thing must have been accumulated or brought onto the defendant's land in the course of some unnatural use of land. The rule does not apply to damage caused by anything which naturally occurs there.

In **Giles v Walker (1890)** a large crop of thistles grew on forest land after it was ploughed by the defendant. Neighbouring lands were affected when the wind carried the seeds with it. The defendant was held not liable under **Rylands v Fletcher** because the thistles grew naturally, and had not been introduced by him.

In **British Celanese v Hunt (1969)** the defendants owned a factory on an industrial estate in which they manufactured electrical components. They negligently allowed metal foil strips stored on the land to blow onto a power line, cutting the supply to the claimant's factory. The defendants were held not liable using **Ryland v Fletcher** but were liable in both negligence and nuisance. It was argued that there was no special risk attached to the storage of the foils and it is submitted that damage was not foreseeable.

2. Non-natural use of the land

Non-natural user has been defined as "some special use bringing with it increased dangers to others, and must not merely be the ordinary use of land or such a use as is proper for the general benefit of the community. It is important that all the circumstances of time and practice of mankind must be taken into consideration..."

In determining non-natural user, the court will look at the activity and the place and how the location is maintained and the relation to its surroundings.

What is a non-natural user of land varies every year. The process of widening the definition of natural user was arrested and even put in reverse by the House of Lords in the case of **Cambridge Water Co v Eastern**

Leather Company. In that case, the trial judge held that the accumulation of chemicals by the defendant was a natural user of the land because the creation of employment in the defendant's tannery was for the benefit of the local community. However, Lord Goff objected to this argument and considered that storing large quantities of industrial chemicals on industrial property was a classic example of non-natural user.

3. Something likely to do mischief

A defendant should be prepared to keep at his peril, anything brought onto his land that is dangerous and is likely to escape and cause injury. In **Transco plc v Stockport Metropolitan Borough Council (2003)**, the defendant council were responsible for the maintenance of the pipe work supplying water to a block of flats. A leak developed which was undetected for some time. The water collected at an embankment which housed the claimant's high pressure gas main. The water caused the gas main to be exposed and unsupported. This was a serious and immediate risk and the claimant took action to avoid the potential danger. It was held by Lord Bingham that the council's use of the land was not non natural and no mischief was actually caused.

4. Escape

The tort will only be committed when damage is caused by a dangerous thing that escapes from the defendant's land. It therefore means that damage caused to someone else while they are on the defendant's land is not compensable under **Rylands v Fletcher.** In **Read v J Lyons (1946)**, the claimant was an inspector of munitions, visiting the defendant's munitions factory. A shell being manufactured there exploded injuring her, as there was no evidence that the defendants had been negligent she claimed under **Rylands v Fletcher.** The defendants were held not liable, on the grounds that although high explosive shells clearly were dangerous things, the strict liability imposed by **Rylands v Fletcher** requires an escape of the thing that caused the injury. The court defined an escape as occurring when something escapes to an area outside the defendant's property where he has no control.

Foreseeability

In **Cambridge Water Co v Eastern Countries Leather (1994)**, Lord Goff established that the harm caused by the escape must be foreseeable in order for damages to be recoverable.

REMEDIES

(1) Damages can be recovered for physical harm to the neigbouring land and to other property that may have been destroyed.
(2) Rylands v Fletcher is a species of nuisance and based on all the authorities, there can be no recovery for personal injury.
(3) Injunction can be granted by the court

DEFENCES

A number of defences have been developed to the rule in Rylands v Fletcher.

1. Consent

Consent of the claimant to the existence or accumulation of a dangerous thing on the defendant's property will be a defence for the defendant where there is no negligence.

2. Common Benefit

The dangerous item may have been maintained for the benefit of both claimant and defendant. In this case, the defendant will not be liable. This is a defence that sounds a lot like consent.

3. Act of a stranger

Where a third party is responsible for the damage and he was not acting under the instructions of the defendant, the defendant will not be liable. In **Box v Jubb (1879),** the defendants were not liable for damage done when their reservoir overflowed, because the flooding was caused by a third party who had emptied his own reservoir into the stream which fed the defendant's reservoir. The defendant will not escape liability for negligence if the act of the stranger is one that the defendant should have foreseen and guarded against.

4. Statutory authority

The terms of a relevant statute will allow the defendant to escape liability if the said terms clearly give them authority to act. Since most statutes do not make provisions for the defence to apply, the court will be called on to interpret the statute in this regard.

In **Green v Chelsea Waterworks Co (1894),** a water main laid by the defendant burst, flooding the claimant's premises. The Court of Appeal held that the company was not liable, because they were not only permitted but obliged by statute to maintain water supply, and occasional bursts were an inevitable result of such duty.

Charing Cross Electricity Co v Hydraulic Co (1914) on the other hand featured similar facts but the defendants were found not to have a defence of statutory authority because the relevant statute did not oblige them to provide water supply but gave them the power to do so.

5. Act of God

The defendant will not be liable where the escape is due solely to natural hazards in circumstances where no human foresight could have conjured up the named hazard. In **Nichols v Marsland (1876) 2 ExD 1**, the defendant was liable when unusual flood rains caused artificial lakes, bridges and waterways to be flooded and damage adjoining land.

The corporation in **Greenock Corporation v Caledonian Railway [1917] AC 556** was liable for damages caused by heavy rains of an unusual nature after they constructed a concrete paddling pool for children in the bed of a stream and obstructed the natural flow of the stream.

6. Default of the claimant

No liability will lie if the escape is the fault of the claimant.

ACTIVITY – NUISANCE

1. "The tort of nuisance can only be established when one balances the rights of the neigbours in their use of land". Discuss this statement, supporting your answer with the use of relevant illustrations.

2. Jackie complains that her eyes get inflamed and her skin itches whenever her neighbor, Mr. Douglas sprays his dogs with pesticide to prevent tick infestation, which he does in his garage every night. She also claims that her two hamsters and her children become very sick from the scents. Discuss whether or not a tort is established and the remedies, if any, available to Jackie.

3. Tash and Layton live next to the Chlorochem Co. Ltd which is a factory that produces toxic chemicals. Tash's father who lives with them has a nervous condition which has worsened because of the constant noise from the factory. Tash loves gardening and has been planting vegetables in her front yard, which she sells to help her son through law school. The plants are doing well and bearing fruit when suddenly Tash notices that they have started to die. They all appear to be burnt.

Advise Tash and her father whether a tort is established and what legal remedies are available to them.

Chapter 23

TRESPASS TO THE PERSON

ASSAULT

An act which intentionally causes a person to apprehend the infliction of immediate, unlawful, force on his person is an assault.

R v Meade and Belt (1823) 1 Lew CC 184 had originally laid down the principle, that 'no words or singing are equivalent to an assault'. The House of Lords in 1997 established a new principle that word can cause a person to apprehend the infliction of unlawful force. This was laid down in the case of **R v Constanza [1997] Crim LR 576**.

Mere words will not constitute assault where they are expressed in such a way that they negative the threat of the defendant. This principle can be found in the case of **Tuberville v Savage (1669) 86 ER 684.**

The claimant must fear that battery is imminent as was seen in **Stephens v Myers (1830) 172 ER 735**, where the defendant made a violent gesture at the plaintiff by waiving a clenched fist, but was prevented from reaching him by the intervention of third parties. The defendant was liable for assault.

BATTERY

Infliction of an unlawful force with intention on another person is a battery. It was stated in **Cole v Turner (1704)** that "the least touching of another in anger is a battery'. There are exceptions to the principle as seen in:

Collins v Wilcock [1984] 1 WLR 1172 - Two police officers on duty in a police car observed two women in the street who appeared to be soliciting for the purpose of prostitution. When the police officers requested the appellant to get into the car for questioning she refused to do so and instead walked away from the car. A policewoman got out of the car and followed the appellant in order to question her regarding her identity and conduct and to caution her, if she was suspected of being a prostitute, in accordance with the approved police procedure for administering cautions for suspicious behaviour before charging a woman with being a prostitute.

The appellant refused to speak to the policewoman and walked away, whereupon the policewoman grabbed the appellant's arm to detain her. The appellant then swore at the policewoman and scratched the officer's arm with her fingernails. The appellant was convicted of assaulting a police officer in the execution of her duty, contrary to s 51(1) of the Police Act 1964. She appealed against the conviction, contending that when the assault occurred the officer was not exercising her power of arrest and was acting beyond the scope of her duty in detaining the appellant by taking hold of her arm. The police contended that the officer was acting in the execution of her duty when the assault occurred because the officer had good cause to detain the appellant for the purpose of questioning her to see whether a caution for suspicious behaviour should be administered.

It was held that the police woman's actions amounted to a battery and the defendant's response was self defence. Her conviction was therefore quashed. In that case, Lord Goff stated that implied consent existed where there was unavoidable touching in crowded spaces, handshakes, touching someone's shoulder to get their attention. Consent was never given to grab the woman's arm.

FALSE IMPRISONMENT

False imprisonment is the intentional restriction of the claimant's freedom of movement however short unless expressly or impliedly authorized by the law. The tort of false imprisonment seeks to protect a person from restraint. If there is an alternative reasonable escape route there will be no false imprisonment. See **Bird v Jones (1845) 7 QB 742** where the plaintiff, attempting to pass in a particular direction, was obstructed by the defendant, who prevented him from going in any particular direction but one that he did not want to take. It was held to be no imprisonment.

Robinson v Balmain New Ferry [1910] AC 295 - In an action for damages for assault and false imprisonment it appeared that the plaintiff had contracted with the defendants to enter their wharf and stay there till the boat should start and then be taken by the boat to the other side. No breach of the defendants' undertaking was alleged, but the plaintiff after entry changed his mind and desired to effect an exit from their wharf without payment of the prescribed toll for exit, and was for a time forcibly prevented from leaving. It was held... that the toll imposed was reasonable and the defendants were entitled to resist a forcible evasion of it.

Can a person be falsely imprisoned without his knowledge? The Court of Appeal and The House of Lords said Yes.

Meering v Graham-White Aviation Co Ltd (1920) 122 LT 44 - A private prosecutor not having the privilege that a police constable possesses of imprisoning a person on mere suspicion that a felony has been committed, false imprisonment results, if the person is detained by the private prosecutor. Arrest, however by a police constable which follows the placing of the case in his hands to do his duty is not an arrest by a private prosecutor, but is an arrest by the police constable. The fact that a person is not actually aware that he is being imprisoned does not amount to evidence that he is not imprisoned, it being possible for a person to be imprisoned in law without his being conscious of the fact and appreciating the position which he is placed, laying hands upon the person of the party imprisoned not being essential.

However, Lord Griffiths did state in the latter case that 'if a person is unaware that he has been falsely imprisoned and has suffered no harm, he can normally expect to recover no more than nominal damages'.

Can an omission to release a person constitute false imprisonment? Not according to the House of Lords, at least where a person has consented to some degree of constraint on their movement.

Heard v Weardale Steel, Coal & Coke Co [1915] AC 67 - A miner descended a coal mine at 9.30 am for the purpose of working therein for his employers, the owners of the colliery. In the ordinary course he would be entitled to be raised to the surface at the conclusion of his shift, which expired at 4 pm. On arriving at the bottom of the mine the miner was ordered to do certain work which he wrongfully refused to do, and at 11 am he requested to be taken to the surface in a lift, which was the only means of egress from the mine. His employers refused to permit him to use the lift until 1.30 pm although it had been available for the carriage of men to the surface from 1.10 pm, and in consequence he was detained in the mine against his will for twenty minutes. In respect of this detention the miner sued his employers for damages for false imprisonment. It was held, on the principle of volenti non fit injuria, that the action could not be maintained.

THE RULE IN WILKINSON v DOWNTON

The rule in **Wilkinson v Downton** relates to the intentional infliction of harm in the form of mental shock. This is not actually a trespass to the person but a separate analogous tort. In a case of the same name, the defendant, by way of a practical joke, falsely represented to the plaintiff, a married woman, that her husband had met with a serious accident whereby both his legs were broken. The defendant made the statement with intent that it should be believed to be true. The plaintiff believed it to be true, and in consequence suffered a violent nervous shock which rendered her ill. It was held, that these facts constituted a good cause of action.

The Court of Appeal upheld this rule in **Janvier v Sweeney [1919] 2 KB 316** - False words and threats calculated to cause, uttered with the knowledge that they are likely to cause, and actually causing physical injury to the person to whom they are uttered are actionable.

The defendants were two private detectives. One of them was designing to inspect certain letters, to which he believed the plaintiff, a maid servant, had means of access. He instructed the other defendant, who was his assistant, to induce the plaintiff to show him the letters, telling him that the plaintiff would be remunerated for this service. The assistant endeavoured to persuade the plaintiff by false statements and threats, as the result of which the plaintiff fell ill from a nervous shock. In an action by the plaintiff against the defendants for damages, it was held, that the assistant was acting within the scope of his employment and that both the defendants were liable. **Wilkinson v. Downton [1897] 2 Q. B. 57** approved.

DEFENCES

CONSENT

Consent may be given by words or even implied from conduct.

According to **Collins v Wilcock**, as a result of social interaction a person is deemed to consent to a reasonable degree of physical contact by all who move in society.

Those who take part in sports that are being played according to the rules also consent to a reasonable degree of physical contact during the course of play, even to the risk of being unintentionally injured. However, there can be no consent to deliberate acts of violence as in **R v Billinghurst [1978] Crim LR 553 - Newport Crown Court: Judge John Rutter: June 12 and 13, 1978** where during a Rugby Football match and in an off-the-ball incident B punched G, the opposing scrum-half, in the face fracturing his jaw in two places. B was charged with inflicting grievous bodily harm contrary to section 20 of the Offences against the Person Act 1861. The only issue in the case was consent. Evidence was given by G that on previous occasions he had been punched and had himself punched opponents on the Rugby field, and by a defence witness Mervyn Davies, a former Welsh International Rugby player, that in the modem game of rugby punching is the rule rather than the exception.

It was argued by the defence that in the modern game of rugby players consented to the risk of some injury and that the prosecution would have to prove that the blow struck by B was one which was outside the normal expectation of a player so that he could not be said to have consented to it by participating in the game.

The prosecution argued that public policy imposes limits on violence to which a rugby player can consent and that whereas he is deemed to consent to vigorous and even over-vigorous physical contact on the ball, he is not deemed to consent to any deliberate physical contact off the ball.

The judge directed the jury that Rugby was a game of physical contact necessarily involving the use of force and that players are deemed to consent to force "of a kind which could reasonably be expected to happen during a game." He went on to direct them that a rugby player has no unlimited license to use force and that "there must obviously be cases which cross the line of that to which a player is deemed to consent." A distinction which the jury might regard as decisive was that between force used in the course of play and force used outside the course of play. The judge told the jury that by their verdict they could set a standard for the future.

The jury, by a majority verdict of 11 to 1, convicted B, who was treated as a man of previous good character and sentenced to nine months' imprisonment suspended for two years.

LAWFUL ARREST

The authority to arrest can be exercised by the police or a private citizen. The Constitution dictates that an arrested person must be told, as soon as is practicable that he is under arrest and should also be told the reason for the arrest. Reasonable force must be exercised by both police and private citizens in effecting an arrest.

SELF DEFENCE

Reasonable force may be utilized to defend self or another person or property from an attack. What is reasonable force is a question of fact and a person may make a mistake as to their right to self defence. When this happens, the law allows a defendant to be judged on the facts as he honestly believed them to be.

R v Williams (Gladstone) (1984) Cr App R 276 - M saw a youth attempting to rob a woman in the street. He gave chase, knocked the youth to the ground and attempted to immobilise him. The appellant, who had not witnessed the attempted robbery, then came on the scene. M told the appellant that he was a police officer, which was untrue, and that he was arresting the youth. When M failed to produce a warrant card a struggle ensued in which the appellant punched M in the face.

The appellant was charged with assault causing actual bodily harm. At his trial his defence was that he had honestly believed that the youth was being unlawfully assaulted by M and that it was irrelevant whether his mistake was reasonable or unreasonable. The judge directed the jury that the appellant had to have an honest belief based on reasonable grounds that M was acting unlawfully. The appellant was convicted. He appealed on the ground that the judge had misdirected the jury.

It was held that if a defendant was labouring under a mistake of fact as to the circumstances when he committed an alleged offence he was to be judged according to his mistaken view of the facts regardless of whether his mistake was reasonable or unreasonable. The reasonableness or otherwise of the defendant's belief was only material to the question of whether the belief was in fact held by the defendant at all. It followed that there had been a material misdirection. The appeal would therefore be allowed and the conviction quashed (see p 413 g, p 414 c to e and p 415 d e g j, post).

Beckford v R [1988] AC 130 - The appellant was a police officer who was a member of an armed posse which was sent to investigate a report that an armed man was terrorising and menacing his family at their house. When the police arrived at the house a man ran out of the back of the house pursued by police officers, including the appellant. There was a conflict of evidence about what then occurred. The Crown alleged that the man was unarmed and was shot by the appellant and another police officer after he had been discovered in hiding and had surrendered, while the appellant claimed that the man had a firearm, had fired at the police and had been killed when they returned the fire.

At the trial of the appellant for murder the judge directed the jury that if the appellant had a reasonable belief that his life was in danger or that he was in danger of serious bodily injury he was entitled to be acquitted on the grounds of self-defence. He was convicted. He appealed to the Court of Appeal of Jamaica, contending that he was entitled to rely on the defence of self-defence if he had had an honest belief that he had been in danger. The Court of Appeal held that the appellant's belief that the circumstances required self-defence had to be reasonably and not merely honestly held, and dismissed his appeal. The appellant appealed to the Privy Council.

Held - if a plea of self-defence was raised when the defendant had acted under a mistake as to the facts, he was to be judged according to his mistaken belief of the facts regardless of whether, viewed objectively, his mistake was reasonable. Accordingly, the test for self-defence was that a person could use such force in the defence of himself or another was reasonable in the circumstances as he honestly believed them to be. It followed that the trial judge had misdirected the jury. The appeal would therefore be allowed and the conviction quashed (see p 426 g, p 431 e f and p 432 e f, post).

NECESSITY

In Re F, a case concerning when medical treatment can be justified when given without consent, Lord Goff having explained public necessity and private necessity stated:

"There is, however, a third group of cases, which is also properly described as founded upon the principle of necessity and which is more pertinent to the resolution of the problem in the present case. These cases are concerned with action taken as a matter of necessity to assist another person without his consent. To give a simple example, a man who seizes another and forcibly drags him from the path of an oncoming vehicle, thereby saving him from injury or even death, commits no wrong. But there are many emanations of this principle, to be found scattered through the books".

Lord Goff went on to say that the present case was concerned with action taken to preserve the life, health or well-being of another who is unable to consent to it. The basic requirements, applicable in these cases of necessity, were "not only (1) must there be a necessity to act when it is not practicable to communicate with the assisted person, but also (2) the action taken must be such as a reasonable person would in all circumstances take, acting in the best interests of the assisted person".

ACTIVITY - TRESPASS TO THE PERSON

1. Petagay is confronted by a girl, Hanna, who accuses her of stealing her boyfriend. Petagay who was already having a bad day at school, gave Hanna a slap across the face. Hanna has reported the matter to her parents who are hopping mad that someone could do such a thing to their daughter. Advise Petagay of:

    a. her liability based on the incident; and
    b. any defence that she may have

2. Mark and Joanna have recently separated. They had a child together. Joanna, the child and Keith were walking along the avenue on which she now lives. Mark approached Joanna and punched her in the head, causing her to lose consciousness and dropped the child. Keith, thinking that Mark was about to attack him, pulled a stick he found nearby and gave Mark several slaps. Gertrude was nearby and thought Mark was a mad man who needed to be restrained. She held onto him and called the police even when Keith tried to explain what had happened, she refuses to release him.

Discuss, with reference to decided cases, the liability of Mark, Keith and Gertrude for assault, battery and false imprisonment.

Chapter 24

LIABILITY FOR ANIMALS

Liability for torts caused by animals are frequently classified as:

1. Liability for cattle trespass
2. Liability for dangerous animals (scienter action)
3. Liability for dogs
4. Liability in negligence

LIABILITY FOR CATTLE TRESPASS

For this cause of action to arise cattle belonging to the defendant must have been intentionally driven onto the plaintiff's property or stray onto the property independently.

The real meaning of the tort has been expressed as follows:

> *If I am the owner of an animal in which, by law, the right of property can exist, I am bound to take care that it does not stray onto the land of my neighbor; and I am liable for any trespass it may commit, and for the ordinary consequences of that trespass; whether or not the escape of the animal is due to my negligence is altogether immaterial.*

The owner of cattle (cows, bulls, horses, donkeys, sheep, pigs, goats and poultry), is liable for any damage done by such cattle having trespassed on the property of the plaintiff. Liability is strict and damages are recoverable for harm to the plaintiff's land and crops, injury to his animals, damage to chattels and any injuries inflicted upon the plaintiff himself. The principle can be found in:

East Coast Estates Ltd v Singh [1964] LRBG 202 where cattle belonging to the defendant strayed onto the plaintiff's land and damaged "pangola grass" which the plaintiffs were cultivating. The defendant alleged that, as he was driving his cattle along the road, rain began to fall and he was forced to drive them into a nearby common whence, through no fault on his part, they strayed onto the plaintiff's land.

It was held that liability in trespass is strict, and the defendant was liable irrespective of any intention or negligence on his part. Crane J said: "the cattle trespass principle is a species of strict liability - one of the oldest grounds of liability in English law...It is clear from his defence that Thakur Singh is urging that he did not deliberately de-pasture his cattle in area "j" and that the trespass is not attributable to any wrongful act of his... On both principle and authority it seems to me that this defence cannot be sustained, for the law is that a defendant is liable for any damage done to another's land by his straying cattle...irrespective of any intention or negligence on his part.

It is a defence to a suit for cattle trespassing that animals stray from the roadway where they are being driven into an adjacent land.

Statutory defence

A defence can be found in section 14 of the Trespass Act in Jamaica which seeks to protect the owner of trespassing cattle where his land is properly fenced:

> *If in any action brought to recover any damages under this Act, the owner of the stock shall prove that his land is enclosed by good and sufficient fences, and that he has adopted all other reasonable and proper precautions for the confinement of his stock, and that they have nevertheless, through some cause or accident beyond his control and which he could not reasonably have provided against,*

> *escaped from his land, the party complaining shall not be entitled to recover any sum unless he can show that he has fenced his land with a fence sufficient to keep out ordinary tame cattle and horsekind.*

Where the plaintiff can show that he fenced his property with a fence that is capable of keeping out tame cattle and horsekind, the statutory defence will be defeated.

In **West v Reynolds Metal Company**, the defence failed because it was held that the defendant's land was not fenced on all sides. The defendant's land bordered on the plaintiff's on two sides, north and east, and both were "enclosed by good and sufficient fences" but this was not enough on the proper interpretation of the statute to give him the protection under the statute as the land has to be enclosed.

Parties to an action in cattle trespass

The general position as it relates to trespass is that only a person with a legal and sometimes beneficial interest in land can sue. This principle also applies to someone suing for cattle trespass.

In **Aziz v Singh**, the defendant's steers had trespassed upon Y's land, where the plaintiff's steers were tethered with Y's permission, and there inflicted fatal injuries upon the plaintiff's animals. The plaintiff's action succeeded on the ground of scienter but, as regards cattle trespass, Verity CJ held that:

> *...the mere acquisition of permission to tie animals upon the land of another confers upon the holder no interest in or right to possession of the land sufficient to ground an action in cattle trespass, nor could the plaintiff plead that he was entitled to damages for the harm he had sustained as a consequence of a trespass on the land of a third party.*

Section 12 of the Trespass Act seems to give a person such as is seen in Aziz the right to sue for cattle trespass. The section is worded as follows: "any injury done by stock trespassing on to the land of other persons". It is submitted that this section can be interpreted to allow non-occupiers to sue for injury or damage that may have been sustained by a cattle trespass.

Trespass from the highway

The owner of land that adjoins the highway is presumed to know and assume the risk of the many dangers that come with the ordinary, non-negligent use of the highway. As such, there is no liability in cattle trespass where without negligence on the part of the person responsible for them, animals stray unto the plaintiff's land and do damage.

Section 13 of the Trespass Act adopted the common law with the following additional protection:

(a) the immunity does not apply where the plaintiff has fenced his land to keep out livestock

(b) the onus is on the defendant to show that his stock were being lawfully driven along the highway, and not on the plaintiff to show the unlawfulness of the defendant's conduct.

LIABILITY FOR DANGEROUS ANIMALS (THE SCIENTER ACTION)

Animals are classified into two groups when dealing with the scienter action:

(a) animals ferae naturae: naturally fierce animals, those that are wild or dangerous, such as lions, tigers, gorillas, bears and elephants; and

(b) animals mansuetae naturae: naturally tame, harmless animals that include domesticated species, such as cats, cows, dogs, donkeys, goats and sheep.

Where an animal ferae naturae causes harm, the owner is strictly liable to the claimant. This will be so whether or not the animal has behaved in a similar manner in the past. Thus, for example, a tiger escapes while being fed by its owner and injures a child.

Liability for harm caused by the animal mansuetae naturae, will be attributed to the owner in the following instances:

(a) the animal is predisposed to behave in a manner that is likely to cause harm; and
(b) it is known that the owner had knowledge of this predisposition.

Scienter has to be proved by the plaintiff. In this context it means that the owner of the animal knew of the animal's predisposition towards harm before the harm took place.

Kodilinye, 2000 has outlined the following principles of liability under the scienter action that have been established by the cases:

(a) whether a species of animal is to be classified as ferae or mansuetae naturae is a question of law for the judge, to be decided either on the basis of judicial notice or expert evidence.

(b) The requisite knowledge of an animal's viscious propensity must relate to the particular propensity that caused the damage. For instance, if a dog attacks a man, it must be shown that the animal had a propensity to attack humans: it would not be sufficient to show a propensity to attack other animals.

(c) In establishing scienter, it is not necessary to show that the animal had actually done the particular type of damage on a previous occasion: it is sufficient to prove that it had exhibited a tendency to do that kind of harm. For instance, in proving a dog's propensity to attack humans, it is sufficient to show that it habitually rushed out of its kennel, where it was chained, and attempted to bite passerby. Thus, the common saying that "every dog is allowed one free bite" is not accurate; though, if the plaintiff can show that the animal did on a previous occasion actually cause the particular type of harm, then his case will presumably be stronger.

(d) Knowledge of an animal's vicious propensity will be imputed to the defendant where it is acquired by someone to whom the defendant delegated full custody or control of the animal; and in certain other cases, it may be inferred that knowledge gained by a third party (for example the wife of the keeper or servant in charge of premises where the animal is kept) had been communicated to the keeper.

(e) For the purposes of the scienter action, it is immaterial where the animal's attack took place; whether, for example, on the plaintiff's land, on the defendant's premises, on the land of a third party, or on the highway or other public place.

(f) In the case of harm caused by an animal mansuetae naturae, the propensity of the animal must be shown to be vicious or hostile. The defendant will not be liable if the animal was merely indulging in a propensity towards playfulness or some other nonaggressive behavior, especially where such propensity is common to most animals of that species, for instance, the frolicking of high spirited horses, or dogs chasing each other or running across traffic.

There is no liability where an animal causes harm when displaying a 'natural' as opposed to a 'mischievous' predisposition. This is illustrated by **McIntosh v McIntosh (1963) 5 WIR 398,** Court of Appeal, Jamaica. The plaintiff was riding his jenny along a bridle track when the defendant's jackass jumped onto it in an attempt to serve it, causing injury to both the plaintiff and the jenny. There was evidence that on a previous occasion the jackass had attempted to serve the jenny while it was in a lying position and had kicked it, and that the defendant knew about this.

It was held that the defendant was not liable, since the jackass, in attempting to serve the jenny, was merely displaying a 'natural' propensity. Lewis JA said

> *The learned trial judge gave judgement for the defendant on the grounds that, first of all, the donkey was a domesticated animal, and secondly, that for a jack to try to serve a jenny was the mere*

exercise of a natural propensity and that even if this were held to be a mischievous propensity, there was no evidence that the jack was known to be in the habit of serving a jenny while it was being ridden.

Learned counsel for the plaintiff/appellant in this case has submitted that the learned trial judge, having found that the defendant was aware that the donkey had previously tried to serve this jenny, ought to have held that this was evidence of scienter of a mischievous propensity and should have given judgment for the plaintiff; or that alternatively, this court ought to allow an amendment to enable him to plead that the jenny had been attacked, and on the basis of the learned judge's finding the court should enter judgment for the plaintiff.

I agree with the trial judge's finding that for a jack to serve a jenny is a natural propensity. The damage which the plaintiff suffered as a result of the exercise of that propensity was merely incidental to what the jack was trying to do - endeavouring to serve the jenny. The donkey, as the learned judge has held, is a domesticated animal, and the authorities show that where a domesticated animal does something which is merely an exercise of its natural propensity, damaged caused as a result is not recoverable.

Who can be sued?

The person who keeps and controls the animal can be clothe with liability even where he is not the owner. In **Mckone v Wood**, an occupier who took care of a vicious dog left on the premises by a previous tenant was held liable for injury caused by the animal. Contrast **North v Wood** where a father was not liable for an injury inflicted by a dog owned and fed by his 11 year old daughter. In the same vein, a school authority was not liable when a dog kept on school premises by the caretaker attacked and injured a cleaner.

Defences

1. Plaintiff's default is used when, for example, a trespasser is bitten guard dog
2. Contributory negligence
3. Teasing an animal
4. Volenti non fit injuria will also be a defence

LIABILITY FOR DOGS

In some jurisdictions, such as Jamaica, statutory provisions such as the Dogs (Liability for Injuries by) Act, imposes strict liability for harm caused by dogs. Under these Acts, there is no need to prove scienter or negligence on the keeper's part and thus an action brought against the owner or the person in control of the dog is more likely to be successful.

LIABILITY FOR NEGLIGENCE

A plaintiff will succeed in negligence only where there was a special risk of injury to others of which the defendant was aware, for example, the owner of dangerous dogs leaves children unattended on his property.

Interestingly, the owner of a property adjoining the highway is not obligated to fence his land so as to prevent his domestic animals from straying onto the highway and causing harm. This is known as the Rule in **Searle v Wallbank.** There are instances where a land owner may be required to fence his property which can be seen in **Ellis v Johnstone,** where it said, "a property may require fencing where a dog dashes on to the road so often that it became, more like a missile than a dog".

Additionally, where the defendant actually takes his animals onto the highway and is negligent in his control of them, he will be liable for any harm suffered consequently.

ACTIVITY - LIABILITY FOR ANIMALS

1. Explain the extent of the liability of owners of dogs for dog bites
2. Explain the concept of Scienter
3. Discuss the concept of negligence as it relates to liability for injury caused by an animal.

Chapter 25

DOCTRINE OF VICARIOUS LIABILITY

The doctrine of vicarious liability is an exception to the general rule in tort law that a person who is responsible for or causes a tort will be personally liable for damage or harm caused as a result.

Vicarious liability speaks to a situation where the liability of a person (the offender) to a third party for the commission of a tort is delegated to another (D) even where (D) may not have participated in the tort and may not have been at fault in anyway. The delegation of the offender's liability to (D) comes about because of the relationship between the offender and (D).

The type of relationship which normally exists between (D) and the offender for the offender's liability to be delegated to (D) is that of master and servant or employer and employee as distinct from employer/ independent contractor.

Vicarious liability may occur in different tortuous contexts. However, we will deal with two instances of vicarious liability in this chapter.

1) Vicarious Liability of an employer for his employee (by far the most common instance of this form of liability)
2) The special cases of vicarious liability of vehicle owners for their drivers, and other intentional torts

THE ELEMENTS OF VICARIOUS LIABILITY – WHAT MUST BE PROVED?

An injured third party who wishes to hold an employer vicariously liable must prove:

a) That the offender was the employer's employee
b) That he (employee) committed a tort
c) That he (employee) committed the tort in the course of his employment

EMPLOYEE VS. INDEPENDENT CONTRACTOR

It is important to distinguish between an employee and an independent contractor as an employer is vicariously liable for the torts of employees committed during the course of their employment but is not generally liable for the torts of independent contractors.

The label used in the contract between the parties

The determination of the work relationship (employee/employer) is normally said to be a question of mixed fact and law, although where identification of the true status depends on the construction of written documents, it may be a question of pure law.

The terms of the contract are not conclusive where liability to third parties is concerned and in any case the contract may be silent or ambiguous on the matter. This must be a factor which is considered by the court in a case of difficulty. As we will see, the court considers all the facts of the case before it, and does not necessarily find any one factor as conclusive. In **Airfix Footwear Ltd. v. Cope [1978] ICR 1210.** A worker who was classified as self-employed by the Inland Revenue was nonetheless found to be an employee for the purposes of employment protection legislation.

Again in **O'Kelly v. Trusthouse Forte plc [1983] ICR 728** bar staff who were called "regular" casual workers, and who worked only when called in to work as required by the employer, were held not to be employees for purposes of claiming unfair dismissal. The workers could refuse any work that was offered to them, and the court of appeal emphasized the lack of "mutuality of obligations" in the relationship.

Note that the label which the parties put on the agreement as independent contractor / employee is not determinative of the relationship. See further **Ferguson v. John Dawson & Partners (Contractors) Ltd [1976] 1 WLR 1213; Warner Holidays Limited v. Secretary of State for Social Services [1983] ICR 440;454; Young and Woods v. West [1980] IRLR 201.**

The Tests Developed to Determine Employee vs. Independent Contractor

A number of tests have been developed by the Courts to assist in determining whether one is engaged under a contract of service (as an employee) or a contract for services (as an independent contractor). These tests are as follows:

i. The Control Test
ii. The Integrated Test
iii. The Economic Reality Test
iv. The Mutuality of Obligations Test
v. The Multi- Factor Approach

The Control Test

The control test was the traditional test for determining whether one is employed under a contract of service or for services. The control test looks at the degree and right of control exercised by the person who has engaged the worker. The greater the degree of control the more likely that the contract was a contract of services and the worker an employee.

Salmond and Heuston, The Law of Torts (21st Edition), puts it thus at p.449

> *"The test for determining who is an employee is the existence of a right of control over the servant in respect of the manner in which his work is to be done. The servant is an agent who works under the supervision and direction of his employer; an independent contractor is one who is his own master. A servant is*

> *a person engaged to obey his employer's orders from time to time; an independent contractor is a person engaged to do certain work, but to exercise his own discretion as to the mode and time of doing it- he is bound by his contract, but not by his employer's orders"*

In **Yewens v. Noakes (1880) 6 QBD 530, 532 – 533** Bramwell LJ regarded a servant as anyone who was subject to the command of the employer as to the manner in which he was to do his work. On the other hand if the employer only determined "what" was to be done rather than the manner of "how" it was to be done, then the person working for him would be an independent contractor.

In **Honeywill and Stein Limited v. Larkin Brothers Limited,** Slesser LJ expressed the test as follows:

> "The determination of whether the actual wrongdoer is a servant or agent on the one hand or an independent contractor on the other depends on whether or not the employer not only determines what is to be done, but retains the control of the actual performance, in which case the doer is a servant or agent; but if the employer while prescribing the work to be done, leaves the manner of doing it to the control of the doer, the latter is an independent contractor."

The Inadequacy of the Control Test

As society evolved the control test became more and more inadequate as a test for determining the employment status of employer/employee. The control test was more appropriate to determine the status of unskilled workers. As society became more modernized and more and more skilled workers emerged the test of whether the master told /controlled the manner in which the work was done became inadequate. It could not be said that a skilled worker employed in his professional capacity was told the manner in which he was to do his job as in some instances the employer may not himself possess that special skill.

In **Morren v. Swinton and Pendlebury BC [1965] 1 WLR 576**, Lord Parker CJ stated:

> "Superintendence and control cannot be the decisive test when one is dealing with a professional man, or a man of some particular skill and experience. Instances of that have been given in the form of a master of a ship, an engine driver, or a professional architect. In such cases, there can be no question of the employer telling him how to do work, therefore the absence of control and direction in that sense can be of little if any use as a test."

See **Gold v. Essex County Council [1942] 2 KB 293** in which the Court of Appeal held that a radiographer was a servant of the hospital that employed him and thus rendered it vicariously liable for his negligence in the course of his duty, even though the hospital authorities were not competent to dictate to him how he should exercise his skill.

The emphasis placed on the control test has been reduced but not abandoned. Other tests and considerations have been developed however the control test is still a relevant factor which the court will have regard to in determining the employment status, but is not the sole decisive factor.

The integration test / The Organisation Test

The difficulties that accompany the control test have led judges to propose alternative approaches. The integration test was proposed by Lord Denning LJ in **Stevenson Jordon and Harrison Ltd v. MacDonald and Evans [1952] 1 TLR 101, 111**. According to Denning

> *"under a contract of service a man is employed as part of the business, and his work is done as an integral part of the business, whereas, under a contract for services, his work although done for the business is not integrated into it but is only accessory to it."*

This test has been little used as a formulae; it is regarded by Street on Torts (9th Edition) at page 486-7 as just another, wider way of looking at control.

The Economic Reality Test

The court's approach of looking to the underlying nature of the relationship between the parties was extended in **Market Investigations Ltd v. Minister of Social Security [1969]2 QB 173**. In this case the appellant company was engaged in market research employing a few full time interviewers and many part-time interviewers selected from a panel of nearly 500 people. In 1966 the company asked the Minister to decide whether a part-time interviewer was employed for the purposes of the National Insurance Acts 1946 and 1965. The minister's conclusion was that the particular interviewer worked under a contract of service (or contract of employment) and not, as the company contended, a contract for services and his decision was upheld on appeal. In the opinion of Cooke J, control, though relevant was not decisive. What mattered more was whether the interviewer could be said to be in business on her own account, or as an employee working for an agreed wage whose employer took the risk of loss and chance of profit.

The economic reality test has since been accepted by the Privy Council in **Lee Ting Sang v. Chung Chi- Keung [1990] 2 AC 374**. The test takes into account such things as the method and frequency of payment, the power of selection, suspension and dismissal and the intention of the parties.

The Mutuality of Obligation

A further approach of the Courts is to examine closely the nature of the "contractual matrix" affecting worker and employer, in order to establish whether there exists the mutuality of obligations which is needed to identify a contract of employment. If there is the existence of mutual obligations to provide work (in the case of the employer) and to accept any work which is offered (in the case of the worker) is in doubt, the relationship may be classified as one of self employment, or otherwise outside the scope of the "employee" concept.

The Multi Factor Approach

It seems that none of these tests on its own is conclusive. The Courts have from time to time explicitly espoused a multi-factor approach to the question of identifying the employment relationship.

See **Ready Mixed Concrete (South East) Ltd v. Minister of Pensions and National Insurance [1968] 2 QB 497, 515, 525.**
In this case a concrete manufacturing company agreed with the owner of a lorry to pay him a fixed mileage rate for transporting concrete. The contract described him as an independent contractor, and he was obliged to maintain his vehicle in good order and at his own expense. He was also free to employ a competent driver whenever necessary. He on the other hand, undertook to make his lorry available whenever the company wanted it to have it painted in the company's colours and to wear the company's uniform. The company also prescribed a special way in which he should present the accounts.

The question whether he was employed within the National Insurance Act 1965 turned on whether or not he was under a contract of service. Mackenna J after a lengthy review of the authorities, decided that he was an independent contractor.
He laid down the conditions of a contract of service as follows:

1) The servant agrees that in consideration of a wage or other remuneration, he will provide his own work and skill in the performance of some service for his master;
2) He agrees expressly or impliedly that in the performance of that service he will be subject to the other's control in a sufficient degree to make that other his master
3) The other provisions of the contract are consistent with its being a contract of service.

In **Ready Mix** the driver owned the lorry and bore the financial risk, and he who owns the assets and bears the risk is unlikely to be acting as an agent or servant. If the man performing the service must provide the means of performance at his own expense and accept payment by results, he will own the assets, bear the risk and be to that extent unlike a servant. The lorry owners contract was one for services and not of services.

The guidelines in **Ready Mix** must not be applied rigidly. In **Market Investigations Ltd. v. The Minister of Social Security** Cooke J said – "No exhaustive list can be compiled of the considerations which are relevant in determining that question nor can strict rules be laid down as to the relative weight which the various considerations should carry in particular cases." Other factors which the Court may take into account are as follows:

a) The degree of control over the worker's work
b) His connection with the business
c) The terms of the agreement between the parties
d) The nature and regularity of the work
e) The method of payment of wages

What emerges from the above is that the courts will take into account a variety of tests to determine the nature of the relationship between the tortfeasor and his employer. How much weight it will attach to each test depends on each case.

THE STATUS OF BORROWED EMPLOYEES

Who is liable in circumstances where E1 the employer of A agrees to lend A to E2 and while A is the temporary employ of E2, A commits a tort which injures B. Which of the employers will be liable to compensate B for his injuries? Is it E1 or E2?

The general principle is that generally the employer will remain liable unless he can prove that at the time the tort was committed he had temporarily divested himself of all control over the servant. In fact there is a presumption in law that the permanent employer remains liable. See the presumption in **Texaco Trinidad Inc. v. Halliburton Tucker Ltd.**

The burden of proof is on the general employer and it is a heavy one for him to discharge.

The leading authority is **Mersy Docks and Harbour Board v. Coggins & Griffith (Liverpool) Ltd [1947] AC**. In that case a harbour authority (the appellants) hired out to X (the respondents), a firm of stevedores, a mobile crane with its operator. The contract expressly provided that the operator was to work for the time being as the employee of X, although the harbour authority retained the power of dismissal. Whilst loading the cargo, the operator of the crane was under the immediate control of X (the Respondents) in the sense that they could tell him which boxes to load, and where to place them, but they had no power to tell them how to manipulate the controls of the crane. In the course of loading a ship a third party (the plaintiff) was injured through the operator's negligent handling of the crane.

The question was whether the harbour authority (the appellant) or the respondent (X) was vicariously liable to the plaintiff who was injured by the negligence of the operator. The answer depended on whether he was the appellant's or the Respondent's servant at the time of the accident. Note that it was not sufficient that the temporary employee (the Respondent) controlled the task to be performed. It had to be shown that it also controlled the manner of performing the tasks. It was easier to infer that the general employer retained control of the manner in which the crane was operated as it was his crane and the driver remained responsible to him for its safe keeping. It was held that the harbour authority was liable as it still controlled the manner in which the crane was worked. The Harbour Authority /Appellants were alone vicariously responsible.

Note that when dealing with "borrowed servants" the court attaches significance to the control test though other factors are taken into account. Other factors include:

1) The type of machinery that has been loaned - the more complicated it is, the more likely the permanent employer will remain liable.
2) The duration of the service under the temporary employer
3) Who pays the employee
4) Who pays his national insurance contributions, income tax and other taxes
5) Who retains the power of dismissal
6) Whether the two employers themselves have attempted to regulate the matter.

See also **Texaco Trinidad Inc. v. Halliburton Tucker Ltd (1975)** Court of Appeal, Trinidad & Tobago as to the presumption against there being a transfer of a servant so as to make the temporary employer responsible for his acts.

THE COURSE OF EMPLOYMENT

An employer will not be vicariously liable to a third party who has been injured as a result of torts committed by the employee, unless the third party can prove that the tort was committed by the employee during the course of his employment. A tort is committed during the course of the employee's employment if:

1) It is expressly or impliedly authorised by the employer
2) It is an unauthorized manner of doing something authorised by his employer or
3) It is necessarily incidental to something which the servant is employed to do or based on developments in case law "closely/sufficiently connected" to the servant's employment.

The question of whether a tort was committed during the course of his employment is one of fact in each case.

Implied Authority

In **Poland v. Parr & Sons** the employee of a company reasonably believed that some children were stealing a company's property and he struck one of them, who was seriously injured. It was held that although his act was unreasonable it was still within the course of his employment, because in the words of Bankes LR "As a general rule a servant has an implied authority upon an emergency to endeavour to protect his master's property if he sees it in danger or has reasonable ground for thinking that he sees it in danger."

The case involved assault and battery by the servant and the notion of implied authority was used as if the act complained could be regarded as one which the employee has the discretion to do, then the employer can be held liable for the wrongful exercise of that discretion. Atkin LJ stated

however the limits of the employee's discretion to protect his employer's property:
"where the servant does more than the emergency requires, the excess may be so great as to take the act out of the class. For example, if Hall (the employee) had fired a shot at the boy, the act may not have been in the interest of the employer but that is not the case."

The principle in **Poland v. Parr & Sons** is where a servant does an act which he has no express authority to do, but which is nonetheless intended to promote his master's legitimate interests, the master will be liable in the event of it being tortuous unless the act is so extreme or outrageous that it cannot be regarded as incidental to the performance of the servant's allotted duties.

Therefore an employee who wrongly arrests someone after a supposed attempt at theft has ceased is not regarded as acting within the limits of implied authority because his motive is no longer protection of property but vindication of justice.

See also **Warren v. Henly's Ltd [1948] 2 All ER 935** - An employer of a garage attendant who attacked one of the customers out of vengeance after accusing him of driving off without paying, was held not liable. The act of the servant was extreme and "not so connected with the acts which the servant was expressly or impliedly authorised to do as to be a mode of doing those acts.

Unauthorised manner of doing something authorised by the employer
An employer will be liable for the negligent acts of his employee if it is an unauthorised mode of doing what the employee is authorised to do. See **Century Insurance Co v. Northern Ireland Road Transport Board** (gasoline lit at gas station). In this case the driver of a lorry negligently threw down a lighted match while petrol was being transferred from the lorry to a tank. An explosion and fire ensued. Viscount Simon held that he was in the course of his employment at the time. Negligence in starting smoke by throwing away a lighted match in the moment is plainly negligence in the discharge of the duties upon which he was employed.

Similarly **Limpus v. London General Omnibus Co.(1862) 1 H & C 526** in which the defendants forbade drivers of buses to race on the road. One driver disobeyed instructions and caused a collision. The Defendants were held liable as the driver was still acting in the course of his employment. Compare however with **Beard v. London General Omnibus Co.**

Distinction in two cases

In **Century** the driver of the petrol tank was employed to deliver gasoline and it was in the process of delivering the gasoline that the tort was committed. In **Beard** the conductor was not employed to drive the bus, but to collect fares. It was in the process of doing something he was not authorised to do (driving the bus) when the tort was committed.

Determining Course of Employment: Factors to consider

1)Authorised limits of time and place – the time and place at which the tort was committed. Was it committed in work hours or on a designated route?

- Where the tort is committed during working hours or within a reasonable time before or after that, the court is more likely to hold the employer liable for it.
- See **Ruddiman & Co. v. Smith (1889) 60 LT 708** – A clerk 10 minutes after office hours turned on a tap in the washroom and forgot to turn it off before going home. His employers were held liable for the consequent flooding of adjoining premises. The use of the washroom by the clerk was an incident of his employment, and the negligent act took place only a few minutes after working hours.

2) Whether a detour by the employee amounts to a "frolic of his own"
In **Joel v.Morrison (1834) 172 E.R.1338** Parke B laid down the principle to be applied in cases where employees drive negligently after making a detour from his designated route.

"If he was going out of his way, against his master's implied commands when driving on his masters business he will make his master liable, but if he was going on a frolic of his own without being on his master's business, the master will not be liable"

It is a question of degree whether a detour amounts to a frolic of his own. One must look at both the extent of the deviation and its purpose. Was the purpose of the deviation for the employer's business or was the servant carrying out his own business

See **Whatman v. Pearson** where an employee who had deviated from his designated route to go home and obtain a mid day meal, left his employer's horse and carriage unattended. The horse ran away and injured a third party. It was held that the since the employee had only deviated a quarter of a mile off his authorised route and the purpose of the detour to obtain refreshment was reasonably incidental to his employment, the employer was liable.

Contrast **Storey v. Ashman** where a driver had been sent to deliver wine and collect empty bottles and on the return journey deviated from his route in order to pick up a cask at the house of a friend and take it somewhere else for the friend's private purposes, the employer was held not liable for the driver's negligent driving on the way to the friend's house, for he was clearly on a frolic of his own.

In **Dunkley v. Howell** See judgment of Graham, Perkins LJ – Court of Appeal of Jamaica.
See the principles set out in **Smith v. Stages [1989] 1 All ER 833**. The speeches in this case offer some general guidance on the issue of "course of employment".

3. Express Prohibition

a) Prohibitions which limit the sphere of employment
b) Prohibitions which merely deal with conduct within the sphere of employment.

> A master may be liable for the torts of his servant even though it was committed while executing an act he expressly forbade.

In **Limpus v. London General Omnibus (1862) 158 E.R. 993** a bus driver had been given express instructions not to race with or obstruct the plaintiff's bus and caused a collision which damaged it, the driver's employers were held liable because the express prohibition did not limit the sphere of the bus driver's employment but merely sought to control his conduct within the scope of his employment.

In **Canadian Pacific Rly Co. v. Lockhart** the defendants expressly forbade their staff from driving an uninsured car on company business and in disobedience one of their employees did so and injured the plaintiff. His employer was held liable as it was not the acting as driver which was forbidden but the non-insurance of the motor car used to execute the employer's work. The prohibition limited the way in which the employee did his work and breach of it would not exclude the employer. Contrast the judgment of Lord Thankerton in the Privy Council case of **Clarke v. William Brewer Co.Ltd** where there was a prohibition which limited the sphere of employment, disobedience of which resulted in the employer not being liable. The prohibition here was that employees were not to drive the employer's truck on Sundays unless they were instructed to do so. In disobedience the employee drove the truck on a Sunday without permission and on his personal business. The company was not liable for the death of another motorist caused by the negligent driving of the employee.

4. Prohibitions against giving lifts to unauthorised passengers

In **Twine v. Bean's Express Limited [1946] 1 All ER 202** the plaintiff's husband T was given a lift in a van driven by X, the Defendant's employee. T was killed by the negligent driving of X. X, the employee had been instructed that no-one, other than those employed by the Defendants should be allowed to travel on the van, and there was a notice to that effect on the inside of the van.

Uthwatt J at first instance held that the Defendant employer was not liable as they owed a duty of care only to persons they could reasonably anticipate would likely be injured by the negligent driving of the van at the time and place in question.

The judgment at first instance was upheld on appeal. The court of appeal noted that though the driver was on his proper route and therefore driving the van in the course of his employment he was doing something simultaneously which was totally outside the scope of his employment, namely giving a lift to a person who had no right whatsoever to be there.

Contrast **Rose v. Plenty** – where contrary to instructions a milkman took a 13 yr old boy on board his milk float to assist him in delivering milk. The boy was injured owing to the milkman's negligence. The employer was held vicariously liable for the milkman's negligence on the ground that the express prohibition merely against boys riding on the milk float merely affected the manner in which the milkman did his job. Lord Denning M.R. further distinguished the case on the ground that the giving of the lift was for the benefit of the employer i.e. to further the employer's business.

Compare **Subhaga v. Rahaman** – passenger was merely unauthorised here – no express prohibition against lifts, no notice placed in the van. Giving of the lift to an unauthorised passenger in this case was merely a wrongful mode of doing what the driver was authorised to do.
Contrast **Battoo Bros. Ltd v. Gittens** - no express prohibition against giving lifts to unauthorised persons but the Court held the employer was not liable.

Note the distinctions in **Battoo Bros Ltd. v. Gittens** which are:

i) The employee charged the passengers a fee of two dollars to take them to their destination
ii) He would have had to deviate for a distance of several miles off his designated route even though the accident happened before he came off his designated route.

iii) Note the reasoning at 1st instant in **Twine v. Bean** was applied about the presence of the passenger being reasonably anticipated by the employer

Intentional torts - "The Test of Sufficient Connection"

It is in the context of intentional torts such as theft, deceit and assaults that the Courts have moved beyond the traditional distinction between authorised acts and unauthorised modes and have applied a test of "sufficient connection" between the wrong committed and the scope of the employee's employment.

Theft

In **Morris v. C.W.Martin & Sons Ltd [1966] 1 QB 716** the plaintiff took her fur coat to a furrier to be cleaned. The furrier did not undertake this type of work, so with the plaintiff's consent, but without acting as her agent, he subcontracted the work to a firm of cleaners, who handed it to one of their employees to clean. The employee stole it and the firm was held liable to the plaintiff. The firm's liability was not for the carelessness in the choice of employee, for there was no reason to suspect his dishonesty. Instead its liability was based on the breach of its non-delegable duty as bailee for reward.

This duty is not strict or absolute but a duty to see that care is taken. Lord Denning pointed out that if the firm could show that it had taken care and that its employees had also exercised due diligence and despite this, the coat had been stolen, it would have been absolved from liability. In the event however the firm could not establish the second part of the proposition, so it was held liable for breach of its own duty and not vicariously. The same primary liability would probably arise of it could be shown that the employer had negligently employed the employee who stole the plaintiff's property.

In **Nahhas v. Pier House (Cheyne Walk) Management Limited [1984] 270 EG 328** the defendant negligently hired an ex "professional thief" to work as a porter in a block of flats. The porter, using the key entrusted to him by one of the tenants, entered the latter's flat and stole some jewellery. The employer was held primarily liable for the theft.

Deceit/ Fraud

There used to be a similar judicial reluctance to make employers liable for the fraud of their employees. It was not until the middle of the 19th century that the possibility of vicarious liability was accepted here too, though for many years it seemed to have been where the employer and not just the employee benefited from the fraud. This qualification was laid to rest in the House of Lords decision of **Lloyd v. Grace Smith & Co [1912] AC 716.**

In this case a solicitor was held liable for the fraud of his managing clerk who having fraudulently persuaded a client to hand over some title deeds, disposed of property for his own benefit. Fraud in such cases such as this involves a deception of the victim by the employee and it is impossible to say whether this deception was in the course of employment before one determines the extent of his authority, whether actual or apparent to do such acts. In **Lloyd v. Grace Smith** there was such apparent authority for the solicitor who took little interest in his firm's affairs had allowed the clerk to deal with such matters and thereby represented that he had authority to do what he actually did. The conclusion therefore seems to be in some cases at least - notably fraud – the employer will be vicariously liable for the employee's fraud only when the latter has acted within his ostensible authority.

In **Dubai Aluminum Co. Ltd v. Salaam [2002] UKHL 48** the issue was whether the firm of solicitors was vicariously liable for the conduct of its senior partner who without knowledge of his partners drafted a series of documents which enabled clients of the firm to defraud the Claimant. The action came before the courts on the issue of contribution between the firm of solicitors, which had settled the action brought by the claimants, and the fraudsters, and proceeded on the assumption (which was never in fact tested) that the senior partner had committed the equitable wrong of dishonestly assisting a breach of fiduciary duty. The House of Lords had to decide whether the senior partner had acted "in the course of the ordinary business of the firm" so as to make the firm vicariously liable for his wrong.

The conduct of the senior partner could not be said to have been authorised by his partners. Lord Nicholls considered that vicarious liability could be established in a case where the wrongful conduct was so closely connected with acts the partner or employee was authorized to do that, for the purposes of the liability of the firm or employer to third parties, the wrongful conduct may fairly and properly be regarded as done by the partner while acting in the ordinary course of the firm's business or the employee's employment. On this basis, since the senior partner was authorized to draft documents of the type which formed the basis of the wrong in this case, the firm was vicariously liable for his wrongs.

Sexual Assaults
The test of "sufficient connection" was also used by the House of Lords case on the liability of an employer for torts involving sexual assault by an employee in **Lister v. Hesley Hall Ltd [2002] 1 AC 215**. Here the warden of a children's home committed a number of sexual assaults on children who were in his care. His employer was unaware of the assaults at the time they were committed, the victims made the relevant complaints, leading to the warden's conviction and imprisonment after an interval of several years. Prior to the case reaching the House of Lords it was held that the employer was not vicariously liable for the assaults on the ground of the warden's acts of sexual abuse could not be regarded as an unauthorized mode of carrying out his authorized duties. The House of Lords overturned the lower courts on this point.

According to Lord Steyn the correct approach is to concentrate on the relative closeness of the connection between the nature of the employment and the particular tort. Since in this case the sexual abuse was inextricably interwoven with the carrying out by the warden of his duties, it was fair and just to hold the employer's vicariously liable.

Lord Millet would similarly have imposed vicarious liability "where the unauthorised acts of the employee are so closely connected with acts which the employer has authorized that they may properly be regarded as falling within the scope of his employment. The advantage of this test in his Lordship's view was that of "dispensing with the awkward reference to "improper modes" of carrying out the employee's duties; and by focusing attention on the connection between the employee's duties and his wrong doing it would accord with the underlying rationale of the doctrine and be applicable without straining the language to accommodate cases of intentional wrongdoing."

In his judgment Lord Clyde suggested that in applying the test of sufficient connection the following three factors should be considered:

(1) A broad approach should be taken to construing the employee's duties, so that "it becomes inappropriate to concentrate too closely on the particular act complained of." Thus an intentional wrong can be seen as one aspect of a larger pattern of conduct which falls within the employee's scope of employment.

(2) The time and place at which a particular wrong is committed are relevant but not conclusive. Thus there might be circumstances under which an employer could be vicariously liable for an act committed during working hours and away from the place of employment, while conversely, "the fact that the act in question occurred during the time of employment and in the place of employment is not enough in itself.'

(3) It is not enough that the employment merely provided the employee with the opportunity to commit the wrong: for example "there must be some greater connection between the tortuous act of the employee and the circumstances of his employment than the mere opportunity to commit the act which has been provided by access to the premises which the employment has afforded.

Assaults/ Intentional Shootings
The landmark decision of the House of Lords decision of **Lister v. Helsey Hall Ltd** was applied by the Privy Council in **Clinton Bernard**

v. Attorney General of Jamaica, Privy Council Appeal No.30 of 2003 (2004) UKPC 47.

The facts of **Clinton Bernard v. Attorney General of Jamaica** are as follows:
At about 9pm on 11 February 1990 the plaintiff, a man aged 32 years, and his parents went to the Central Sorting Office in Kingston to make an overseas call. He joined a queue of about 15 people who were waiting to phone. Eventually his turn came. The plaintiff dialed. Suddenly a man intervened. According to the plaintiff's oral evidence the man announced "police" and demanded the phone which the plaintiff was then using. According to the oral evidence of his mother the man said "I am going to make a long distance call" and added "boy leggo this, police". The man making the demand was in fact Constable Paul Morgan ("the constable"). The plaintiff refused to release the phone. The constable said "boy me naw join no line, give me the phone".

It is convenient here to interpose the fact that at the trial a police sergeant, a witness called on behalf of the Attorney-General, testified that –
"If there is an emergency situation and [an] officer needs to use the phone I would consider it normal for him to go to the head of the line and demand to use the phone as a matter of urgency." In any event, the plaintiff was determined not to let go of the phone. The constable slapped the plaintiff on the hand and then shoved him in his chest. When the plaintiff still resisted the constable took two steps backwards, pulled out a service revolver, pointed it at the plaintiff, and fired at his head at point blank range. The bullet hit the plaintiff to the left side of his head, leaving entry and exit wounds in his skull.

The injury rendered the plaintiff unconscious for a short period. He was taken to a nearby hospital by ambulance. The plaintiff awoke in the casualty department of the hospital. He was surrounded by police officers who included Constable Morgan. In the hospital Constable Morgan placed the plaintiff under arrest for allegedly assaulting a police officer and handcuffed him to his bed.

Criminal charges were brought against the plaintiff. After a few months these charges were withdrawn. In the meantime the constable was dismissed from the Jamaica Constabulary Force with effect from 17 March 1990. The ground of his dismissal was that he had been absent from duty for over 48 hours.

At first instance in the Supreme Court McCalla J held that the Crown (Attorney General) was vicariously liable for the tort of the constable:

> *"The First Defendant demanded the use of the telephone by identifying himself as being a police officer albeit in a most crude and vulgar manner. The witness for the defence has admitted that it would be within the scope of a police officer's duty to demand the use of a telephone as a matter of urgency if the necessity arose.*
>
> *Although no evidence has been adduced that at the relevant time the first defendant was on duty, in the absence of evidence to the contrary the reasonable inference to be drawn is that his demand was somehow connected to his duties.*
>
> *The act of shooting the plaintiff was unlawful and clearly did not fall within any of his prescribed duties but was nevertheless in furtherance of his demand. He subsequently arrested and charged the plaintiff for assaulting him and by that act he could only have been asserting that at the material time he was executing his duties as a police officer.*
>
> *In these circumstances I find that the Attorney-General is vicariously liable for the action of the first defendant. The plaintiff has established his case on a balance of probabilities and the defence fails."*
>
> *The Court of Appeal, with evident reluctance, felt compelled to allow the appeal. Bingham JA said:*

> *"In the instant case, the constable was in possession of a service revolver issued to him by his superior officer which could be regarded as authorising him to be at large in carrying out his sworn duty to uphold the law. By his unlawful action in shooting and injuring the respondent the constable could not be seen as acting in the lawful execution of his duty. His conduct was of such a nature as fell outside the class of acts authorised by section 13 of the Constabulary Force Act, and did not render the state as his employer vicariously liable to the respondent."*

The Privy Council disagreed with the reasoning of the Court of Appeal and upheld the Supreme Court decision of McCalla J that the Attorney General was vicariously liable.

The Privy Council held that in the case of intentional wrongs, the correct approach to determine whether the employer (in this case the Crown) is liable for a shooting committed by an employee (in this case, an armed member of the Jamaica Constabulary Force) is to concentrate on the relative closeness of the connection between the nature of the employment and the particular tort, and to ask whether it is just and reasonable to hold the employer vicariously liable.

According to the Privy Council:

> *"Three features of the case must be considered. It is of prime importance that the shooting incident followed immediately upon the constable's announcement that he was a policeman, which in context was probably calculated to create the impression that he was on police business. As a matter of common sense that is what he must have intended to convey. It may be that the plaintiff, and others in the queue, viewed this invocation of police authority with some scepticism. But that purported assertion of police authority was the event which immediately preceded the shooting incident. And it was the fact that the plaintiff was not prepared to yield to the purported assertion of police authority which led to the shooting:*

compare Weir v Bettison (CA) [2003] ICR 708, para 12, per Sir Denys Henry.

Approaching the matter in the broad way required by Lister, the constable's subsequent act in arresting the plaintiff in the hospital is explicable on the basis that the constable alleged that the plaintiff had interfered with his execution of his duties as a policeman. It is retrospect ant evidence which suggests that the constable had purported to act as a policeman immediately before he shot the plaintiff.

Moreover, one must consider the relevance of the risk created by the fact that the police authorities routinely permitted constables like Constable Morgan to take loaded service revolvers home, and to carry them while off duty. The social utility of allowing such a license to off duty policemen may be a matter of debate. But the state certainly created risks of the kind to which Bingham JA made reference. It does not follow that the using of a service revolver by a policeman would without more make the police authority vicariously liable.

That would be going too far. But taking into account the dominant feature of this case, viz that the constable at all material times purported to act as a policeman, the risks created by the police authorities reinforce the conclusion that vicarious liability is established.

Cumulatively, these factors have persuaded the Board that the trial judge was entitled to find vicarious liability established and that the Court of Appeal erred in allowing the appeal."

The Privy Council decision in **Clinton Bernard v. The Attorney General** was also followed by the Board in **Inez Brown v. David Robinson & Sentry Services Co. Limited [2004] UKPC 56 delivered 14th of December 2004.**

Inez Brown v. David Robinson & Sentry Services Co. Limited [2004] UKPC 56

> Material Facts - On 8 October 1985 Paul Reid, a young man of 17 years, was shot and seriously injured by the first-named respondent David Robinson, an employee of the second respondent, a security company named Sentry Service Co Ltd ("the company"). He was taken to hospital suffering from paraplegia and died on 20 January 1986 from septicaemia resulting from his wounds.

On 8 October 1985 Paul Reid went to Sabina Park, Kingston to see a football match. Robinson was on duty at the gate at which he sought entry. The match had already started and the line of people waiting to get in began to push and became unruly. Robinson tried to restrain the crowd and struck some of them with his baton, including Reid, who pushed him and then ducked under the rails and ran off. Robinson gave chase after him in hot pursuit, pulled out his firearm and fired a shot. He caught up with him some little distance away from the gate to the ground and both men dodged around some parked cars. Reid stopped, held his hands in the air and said that he would not run as he had done nothing. Robinson said words to the effect "You want me shoot you boy? You want me kill you?" Reid replied "after you can't shot mi because mi nuh do nuttin". Robinson then shot Reid from about two paces distance. Reid fell and Robinson bent over him, pointing his gun, and said twice "You want me kill you bwoy?" The crowd which gathered became hostile and Robinson fired a shot in the air to scare them. A soldier then intervened and Robinson was eventually disarmed by a police officer.

Robinson gave evidence that Reid had stabbed at him with a knife at the gate to Sabina Park and again when he caught up with him, but the judge regarded his account as unreliable and untruthful (page 76 of the record) and rejected the evidence that Reid had stabbed at Robinson on the road after the chase.

Judgment

At first instance the Supreme Court held that the employer was vicariously liable. According to the judge at 1st instance:

> *"I find that Robinson was engaged to ensure that only authorised persons were allowed to enter the park, and therefore he had a duty to prevent unauthorised persons from entering. His duties included protecting the life and property of patrons, the identification, restraint and apprehension of those causing damage to property, injury to persons or threatening the lives or health of patrons and of course himself, so that where damage occurred recompense could be made and offenders prosecuted. In seeking to restrain and/or apprehend undesirable and unruly persons he was entitled to use reasonable force including a baton and a firearm. Implicit in all this was a discretion to decide whether and if so when he should use force and as to the degree (including the discharge of his firearm) which would be appropriate in any circumstance where he ought to control a disturbance."*

The judge set out at pages 86-7 of the record the test which he applied for determining whether the company was vicariously liable for Robinson's acts:

> "A master is liable for the tortious act of his servant done in the course (or scope) of his employment. It is deemed to be so done if it is (a) a wrongful act authorised by the master or (b) it amounts to an unauthorised mode of performing an authorised act. Such latter acts to fix the master with liability must be sufficiently connected with the authorised act as to be a mode of doing it. **Poland v Parr (John) & Sons [1927] 1 KB 236 at 240.**"

The judge at 1st instance then examined in some detail a number of previous cases and concluded that Robinson's conduct was an unauthorised act which was within the scope of his duty to preserve order at one of the gates to Sabina Park.

The Court of Appeal overruled the decision at 1st instance. The Privy Council overruled the decision in the Court of Appeal and held that the employer's were vicariously liable. According to the Privy Council paras 12-17 of judgment:

- "When one substitutes the test of whether Robinson's acts were so closely connected with his employment that it would be just and reasonable to hold his employer liable, the answer seems clear to their Lordships. They are satisfied that when one applies this test the employer was vicariously liable for the shooting and the judge was quite justified in so holding. They are unable to agree that it fell on the side of the line that would make it an act of revenge or "private retaliation", as the Court of Appeal held. Their Lordships are accordingly of the opinion that the appeal should be allowed.
- The present case is in their view distinguishable on the facts from Attorney General of the **British Virgin Islands v Hartwell [2004] 1 WLR 1273**. In that case Lord Nicholls of Birkenhead summarised at para 17 the actions of the police officer who shot the claimant in the following terms:

"From first to last, from deciding to leave the island of Jost van Dyke to his use of the firearm in the bar of the Bath & Turtle, Laurent's activities had nothing whatever to do with any police duties, either actually or ostensibly. Laurent deliberately and consciously abandoned his post and his duties. He had no duties beyond the island of Jost van Dyke. He put aside his role as a police constable and, armed with the police revolver he had improperly taken, he embarked elsewhere on a personal vendetta of his own. That conduct falls wholly within the classical phrase of 'a frolic of his own' and his Lordships are accordingly of the opinion that the appeal should be allowed."

British Virgin Islands v Hartwell [2004] 1 WLR 1273

On 2 February 1994 Police Constable Kelvin Laurent was the sole police officer stationed on the island of Jost Van Dyke in the British Virgin Islands. It was the last day of his three day tour of duty on the island. Jost

Van Dyke is a small island with a population of about 135 people. Laurent was still on probation.

He was subject to daily supervisory visits by a police sergeant from the West End police station on the nearby larger island of Tortola. As the officer in charge of the Jost Van Dyke police substation PC Laurent had a key to the substation's strongbox. Kept in this metal box were a .38 caliber service revolver and ammunition.

The Royal Virgin Islands Police Force is not an armed force. Police officers do not normally carry arms. Guns are kept in police stations and only issued to police officers when needed.

During the evening of 2 February 1994 PC Laurent abandoned his post. He left the island, taking with him the police revolver and ammunition. He went five miles by boat to West End, Tortola. He then travelled nine miles by road across Tortola to Road Town and from there 13 miles by boat to the island of Virgin Gorda. Presumably he was not wearing his police uniform.

PC Laurent next made his way to the Bath & Turtle bar and restaurant at The Valley where his partner, or former partner, and mother of his two children, Lucianne Lafond worked as a waitress. The bar was busy and full of local residents and tourists. It was a popular evening, with a band playing. At about 10.30 pm Laurent entered the bar in search of Ms Lafond. He wanted to see if she had anyone with her. In the bar was Hickey Vanterpool who, so it was said, was associating with Ms Lafond. Without further ado and without any warning Laurent fired four shots with his police service revolver. He was, apparently, intent on maiming Mr Vanterpool and, possibly, Ms Lafond herself. Two of the shots caused minor injuries to Ms Lafond and a tourist. A further shot struck and caused serious injuries to Craig Hartwell, a customer at the pub, who was standing near the doorway. Mr Hartwell was a British resident visiting the island.

Laurent was prosecuted and pleaded guilty to charges of unlawfully and maliciously wounding Mr Hartwell and Ms Lafond and having a firearm with intent to do grievous bodily harm. He was sentenced to five years' imprisonment and dismissed from the police force. Mr Hartwell then brought these civil proceedings against Laurent and the Attorney General as the representative of the Government of the British Virgin Islands.

Judgment

On Appeal to the Privy Council it was held that the Attorney General was not liable. According to the Privy Council "The immediate cause of Mr Hartwell's injuries was the deliberate, reckless act of Laurent firing his revolver in the crowded bar. Laurent was consumed by anger and jealousy at the sight of Ms Lafond in company with Mr Vanterpool on the fateful evening. He fired shots at one or other or both of them. So this is not a case where a police officer used a service revolver incompetently or ill-advisedly in furtherance of police duties. Laurent used a service revolver, to which he had access for police purposes, in pursuit of his own misguided personal aims.

The applicable test is whether PC Laurent's wrongful use of the gun was so closely connected with acts he was authorised to do that, for the purposes of liability of the Government as his employer, his wrongful use may fairly and properly be regarded as made by him while acting in the ordinary course of his employment as a police officer.

The connecting factors relied upon as satisfying this test are that Laurent was a police constable on duty at the time of the shooting (working his three day shift on Jost Van Dyke), that his jurisdiction extended to Virgin Gorda, and that before leaving Jost Van Dyke he had improperly helped himself to the police revolver kept in the substation on that island.

These factors fall short of satisfying the applicable test. From first to last, from deciding to leave the island of Jost Van Dyke to his use of the firearm in the bar of the Bath & Turtle, Laurent's activities had nothing whatever to do with any police duties, either actually or ostensibly. Laurent deliberately and consciously abandoned his post and his duties. He had no duties beyond the island of Jost Van Dyke. He puts aside his role as a police constable and, armed with the police revolver he had improperly taken, he embarked elsewhere on a personal vendetta of his own. That conduct falls wholly within the classical phrase of "a frolic of his own"."

VEHICLE OWNERS AND CASUAL AGENTS

An critical extension of the doctrine of vicarious liability has been developed on the grounds of public policy in order to fix liability upon the owner of a vehicle for damage caused by the negligent driving of that vehicle by persons who are not servants/employees but merely casual agents of the owner such as the owner's wife, son, daughter, friend or stranger where the agent acts wholly or partly for the purposes or business of the vehicle owner.

There is a presumption of service or agency. This means that the driver of a vehicle will be presumed to be the servant or agent of the owner of the vehicle. The fact of ownership of the vehicle is prima facie evidence that the vehicle was being driven at the material time by the servant or agent of the owner. It is for the defendant to rebut this presumption.
Note the vehicle owner is only liable where the causal agent was driving for some purpose of the owner.

LIABILITY FOR INDEPENDENT CONTRACTORS

There are exceptions to the general principle of non-liability for torts of independent contractors. They are as follows:

a) Authorisation of Tort
b) Torts of Strict Liability
c) Where the duty to take care is non- delegable

Authorisation of Tort

Where the employer directs or instigates an independent contractor to commit a tort, both the employer and independent contractor will be liable for it. This principle applies equally to servants/ employees and employer.

Negligence / Non-Delegable Duty of Care
A non- delegable duty is one which cannot be delegated to a third party. The employer does not discharge his duty of care by merely appointing, instructing or supervising a competent contractor.

How does one determine if the Duty is Non-delegable?
Non-delegable duties arise where the work is

a) intrinsically / inherently dangerous
b) hazardous and involves a high risk requiring special precautions

ACTIVITY - VICARIOUS LIABILITY

(1) Define the term "vicarious liability"

(2) Identify two differences between "a servant" and an "independent contractor"

(3) By referring to one decided case, illustrate the meaning of the term "in the course of employment

(4) What is the meaning of the phrase "a frolic of his own"?

(5) Mr Cranston, an employee of Flamingos night club, in London, was employed as a bouncer to keep order at the club's doors, and to break up scuffles and fights. On 18 July 2015, an incident occurred involving a customer, Mr Fitzgerald, and Mr Cranston, who threw a friend of his across a room. Mr Pollock had given Mr Cranston instructions to "impress upon Mr Fitzgerald that Mr Cranston was prepared to use physical force to ensure compliance with any instructions that he might give to Mr Fitzgerald or any of his companions".

Subsequently, on 24 July, Mr Mattis was attending the club with a friend, Mr Cook. Mr Cranston was instructed that Cook should be barred from the club, and was ejected. A week later, Mr Mattis attended the club with other friends, at around 11:15pm. Mr Cook turned up with Mr Fitzgerald, at around 1am, and upon seeing them, Mr Cranston violently assaulted Mr Cook and one of his friends. Upon witnessing this, Mr Mattis attempted to pull Cranston from Cook, whereupon several other customers surrounded Cranston, who was forced to flee. Upon arriving back at the club, he grabbed Mr Mattis, and stabbed him in the back. As a result, Mr Mattis was rendered paraplegic.
Discuss the principles of vicarious liability and determine the extent of the employer's or employee's liability.

Chapter 26

OCCUPIER'S LIABILITY

In Barbados and Jamaica, occupiers liability is governed by statute. Jamaica relies on the Occupiers" Liability Acts 1969 (OLA). Elsewhere in the Caribbean it is governed by common law principles.

The Acts prescribe that the occupier of premises owes a, common duty of care to take reasonable steps to ensure that lawful visitors to his premises are reasonably safe for the purposes for which they are permitted to be there.

Section 4(6) of the Occupiers' Liability Act of Barbados and section 3(6) of the Jamaican Act dictates that where the occupier employs an independent contractor to do work on the premises, he will not be liable for the contractor's negligence, provided he took steps to satisfy himself that the contractor was competent and that the work was properly done.

Very close attention must be paid to the exact words of the Act to set the limits of the ambit of liability. Different categories of entrants are owed different standard of care:

(a) **Contractor** because the occupier's freedom to use the land as he sees fit is to be balanced against the rights of the contractor.
(b) **Invitees** - people invited to the land - were owed the next highest standard of care because they had some mutual interest of a business or material nature with the occupier.

(c) **Trespassers** - persons who come on the land without permission
(d) **Licensees** – persons who had permission to enter the land for some purpose on their own are the next category.

The doctrine 'Occupier' is the same as at common law. The test in ***Wheat v E. Lacon [1966] AC 428*** Lord Denning Held: '…Wherever a person has a sufficient degree of control over premises that he ought to realise that any failure on his part to use care may result in injury to a person coming lawfully there, then he is an "**occupier**" and the person coming lawfully there is his "**visitor**".

Lord Denning divided the law into four categories as follows:

(1) Where a landlord lets premises, by demise, the landlord is regarded as having parted with all control over the premises that the tenant is the occupier.
(2) Where a landlord lets part of a building but retains other parts such as a common staircase, then the landlord remains liable as an occupier for the parts of the building he has retained ***Miller v Hancock [1893] 2 QB 177.***
(3) Where a landowner licenses a person to occupy his premises on terms which do not amount to a demise and the owner still has the right to enter on to the premises to do repairs then the owner remains sufficiently in control to be an occupier. (see **Wheat**)
(4) Where an occupier employs independent contractors to do some work on his premises, the owner is generally still sufficiently in control to be an occupier. There can be more than one occupier at the same time.

The four categorization noted above are helpful, but it is not exhaustive as confirmed in ***Harris v Birkenhead [1976] 1 WLR 279***

Visitors

The duty owed by the occupier is to his 'visitors'. A lawful visitor is either an invitee or a licensees. Vistors are allowed on the premises through implied or express authorization. Express authorization depends on proof that the occupier did in fact give permission while the existence of implied permission rests on the person who alleges that it exists. An example exists where an officer seeking entry to a private dwelling house has implied permission. In ***Robson v Hallett [1967] 2 QB 393***

It was held that a person who enters upon the premises of the occupier for the purpose of communicating with the occupier is treated as having implied permission until the visitor knows or ought to have known that the permission is revoked. Once his permission is revoked he has a reasonable time to leave the premises before he becomes a trespasser.

In ***Edwards v Railway [1952] AC 737*** where a boy climbed through a boundary fence to retrieve his ball and was injured by a train. The House of Lords held that repeated trespass does not turn a person into a licensee. There must be evidence of the landowner's express consent or conduct of which he cannot say he did not give permission. Generally, persons who enter premises for any purpose in the exercise of a right conferred by law are to be treated as having permission by the occupier to be there for that purpose whether in fact they have permission or not.

Limitation on permission: The occupier may limit permission in three ways:
i. An occupier may give the visitor permission to enter some parts of his premises but not others. In **The Calgarth [1927] P 93** Scrutton LJ "when you invite a person into your house to use the stairs, you do not invite him to slide down the banister."

In ***Gould v McAuliffe [1941] 2 All ER 527*** the plaintiff got lost looking for an outside toilet and was attacked by the defendants' dog. The defendants argued that the plaintiff was a trespasser. It was held that the gate was not locked and there was no notice that the yard was private or that there was a dangerous dog there. If the occupier wishes to put limitations on the visitors he must bring it to his attention.

ii. The purpose for which the visitor come on the land. In ***R v Smith and Jones [1976] 1 WLR 672*** a son broke into his father's house and stole a

TV, and at the trial the father said he was not a trespasser. Under the Theft Act 1968 he was a trespasser as when he entered he was in excess of the permission given to him, or was reckless whether his entry was in excess of that permission.

iii. An occupier who intends to permit persons to enter his premises for a limited time only, must give the person clear indication that his permission to be on the premises is subject to a time limit.

There is no exhaustive definition of 'premises' but can include land, houses, buildings, vessel, vehicle or aircraft - fixed or movable structure. In **Bunker v Brand [1969] QB 480**, it was said that this definition includes pylons, grand stand, lifts and even tunnels.

The duty owed by an occupier to a visitor is the common duty of care to take such care as in all the circumstances of the case is reasonable to see that the visitor will be reasonably safe in using the premises for the purposes for which he is invited or permitted.

In ***Jolley v Sutton LBC [2000] 3 All ER 409*** it was held that if damage is foreseeable then there is liability even if the way in which it is caused is not foreseeable. Danger must not only be done from the state of the premises but also to things done or permitted to be done of them. It is the visitor that must be reasonably safe.

The duty to take care as is reasonable in the circumstances involves consideration of issues to those involved in a common law negligence action.

In ***Sawyers v H and G Simonds (1966) 197 EG 877*** The claimant slipped and injured his hand on broken glass in the defendant's hotel. In court it was not proved that the defendant was negligent based on the time it took to remove the broken glass.

Children

An occupier must be prepared for children to be less careful than adults.

In ***Glasgow v Taylor [1922] 1 AC 44*** a 7 year old child ate poisonous berries in a park and later died. It was held that the defendants were liable as the berries were tempting to the child.

Common calling

An occupier may expect that a person in the exercise of his calling, will appreciate and guard against any special risks ordinarily incident to it, so far as the occupier leaves him free to do so.

In ***Roles v Nathan [1963] 1 WLR 1117*** two chimney sweeps were killed by carbon dioxide on the occupier's premises. It was held that the occupier not liable as they were reasonably expected to take care of themselves.

The fact that the visitor has a particular skill is not sufficient to discharge the duty of care owed to the visitor. In ***Salmon v Seafarer [1983] 3 All 729***, it was the decision of the court that an occupier owes the same duty of care to a fireman as to any other visitor, and the argument that the duty was limited to protecting the fireman from special risks not associated with normal fires was rejected.

Warning of danger

Warning of the danger must be given by the occupier. It must be given in clear terms because an inadequate warning may lead to the imposition of liability. The fact that the occupier has gone to the trouble of putting up a warning sign suggest he is aware of the danger and his failure to take sufficient steps to bring the danger to the attention of the visitor is a breach of duty on his part.

A warning may in combination with some other factor (such as handrails) be sufficient to discharge the duty upon the occupier. There is no need to warn of obvious danger: ***Staples v W. Dorset (1995) The Times 28 April*** – no need to warn a visitor of obvious, visible algae on a stone surface.

Defences

1. Volenti non fit injuria; and
2. Contributory negligence

The following defences of excluding liability and warning are also available under the relevant Acts in both Barbados and Jamaica.

Excluding liability

The relevant statute allows the occupiers to exclude liability "by agreement or otherwise". Frequently we enter parking lots or university properties only to see signs strategically posted that all persons park at their own risk. You would have seen in the earlier chapter how excluding liability works in practice.

Warning

Merely giving a warning of a danger to a visitor will not be sufficient to "absolve" the occupier unless the warning is such as "to enable the visitor to be reasonably safe".

Common law liability

The common law makes the distinction between an invitee and a licensee on a property. An invitee is a person who enters premises to do business with the occupier (for example, a client visiting the office); a licensee is one who merely has permission to enter (for example, a guest at your mother's birthday party). An occupier owes an invitee a duty to exercise reasonable care to prevent damage to the invitee from any "unusual danger" known to the occupier, or which should have been known to him.

The licensee on the other hand, must "take the premises as he finds them" because the occupier only has a mere duty to warn about concealed dangers and traps.

Liability to trespassers

In ***British Railways Board v Herrington*** [1972] 1All ER 749 it was established that the occupier owes a duty of "common humanity" to a trespasser even though no duty of care is owed generally. This trespasser can be a burglar, a curious child, or an adult that has lost his way onto the premises of the occupier. A person is a trespasser if he has no permission to be on the premises of another and the House held that a person trespassed at his own risk. Notwithstanding, an occupier's duty is not limited to not harming the trespasser intentionally or recklessly but should take reasonable steps to enable the trespasser to avoid danger. The duty however, arose only where the probability of danger was such that the occupier ought to act in "common humanity". Common humanity has not been defined but appears to have taken on a pragmatic approach, relaxing the duty of the occupier according to the circumstances.

ACTIVITY – OCCUPIER'S LIABILITY

Mr Corrudus lives on an old property that was once a fort. He has made it into a tourist attraction and so it is open to the public on a daily basis. He has however posted signs that read "Visitors enter at their own risk. Owner is not liable for any injuries that anyone may suffer". Some areas are not opened to the public and are also marked with notices that read: "Staff and Owner Only". Other buildings are also marked as dangerous and that children should be monitored by their parents.

Mohamed visits the property, accompanied by his infant son. While visiting the various relics, the son disappears and eventually slips. This causes him to fall a great distance into an area that was once used as a cane mill. He suffers a broken hand and leg.

Advise Mr Corrudus of his liability, if any, to Mohamed and his son, referring to the law in a named Commonwealth Caribbean country. Give reasons for your answer.

Chapter 27

REMEDIES IN TORT

Damages and Injunctions are the remedies that are most frequently awarded and recommended.

DAMAGES

Damages are monetary awards meant to compensate the claimant allowing him to be restored to the position he would have been in had the tort not been committed as far as money can do so.

TYPES OF DAMAGES

i. Nominal and contemptuous

Nominal damages are awarded when the claimant proves his case but has not shown any actual loss. A claimant may have been successful and is thus awarded with contemptuous damages by the court. These are extremely small monetary compensation which may be awarded if the court considers that the case should not have been brought to court and could have been settled by other means.

ii. General and special

General damages are meant to compensate the claimant for nonmonetary part of the injury suffered. It is often awarded, for example, for pain and suffering for which there is no exact dollar value which can be calculated. In the case of Domsalla **v Barr [1969] 3 All ER 487** special damage was referred to as those damages that can and must be proved. A doctor's or hospital receipt is evidence of a special damage. The expenses which the plaintiff has actually incurred up to the date of hearing constitute special damages. General damages are such damages as the law will presume to have resulted from the defendant's tort. The heads of General damages usually include: Pain and suffering, loss of amenities, loss of expectation, life and loss of future earnings.

General damages are usually assessed according to guidelines laid down in **Cornilliac v St Louis (1965) 7 W.I.R. 491 at 495.**
Guidelines:

a. the nature and extent of the injuries sustained;
b. the nature and gravity of the resulting physical disability;
c. the pain and suffering which had to be endured;
d. the loss of amenities suffered; and
e. the effect of on pecuniary interest

iii. Aggravated
The manner in which the tort was committed is important in the assessment of damages. Aggravated damages may be awarded where there was significant injure to the claimant's dignity and pride. These damages are compensatory in nature but are higher than other compensatory awards because they reflect the serious injury to the claimant's pride. Aggravated damages have been commonly awarded in actions for defamation and trespass. The availability in other torts have been restricted by the judgment of the Court of Appeal in **AB v South West Water Services [1993] 1 ALL ER 609**

iv. Exemplary
Exemplary damages are punitive in nature. According to **Rookes v Barnard [1964] AC 1129**, they are awarded in the following instances:

(a) Oppressive, arbitrary or unconstitutional action by servants of the government.
(b) Where the defendant's conduct has been calculated by him to make a profit for himself which may well exceed the compensation payable.

INJUNCTIONS

The remedy of injunction is a critical weapon in the claimant's armoury in many tort claims. A remedy in damages alone may sometimes be insufficient or inappropriate to completely validate the claimant's right. An injunction is an order by the court to a party to do or refrain from doing a particular act. Types of injunctions include: Mandatory and prohibitory, Perpetual and interlocutory injunctions; Injunctions without notice and Quia Timet Injunctions.

(i) Mandatory and Prohibitory

A mandatory injunction requires the defendant to do a positive act in order to terminate a state of affairs which amounts to a tort. A mandatory injunction may require **A** to pull down a Gazebo which interferes with the claimants right to his share of property. Prohibitory injunctions may be issued against a particular person or business with the purpose of restricting or refraining them from carrying out an act.

(ii) Interlocutory and Perpetual Injunctions

Interlocutory and Perpetual injunctions are also called interim injunctions. Perpetual means that the order finally settled the present dispute between the parties, being made as the result of an ordinary action, the court having heard in the ordinary process the arguments presented on both sides. Interlocutory injunction may be mandatory or prohibitory and usually has a speed efficiency effect.

(iii) Quia Timet Injunctions

A quia timet injunction may be issued to restrain a tort which has not yet been committed, but commission of which is threatened. It can be used in instances where a landlord threatens to distrain.

ACTIVITY – DAMAGES

1. Distinguish between general and special damages; aggravated and exemplary damages.
2. Determine whether Damages is adequate compensation in all circumstances. Use decided cases to support your response.
3. Classify the various injunctions available as remedy.
4. Your neighbor breaches your right to quiet enjoyment of your property by keeping and selling exotic birds that are always chirping and fluttering. Discuss the type of Injunction that may be available to you.

Chapter 28

DEFENCES IN TORT

1. Voluntary assumption of risk *(Volenti non fit injuria)*

A man who goes rock climbing and tumbles to the ground from approximately 100 feet has no one to blame but himself. When he participates in such an event that is known to be so risky he generally cannot sue for damages and it is assumed that he was aware of the risk involved in that kind of activity and has volunteered to accept it. This is a defence which operates to completely absolve the defendant of all liability as the claimant consented to the risk of harm.

The requirements of the defence are:

i. a voluntary assumption of risk
ii. an agreement to take the risk
iii. a decision made with full knowledge of the nature and extent of the risk or dangers.

2. Participation in illegal activities

There is no compensation for injury sustained as a result of participation in an illegal activity. This is so even where the wrongdoer was negligent. Examples of this dilemma can be seen where a trespasser slips and breaks his leg in an open manhole on an occupier's property.

3. Inevitable accident

The burden of proof is on the defendant to show that an even was beyond his personal control, and that an accident was unavoidable even where great skill and care was exercised. It is an accident that is certainly not caused by negligence.

4. Contributory negligence

This is a defence in which the defendant tries to get the plaintiff to share the liability. The defendant will argue that the claimant contributed to his injuries. It may be that the plaintiff's actions made the accident more likely to happen or made the injuries more serious. Have a look at the relevant causation cases.

ACTIVITY – REMEDIES

1. Give illustrations or instances when at least three (3) defences you learnt become available to a defendant.
2. Analyse one defence that you have explored so far and make at least two (2) recommendations regarding reform of this defence.

Bibliography

Elliott, C. and Quinn, F. Tort Law, 7th ed, Prentice Hall Publishers

Gary, K.J and Symes, P.D. *Real Property Real People*, Buttersworth, 1981

Kodilinye, G. *Commonwealth Caribbean Property Law*, Cavendish, 2000

McKendrick Ewan, *Contract Law*, 11th edition, McMillan Publishers, 2015

Pollock, F., *Pollock's Principles of Contract*, 13th edition, 1950

Riddall, J.G. *Introduction to Land Law*, Buttersworth, 1979

Salmond and Heuston, *The Law of Torts* (21st Edition), p.449

Murphy, J and Witting, C. *Street on Torts* (9th Edition) p. 486 -7

Treitel, G. *The Law of Contract*, 13th ed, Sweet & Maxwell, 2011

Defamation Act, 2013 (Jamaica)

Website: www.lawteacher.net (July 2012)

Printed in the United States
By Bookmasters